Supersenses

Supersenses

Our Potential
for Parasensory Experience

CHARLES PANATI

NYT

Quadrangle/The New York Times Book Co.

Permission to reprint from the following sources is gratefully acknowledged:

From *Beyond Hypnosis: Explorations in Hyperempiria,* by Donald Gibbons. Reprinted by permission of the publisher, Power Publishers, Inc.

From *Four Quartets,* copyright 1942, 1943 by T. S. Eliot; renewed, 1970, by Esme Valerie Eliot. Reprinted by permission of Harcourt Brace Jovanovich, Inc.

From "The Pleasures of Dying." Reprinted by permission from *Time,* The Weekly Newsmagazine; Copyright Time Inc.

From *The Psychic Feats of Olof Jonsson* by Brad Steiger. Copyright © 1971 by Brad Steiger and Olof Jonsson. Published by Prentice-Hall, Inc., Englewood Cliffs, New Jersey.

From *Psychic Magazine.* Reprinted by permission of Psychic Magazine, Inc., 680 Beach Street, Suite 418, San Francisco, California 94109.

"The Rhythm" copyright © 1962 by Robert Creeley is reprinted by permission of Charles Scribner's Sons from *Words* by Robert Creeley.

From *Transcendental Meditation* by Jack Forem. Copyright © 1973 by Jack Forem. Reprinted by permission of the publishers, E. P. Dutton & Co., Inc.

Book design: Mary M. Ahern

LIBRARY OF CONGRESS CATALOGING IN PUBLICATION DATA

Panati, Charles, 1943–
   Supersenses.

   Bibliography: p.
   1. Psychical research. I. Title.
BF1031.P24 1974   133.8   74–77937
ISBN 0–8129–0472–9

To
　　Mary,
　　　Ron,
　　　　and
　　　　　Marc
for listening

Contents

Acknowledgments

There are many people to whom I am indebted: those who introduced me to the field as it exists today, those who gave freely of their time to explain and demonstrate their experiments, and those who generously provided me with yet unpublished papers.

With gratitude I acknowledge Dr. Montague Ullman, Dr. Stanley Krippner, and Mr. Charles Honorton of the Division of Parapsychology and Psychophysics at the Maimonides Medical Center; Dr. Charles Tart, University of California; Dr. William Tiller, Stanford University; Dr. Robert Ornstein, Langely Porter Neuropsychiatric Institute; Dr. Lawrence LeShan, New York City; Dr. Burton Glick, Elmhurst Hospital, New York; Dr. William Braud and his wife, Lendell, University of Houston; Dr. Robert Van de Castle, University of Virginia; Dr. J. B. Rhine, Foundation for the study of the Nature of Man; Dr. Karlis Osis, American Society for Psychical Research; Dr. Kenneth Keeling, University of Waterloo, Canada; Dr. Richard Dobrin and Dr. Carl Kirsch, Institute for Bioenergetic Analysis; Dr. Edgar Mitchell, Institute of Noetic Sciences; Mr. Douglas Dean, Newark College of Engineering; Dr. Thelma Moss and Mr. Kendell Johnson, University of California; Dr. Gertrude Schmeidler, City College of New York; Dr. Justa Smith, Human Dimension Institute; Dr. Harold Puthoff and Mr. Russell Targ, Stanford Research Institute; Dr. Harry Hermon, Maimonides Medical Center; Dr. William Roll, University of Virginia; and Dr. Jean Houston and Mr. Robert Masters, Mind Research Foundation.

I also wish to thank the staff of the Parapsychology Foundation, New York, for their research assistance and New York University for the opportunity to present a good portion of the material in this book to their students in a colloquium.

For permission to print copyrighted material I am grateful to the American Society for Psychical Research, Ingo Swann, Thelma Moss and Kendell Johnson, Donald Gibbons, and *Newsweek* magazine.

Finally, I wish to offer warm thanks to Mrs. Judith Skutch, President of the Foundation for Parasensory Investigation, New York, for her time, intelligent suggestions, and most valuable introductions.

Supersenses

Impossible Things

*"There is no use trying," Alice said. One
can't believe impossible things."*

*"I daresay you haven't had much practice,"
said the Queen. When I was your age I always did
it for half-an-hour a day. Why, sometimes I've
believed as many as six impossible things before
breakfast."*

Lewis Carroll, *Alice's Adventures in Wonderland*, 1865

Impossible things, as history constantly reminds us, have an uncanny way
of becoming possible when given enough time. Of course, it is seldom the
events themselves which change, only our attitude toward them. Such a
change of heart is particularly evident today in the field of parapsychology,*
the ambitious discipline which deals with many events once tainted by
occultism and talk of the supernatural. In terms of present-day research the
field can be conveniently divided into five major categories:

Telepathy—the direct interchange of information between two or more
minds

Clairvoyance—the acquisition of information by a mind from an inanimate
object—for example, deciphering the contents of a sealed letter

Precognition—the acquisition of information about some future event by a
mind

Psychokinesis—the placing of an object in motion by volition alone

Psychic Healing—treatment of disease by an "unconventional" interaction
between a "healer" and a patient.

*The word *parapsychology* was coined by the German philosopher-psychologist Max
Dessoir in 1889; in Greek *para* means *besides*.

Throughout this book these five phenomena are referred to collectively as "paranormal events" or, to use a shorter and increasingly popular expression, "psi events."* It should be made clear that dubbing these five phenomena "paranormal" does not imply that they have some sort of supernatural origin, nor does calling the mode of perception through which a person becomes aware of such information "parasensory" imply some unearthly talent. The prefix *para* is used merely to indicate that the precise mechanism underlying the phenomena lies beyond our present understanding of normal sensory perception.

Today more than a dozen university laboratories, even more research centers, and the federal government are actively engaged in parapsychological research. The researchers are conventionally trained physicists, chemists, neurobiologists, psychologists, psychiatrists, and physicians—each bringing the powerful tools of a specific discipline to the psi challenge. Under this interdisciplinary attack paranormal phenomena, for the first time in history, are beginning to relinquish their secrets—secrets which are already changing our views of humankind and human interactions with the universe.

Some scientists are working under the premise that parasensory abilities are latent within us all and concentrating their studies on ordinary people, not psychics. Through hypnosis, drugs, dream experiments, and modern techniques of sensory bombardment and deprivation, these researchers are finding that certain mental states are more conducive to parasensory happenings than others.

Other laboratories are focusing on individuals who possess manifest psychic talents. While a psychic mentally transmits an image or levitates an object from across the room, today's psi researchers do more than just observe and statistically record the success or failure of such feats as their predecessors once did. In modern experiments the psychic subject is wired to a complex array of physiological monitoring equipment which continuously follows the rise and fall of such parameters as blood pressure, respiration rate, the skin's electrical conductivity, and brain-wave emanations. Scientists are finding that the acquisition of parasensory information, whether through telepathy, clairvoyance, or precognition, the motion of objects by psychokinesis, and the efforts of the psychic healer are all accompanied by measurable, and sometimes gross, psychophysical alterations in the human body.

*The term *psi* is borrowed from physics where it denotes an intangible field or immaterial substratum of matter.

Still other researchers are measuring lactate levels, enzyme activity, and blood hemoglobin values in the bodies of their subjects as they seek evidence of fundamental changes in body chemistry that might accompany paranormal phenomena. The question today is no longer whether parasensory perception is real or imaginary, but under what conditions it manifests itself. And once these variables are known, be they particular brain-wave patterns, muscular relaxations, or hormonal secretions, can one learn to induce them at will through biofeedback training to awaken psychical abilities?

A little more than a decade ago the research reported in this book would have been impossible to conduct. The technology was not lacking, nor was there a paucity of qualified scientists. The equipment and the men were there—but the will was not. Parapsychology was a taboo field, and psi research was an open invitation to professional suicide. Simply, the subject suffered from an embarrassing ancestry. True, chemistry was born out of the dubious efforts of alchemists, surgery from the butcherous works of barbers, and astronomy from the early sky-gazing of astrologers. But parapsychology had to break away from a shadier lot: witches, sorcerers, and charlatans. It also had to live down such systems of divination as hippomancy (forecasting events from the stamping of horses), aeromancy (from the shapes of clouds), capnomancy (from patterns of smoke rising from a fire), and tiromancy (from reading the holes in Swiss cheese). Understandably, it's been a hard, often embarrassing, struggle toward respectability, and the victory is not yet fully won.

Beyond the operational hurdles, parapsychology has had to surmount a monumental conceptual barrier. For centuries legitimate scientists did not deal with phenomena existing at the outer fringes of human consciousness. Indeed, consciousness itself was not considered a legitimate field of scientific study. In 1913 psychologist John Broadus Watson proclaimed that "the time has come when psychology must discard all references to consciousness . . . Its sole task is the prediction and control of behavior."[1] Paranormal phenomena, with their roots anchored in consciousness, thus became more a subject for mediumistic shenanigans than scientific scrutiny.

As Watsonian Behaviorism caught on like a dry brush fire, growing and evolving through its various forms, any serious efforts to investigate psi events were thwarted. It was the brave scholar, then (or the crazy one, as some saw it), who would dare cast an eye toward the paranormal. Nevertheless, many of the people who did had impeccable credentials: the eminent classic scholar Henry Sidgwick; Lord Rayleigh, the great physicist; Nobel laureates Charles Richet and Henri Bergson; and William James, the father of American psychology. These men believed that the human mind had modes of perception beyond the five somatic senses, and they tried to give parapsychology the respectability it so badly lacked. To appreciate where the field is today, how it got there, and what personal and theoretical opponents it had to battle, it is necessary to step back in time, back to the 1880s, and scan the three phases which constitute parapsychology's past.

The early pioneers took the only research approach they could, given the conditions of the times: field work. It entailed collecting, collating, and studying reports of spontaneous paranormal happenings involving cobblers, aristocrats, and anyone else who thought he had a tale to tell. The researchers sought common denominators from these cases which might cast some light on the conditions under which parasensory perception occurs. This was the Field Work Phase of parapsychological research, and though its intentions were noble, the collected psi reports were so awash with subjectivity that they convinced no one of anything. In fact, the attempts of early scientists to lend their scholastic training to paranormal investigation met with immediate hostility and ridicule. The formation of the Society for Psychical Research in 1882, an organization with a scientific bent, brought thunderous criticism from the scientific community. As Sidgwick reported: "We were told somewhat roughly that being just like all other fools who collected old women's stories and solemnly recorded the tricks of imposters, we only made ourselves the more ridiculous by assuming the aims of a scientific society and varnishing this wretched nonsense with technical jargon."[2]

By the late 1920s, with paranormal phenomena still regarded by most scientists as "impossible things," psi investigators shifted the emphasis of their research from the Field Work Phase to what could be called the Qualitative Phase. Basically, the new experiments, done in England and the United States, involved an agent (sender) who drew a figure, number, or word in one room while a percipient (receiver) in another room wrote down his or her impressions. Two diagrams were thus produced which could be compared to see if parasensory communication had occurred. The idea itself isn't bad; fraud was easily controlled, and any number of skeptics could witness the experiment. But there is a hitch to the experiments conducted in this phase of psi research: How does one objectively evaluate the likeness between the agent's drawing and the percipient's impression of it? If the agent draws a heart with an arrow piercing it, and the percipient sketches a line intersecting a circle, is that close enough to be counted as a "hit," or is it a "miss"? How close is the figure 8 to a 3; the word *apple* to *ape?*

Clearly, there is no unequivocal way to measure the results of such an experiment. And, as the Field Work Phase had fallen on deaf ears, so too did the Qualitative Phase of psi research.

But in the early 1930s one man thought he had the psi research problem licked. His method would convince the most hardened skeptic, he believed. The man was J. B. Rhine of Duke University; his approach was to use a deck of cards or a die as the target, and to treat the experimental results to statistical analysis. If the agent concentrated on the queen of hearts and the percipient claimed he or she telepathically saw the queen of hearts, it was a clear hit, with unarguable odds of fifty-two to one against chance occurrence. If a die in a sealed box were shaken and a subject clairvoyantly guessed before the box was opened that the uppermost face was a **3**, there was no ambiguity in determining whether the subject was right and in dealing statistically with the outcome. What could be simpler? What could be more precise? More foolproof?

In the late 1930s Rhine began reporting phenomenal success using college students as subjects in his card-guessing experiments. His results were too phenomenal for many observers. Perhaps if Rhine's success had been moderate, he would have drawn favorable attention from science, and parapsychological research might have had a different evolution. But so amazing were his reported successes, often with odds of over a million to one against chance, that he came under a wild barrage of attack.

First his professional colleagues challenged his statistical evaluation methods. His mathematics was faulty, they insisted. But soon the American Institute of Mathematical Statistics perused his calculations and issued a statement: "On the statistical side, recent mathematical work has established the fact that, assuming that the experiments have been properly performed, the statistical analysis is essentially valid. If the Rhine investigation is to be fairly attacked, it must be on other than mathematical grounds."[3]

Rhine's critics wasted no time in finding other grounds; thunderous shouts of fraud arose claiming that Rhine had altered the numbers, fiddled with the tally sheets. Many psi researchers, both at home and abroad, quickly adopted Rhine's simple experimental method, hoping to come to his aid by duplicating his phenomenal results. But the situation only worsened. No one could achieve the level of success that Rhine consistently reported. Another dark cloud hung over the field of parapsychology.

Some researchers, in going over their calculations, found that certain subjects were not guessing the target card but the one directly after it in the deck—a sort of "psi offset effect," as they called it. Others found that certain

subjects who missed target calls did so more frequently than chance allowed, which also represented statistically significant scoring. This became
known as the "psi missing effect." Still, no one else's scores soared as high
as Rhine's.

To account for the differences between Rhine's results and those from
the rash of other card-guessing experiments that had erupted, psychologist
G. N. M. Tyrrell suggested that the interpersonal relationship between
subject and experimenter was an important variable.[4] Certain pairs of individuals had what it took, others did not. Rapport was important. So too
was an individual's personality structure, according to psi researcher
Whately Carington.[5] And psychologist Dr. Gertrude Schmeidler suggested
that a subject's attitude toward the paranormal, whether the person was
a believer or a scoffer, was a critical issue.[6]

Today we know that all of these suggested variables are crucial in a
psi experiment. A hardhearted disbeliever *does* make a poor subject, perhaps for the same reasons that a negative attitude in business, love, or life
makes for repeated failure. We know that the lack of rapport between a
sender and a receiver *can* ruin a psi experiment, just as it can a marriage.
Rhine's supporters argue that he had a fiery, ebullient personality, and
what's more, he was thoroughly convinced of the reality of what he was
doing. Was he able to infect subjects with his fever and awaken their
parasenses, the way any good teacher can sharpen the senses of a student?

Many historians of parapsychology feel that this was largely the case,
that Rhine was a special person, and that the Statistical Phase of psi
research, largely dominated by Rhine, was honestly conducted. Others
disagree. They contend that Rhine's abundant enthusiasm did not so much
infect his subjects as it did his calculations. But despite the integrity, or lack
of it, which characterized the card-guessing era, Rhine and his followers
fought a losing battle from the start. Their research into the paranormal
aspects of the human mind collided head-on with a new, rising form of
behaviorism—the Skinnerian variety.

With the ascent of Harvard's B. F. Skinner to international influence
in the 1950s and 1960s, the paranormal workings of the mind sank still
deeper into the occult ash. Skinner's view of the mind, expressed in his
standard work, *Science and Human Behavior,* and shared by most psychologists at the time, was that the term *mind* stands for a nonexistent
entity "invented for the sole purpose of providing spurious explanations."
For psi researchers, whose study was the sensitive progeny of consciousness,
Skinner's pronouncement was a clobbering blow. And Skinner went further: "Since mental or psychic events are asserted to lack the dimension of

physical sciences, we have an additional reason for rejecting them."[7] Of course, what Skinner chose to overlook in making that particular comparison between psychology and the physical sciences (as we shall soon see in more detail) is that with the birth of modern physics—Relativity and Quantum Theory—in the early 1900s, the physical sciences had lost their classical concreteness. They themselves, forced to accept such concepts as antimatter, time reversal, and acausality, entered into an area of what can be called the "parapsychical." Nevertheless, with Skinnerian Behaviorism in the saddle, serving as the mainstream of psychological thought, it is little wonder that university psychology departments frowned at the very mention of paranormal phenomena. In fact, modern psychologists with purely behavioral viewpoints still frown. As recently as 1971 Skinner wrote, in his best seller *Beyond Freedom and Dignity:* "The dimensions of the world of mind and the transition from one world to another do raise embarrassing problems, but it is usually possible to ignore them and this may be good strategy, for the important objection to mentalism is of a very different sort. The world of the mind steals the show."[8]

Steals the show, indeed. This is precisely what is happening today. The subject of human consciousness has moved into the center ring, and standing foremost in the spotlight are paranormal phenomena.

Why such a complete turnabout? Why is the occult becoming a science? There are two major reasons: a change in research methodology ("hardware") and a new working philosophy ("software"). The use of such conventional hardware as electroencephalographs, temperature sensors, and galvanic skin resistance devices makes modern psi research parallel that of established branches of science. It is not as easy to discard the statistics sheet of a psi experiment when it is accompanied by a record of the physiological changes the subject experienced while performing psychically.

The second reason for the emerging respectability of parapsychology has to do with the new willingness among psychologists to study Altered States of Consciousness (ASCs)—such conditions as dreaming, hypnotic and hyperaroused trances, and sensory deprivation. Historical psi literature contends, and modern experiments confirm, that parasensory perception seems to be a manifestation of various altered states of the mind, not a phenomenon of normal "wakeful consciousness." A recent experiment can illustrate this point. Student volunteers were divided into percipient–agent pairs for a telepathy test. The two halves of a cut ping-pong ball were placed over the eyes of each percipient, and a bright red light was set six inches in front of him or her. The percipient's ears were covered by a headset which played uninterrupted white noise—the static one would hear by tuning a radio to a band between broadcasting stations. Sight and sound are the senses we rely on most heavily. Under the experimental conditions, when the eyes and ears are deprived of patterned information from the real world and surrounded by a continuous field of meaningless stimuli, wakeful consciousness is irresistibly lost. The mind of a person isolated from normal sensory inputs turns inward toward imagery and thought. In the experiment, an agent in a room thirty feet down the hall from the percipient attempted to transmit the face from a randomly selected picture. More than half the students who served as percipients were able to describe the target picture, something they could not do in their normal wakeful state.*

It is hard to deny that parapsychology has come of age; the indicators are everywhere. *New Scientist* magazine, which has a highly technical audience of scientists and technicians, took a fall 1972 poll of their readers' attitudes toward psi research. Over seventy percent of those polled indicated that they believe the field of parapsychology to be a legitimate area of scientific research and one that has too long been overlooked. Staid technical journals are now publishing parapsychological research papers, and in December, 1969, the Parapsychological Association was accepted into the prestigious American Association for the Advancement of Science. (This acceptance was due in large measure to the support of the anthropologist Dr. Margaret Mead, who has been interested in psi research for many years.)

In 1972, the American Psychiatric Association expressed a healthy attitude toward paranormal research by turning part of its 125th annual meeting in Dallas into a symposium entitled "Science and Psi: Transcultural Trends." Currently, the association is considering formation of a special task force on psi research to investigate its future uses in clinical psychiatry.

But psychiatrists and psychologists are not the only "establishment scientists" who have taken an interest in the new parapsychology; even more physicists and engineers have entered the field. While psychiatrists and psychologists have turned to psi research with the hope of parting the dark curtain which cloaks the subconscious mind, physical scientists are enticed by the prospect of finding a hitherto unknown form of energy— psychic energy—which presumably mediates psi occurrences. In March, 1972, the Stanford Research Institute, a giant think-tank in Menlo Park, California, which performs high-caliber research for both the Department

*Experiments conducted by Charles Honorton at the Maimonides Medical Center in Brooklyn, New York. Published in the April, 1974, issue of the *Journal of the American Society for Psychical Research.*

of Defense and industry, took its first plunge into psychical research with the testing of two talented psychics. What the scientists witnessed during the several months of this study left them thrilled, if somewhat dumbfounded. The official word from the Institute was: "We have observed certain phenomena with the subjects for which we have no scientific explanation. All we can say at this point is that further investigation is clearly warranted."[9]

Scientists entering parapsychology are presumably spurred on by innate intellectual curiosity. The federal government's interest in psi, on the other hand, must be attributed in large part to the Soviet Union's attitude toward psi research in recent years. In 1955 an official Soviet publication defined parapsychology as: "the non-scientific idealistic consideration about supernatural abilities of perception phenomena."[10] By 1970, however, the Soviets had done a complete about-face. The same publication gave the following definition: "Parapsychology is the area of psychical and biophysiological research dealing with the informational and energetic possibilities of living organisms. Parapsychology considers the newest forms of sensitivity, the results of those sensitivities and possibilities in the human organism."[11] The change of heart came in 1963 when the Kremlin issued an edict that top priority was to be given to psychically related sciences. Part of the Soviet impetus undoubtedly stems from the possibility of harnessing psi for military purposes, but another part has to do with the use of telepathy as a superior means of communication in their cosmonaut program. To date, all experimental evidence, U.S. and Soviet alike, suggests that telepathic transmission does not suffer the attenuation of ordinary electromagnetic waves over distance. Clearly, this fact could revolutionize the communications field. Today, the Soviet Union has more than twenty-five centers for the study of parasensory perception with an annual budget in excess of twenty million rubles (about twenty-one million dollars).[12]

The sizable Soviet effort in psi research has sparked the interest of several government agencies in this country. Among them is the National Aeronautics and Space Administration (NASA), whose interest is twofold. First, there is the straightforward hope of one day using telepathy between earth and spacecrafts, and from one craft to another. U.S. space shots now reach Jupiter (round-trip radio communication takes ninety minutes) and soon will venture beyond our own solar system; communication time between earth and a spaceship grows ever longer. Psi research could prove to be a boon in this area. NASA's second interest in psi is more futuristic. When the day comes that we do encounter intelligent life in outer space (and most scientists believe this is inevitable), how will we communicate with these extraterrestrial beings? No one believes the interchange will be verbal. Some scientists feel the "talk" might consist of mathematical notations because of their abstract mimicry of nature. But this may still be presuming too much. Perhaps the only common language will be in preverbal, prewritten thoughts—intangible, universal patterns that might be directly read telepathically. One high NASA official described the space industry's interest in psi research:

> Until recently these phenomena have in general been ignored by Western scientists; however the many hypotheses involved are now receiving attention in world literature.
>
> Specific U.S. experiments in energy-transfer phenomena, or the relationship between the physical fields of particles and the non-demonstrable "personal" psi plasma field, are being carried out or planned under various advanced concepts.
>
> . . . To Western scientists and engineers the results of valid experimentation in energy transfer could lead to new communications media and advanced emergency techniques, as well as to biocybernetical aids for integrating with a conceptual design of an ultimate operational flight system.[13]

If man's psychical senses are to be awakened, there are many scientists and agencies today who would like to sound the alarm. Within the last few years the National Institute for Mental Health in Bethesda, Maryland, has begun issuing government grants for psi research. Thus far funds have been granted for studies in precognition, telepathy, and clairvoyance; several dozen more proposals are under consideration. The government funding of psychical research is an unprecedented move and a clear indication of where psi research is heading.

The computer age began in the 1950s, the space age in the 1960s, and the psychic age has begun in the 1970s. Paranormal phenomena are no longer being viewed as impossible things. They have finally moved off the magician's stage and come full swing into the scientific laboratory. What is happening there, and its implications for dramatically reshaping our image of ourselves and our place in the universe, are the subjects of this book.

Charles F. Panati
New York City, January, 1974

I

The Dream Scene

Human kind cannot bear very much reality.

T. S. Eliot, "Burnt Norton"

Dream Consciousness

During the fall of 1894, the great Russian pianist-composer Anton Rubinstein was living in Peterhof, Germany. It was a cold fall that year, which did not help the musician's failing health. For weeks he had been ill, periodically confined to bed, and on the evening of November 20 Rubinstein took a turn for the worse.

In Paris that same evening, a former student of the great musician, William Nichia, who had not seen his mentor for many years, had a frightening dream. The face of Rubinstein, grotesquely contorted and framed in pain, approached him in awesome reality. When Nichia jumped up and turned on the lights, the dream was gone. But he could not shake its nightmarish impact.

The next morning Parisians read of Rubenstein's death. Later that day Nichia learned through a friend that the pianist had suffered a heart attack and suffocated. Rubinstein had died with a horrible, agonizing cry at the very time of Nichia's dream.[1]

Parapsychological literature is filled with such anecdotal dream material. Dreams of accidents, illness, and death which contain telepathic or precognitive flashes are well recorded back to the time of Julius Caesar, whose wife foresaw his bloody murder in a dream. Although these tales can never constitute scientific proof of the paranormal, their sheer quantity suggested a tempting hypothesis to early psychical researchers: Perhaps dream consciousness is a mental state highly amenable to psi happenings. In 1960, Carl Jung voiced this belief, based on lifelong experience with

13

patients' dreams. "I have found," wrote Jung, "that telepathy does, in fact, influence dreams, as has been asserted since ancient times . . . I would not, of course, assert that the law behind them is anything 'supernatural,' but merely something which we cannot get at with our present knowledge."[2] A few years later a detailed study of over 7,000 spontaneous psi cases from the Rhine files strongly supported the hypothesis,[3] but this still was not proof. A repeatable experiment was needed, a test that could be duplicated in any laboratory, by any researcher, under carefully controlled conditions. Only this would turn the heads of skeptics, ensure scientific acceptance, and open the doors to government funding. One man who had set out to devise this ideal experiment was psychiatrist Dr. Montague Ullman.

Since graduating from medical school in 1938, Ullman had been fascinated with the intricacies of the dream state. Little was known then of the physiology of dreaming, but Ullman, who today is director of the Maimonides Medical Center in Brooklyn, felt certain that the dream state had rich psychical potential. He was well acquainted with psychiatric reports that during psychoanalysis a patient's dream often contains information about the therapist's life which the patient has no recourse for knowing.[4] Once Ullman began psychiatric practice, he experienced many such instances firsthand. As he says, "It seemed to me that I was on the receiving end of a number of presumptively telepathic dreams of patients. They dreamed about details of my own personal life that they could not have had any access to or could not have inferred."[5] In one case, a patient undergoing psychoanalysis revealed this dream to Ullman:

> I'm in a hotel room . . . I was wrapping up a few of the samples that had been on exhibit and was preparing to leave. Someone gave me, or I took, a chromium soap dish. I held it in my hand and I offered it to him. He took it. I was surprised. I asked him, "Are you a collector too?" Then I sort of smirked and said knowingly, "Well, you're building a house." He blushed. He smirked and kept on smoking his cigar.[6]

What the patient did not know was that Ullman had recently had a new home constructed, and an extra chromium soap dish had been shipped to his house by mistake. He did not mention the fact to anyone and kept the extra dish. Just a week before the patient's dream, some workmen at the house had spotted the extra dish and made a snide remark which had embarrassed Ullman.

Such personal incidents fired Ullman's desire to probe dream consciousness scientifically for its psychical potential. But soon he found, as other researchers had, that there were intractable problems. How do you bring the dream from the psychiatrist's couch into the scientist's laboratory? How do you replace subjective psychiatric analysis with objective scientific fact? The evanescent nature of dreaming seemed to preclude scientific probing. Dream consciousness appeared from all observations to be a capricious state of the mind. Some individuals experienced it often, but the majority of the populace seemed to dream rarely or not at all. Some reported colorful, pleasant dreams; others had bizarre dreams of sufficient reality to evoke sweating and bruxism. Still other individuals experienced sleeptalking, sleepwalking, or sexual dreams that culminated in nocturnal orgasm. How could such a random phenomenon be rigorously studied? If the future of psi research rested on catching and taming dreams, the days ahead looked bleak.

There was another hopeless aspect: Dream theory at that time held that dreaming only occurred in the fleeting seconds prior to awakening, when a full-blown episode passed in a flash, leaving little time for experimentation. In addition, many scientists scoffed at the whole idea, firmly believing that dreams were totally devoid of meaningful information, "children of an idle brain, begot of nothing but vain fantasy," as Mercutio declares in *Romeo and Juliet.*

From an experimental standpoint, then, dream consciousness seemed to be a transient and nebulous concept, hardly a suitable subject for scientific scrutiny.

Breaking Ground

But in 1952 the dream scene underwent a dramatic change. In April of that year, a graduate student at the University of Chicago made a revolutionary discovery. Using an electroencephalograph (EEG) to electronically monitor the brain waves of sleeping subjects, he found that their eyes moved rapidly in the sockets for several minutes at a time. The rapid eye movements (REMs) were not random, but displayed considerable pattern throughout the night. Other researchers soon found that during a typical seven-hour night's sleep, anywhere from four to seven REM cycles occur. More importantly, the REM periods were conclusively related to dreams in progress. The sleepers' eyelids fluttered as though they were shutters to the world of dreams. For the first time the phenomenological dream had entered the scientist's laboratory. Ullman excitedly kept abreast of the day-to-day happenings in dream research; already he saw what he had been waiting for.

Subjects awakened during strong REM cycles related dreams in which they were active participants. They were being chased, running, playing tennis, or engaging in sexual acts. On the other hand, subjects awakened from weak REM activity reported being passive observers in their dreams. One significant find, essential to the psi–dream research that followed, was that if a dreaming subject were awakened during REM activity or immediately thereafter, he or she had excellent dream recall. This was true whether the subjects regarded themselves as dreamers or not. However, subjects awakened as little as five minutes after a REM burst could not remember having dreamed.

From such early EEG observations on dream consciousness it became apparent that if the dream state is indeed a psi-favorable condition, then parasensory information could register with a sleeping subject at several distinct phases during the night—phases that could be accurately observed and measured.

Also important from a parapsychological standpoint was the observation that each REM cycle during a night's sleep was found to exhibit its own characteristic features. The first REM period, which begins approximately an hour after a person falls to sleep, lasts only about ten minutes. Then, after a period of relative mental quiescence, the brain starts up again, this time with dream consciousness lasting about twenty minutes to half an hour. Each succeeding period throughout the night lengthens until near morning the brain may be in the dream mode for an hour or longer.

The average person has no voluntary control over these stop-and-start dreams; they simply occur, flowing naturally from deep within all of us. But rare individuals have been known to awaken after each REM phase. One person who apparently had this ability was Robert Louis Stevenson. He discovered early in life that he could dream complete stories, waking up and going back to sleep again if he had to continue an incomplete episode. During one evening's dreams he pieced together a tale in which a criminal, pursued by the police, imbibed a fuming potion and presently changed his appearance. The dreams, artistically woven, eventually were published as *Dr. Jekyll and Mr. Hyde.*[7] Needless to say, such control of dream mentation is extremely rare.

Much of the emerging new evidence on dreaming flatly contradicted views long held by the prominent schools of psychiatry and psychology. A storm of controversy ensued. Whereas both Freud and Adler had held that the length of time an individual dreams is proportional to the number and intensity of the individual's personal experiences and problems, the new laboratory data showed otherwise. With slight variation, all of the people studied dreamed in similar and predictable amounts—saints and sinners, paupers and kings; dreaming is a universal phenomenon.

The new evidence on dreaming provided psi researchers with just the pinch of objectivity they needed to pry open the psychical doors of the mind. If dream consciousness was a highly psi-favorable state as the literature proclaimed, then from a first approximation at least it appeared that all people had an equal potential to experience paranormal events.

On June 6, 1960, Dr. Ullman, assisted by psychologist Dr. Karlis Osis and engineer E. Douglas Dean, began some preliminary studies at the Parapsychology Foundation in Manhattan. Although ordinary people with no spectacular history of paranormal events were used in almost all these pilot tests, the first subject was the renowned psychic Eileen Garrett. Mrs. Garrett, then in her early sixties, had a long history of psychic experiences dating back to her childhood in County Meath, Ireland. Although she had been studied for over thirty years by other scientists, this was to be a wholly different type of test. In beginning their experiments with one of the century's foremost psychics the researchers may have shown a lack of confidence in their project, but that bit of self-doubt soon proved to be unwarranted. In fact, this woman's potent talents were to give the researchers a surprise they had not anticipated.

On the evening of June 6, Mrs. Garrett reported to the laboratory. She was placed in a room and seven electrodes were attached to her head with conductive paste: two near her eyes, one at the front and one at the back of her skull, two ear reference electrodes, and one electrical ground. These connections wired her to an EEG, which would tell the researchers when and to what degree she was dreaming. Once a dream cycle began, one researcher was to call a friend of Mrs. Garrett who was serving as the agent in the experiment from her home several miles from the laboratory. At that time the agent would randomly select one of three envelopes which would serve as the evening's target, and attempt to transmit its contents to Mrs. Garrett. The envelopes, prepared in advance by Dr. Osis, contained color prints taken from a current issue of *Life* magazine. No one, not even Osis, knew in advance what the target picture would be.

As Ullman and the others watched the EEG readout, they were somewhat disappointed. Mrs. Garrett did not enter full dream consciousness that night. Without the long REM periods, Ullman decided that the experiment should be postponed until another evening when the psychic showed a more normal sleep pattern. The agent was never called, and no envelope was selected to be opened.

But when Ullman awakened Mrs. Garrett he was surprised to learn that she remembered a dream: She had been watching horses running up a hill, and this reminded her of the movie *Ben Hur*. The dream meant nothing to Ullman, but Osis immediately saw its significance. One of the three color prints he had sealed in the envelopes was a picture of the spectacular *Ben Hur* chariot race taken from an advertisement for the movie.[8]

Subsequent tests with Mrs. Garrett and with several other subjects pleased Ullman and his colleagues, for they suggested that dream consciousness was indeed a highly psi-favorable state. But these initial runs did not constitute scientific proof of the phenomenon. Tighter controls were needed to eliminate the possibility of sensory clues and cheating, and there had to be some independent means of judging the results—a rigorous statistical method for evaluation. These things were necessary if the experiments were ever to be accepted by the scientific community. But at least the ground work had been laid.

A Favorable State

Frontier research proceeds slowly. Usually results just trickle in, which is one important reason why funding for pure research is so difficult to obtain. But this snail's pace is necessary if the right questions are to be asked and the right roads explored. In psychical research, with its critics poised to attack, this is particularly true. Taking a few wrong turns, running your subjects down a few blind alleys, or hastily announcing inconclusive results can do irreparable damage to the future of psi research. If the dream pilot-studies were correct—and everyone concerned with them was convinced of that—a big question now demanded an answer: *Why* is dream consciousness so amenable to paranormal occurrences? What is the neurophysiological state of the brain that opens the mind to parasensory information? Are the favorable factors environmental or genetic? These are hard questions to answer, but they are the road signs which steer psi research in a progressively forward direction.

Dreaming is an ASC which is distinct from either the waking or the sleeping state. Whether we drift into the dream world for wish-fulfillment, social problem-solving, or an honest glimpse of the unshielded self is still unknown, but today one thing can definitely be said for dream mentation: It is a unique state of the mind both neurophysiologically and psychologically. Dreaming has a Janus-faced identity—from different vantage points it offers different features. Psychically, this turns out to be the dream's most salient characteristic. Its deep, dark face emerges from behavioral considerations, while its active, alert face is revealed in physiological factors.

From a behavioral standpoint, it appears that dream consciousness is a profoundly deep level of sleep from which external stimuli are excluded. Slight noises, gentle touches, and unpleasant odors, all stimuli which could awaken an individual from nondream sleep, pass the REM-dreamer undetected. If the criterion of the depth of sleep hinges on a behavioral response to external stimuli, dream consciousness is a period of deep sleep.

From a physiological standpoint, however, the dream state appears to be the lightest phase of sleep. In fact, on many observable accounts it equals or exceeds the state of wakeful consciousness. During dreaming the neurons —the single nerve cells which provide the two-way communication between the brain and the body—can fire electrical discharges at a rate slightly faster than during wakefulness. This fact indicates that the brain's relative unreceptiveness to external stimuli is not due to diminished activity. On the contrary, the dreaming brain is neurophysiologically "hot." The brain is not alone in reflecting all signs of being "awake" during dreaming, for similar signs are shown by the body. There is a noticeable rise in heart rate, body temperature, and respiration; in males, more than eighty percent of the evening's dream time is spent with an erection—this is true whether or not the dream has any manifest sexual content.[9]

Thus, while the brain and body of the dreamer show all signs of being awake, he or she is in a world immune to external stimuli. The dream state can be likened to that of a small boy who is avidly watching his favorite television program. When his concentration is focused, his interest keen, the child's internal bodily processes are active, perhaps even accelerated above their normal waking level. But this pinpointed concentration also diminishes his awareness of external stimuli. He may be called and not hear his name because he is so thoroughly entrenched in an ASC. One of the most important aspects of dream consciousness is the internally active brain, shielded from the daily bombardment of sights, sounds, smells, and touches.

It seems feasible that if parasensory information were ever to register with the brain, at least one ideal time would be during REM sleep. Not only is the brain shut off from the external world, but it is electrochemically primed to handle vast amounts of information. In the language of communications engineering, dream consciousness represents a mental state in which the signal-to-noise ratio is greatly enhanced. The noise of everyday wakefulness has been described by the eminent philosopher C. D. Broad as the "multitude of sensory impressions raining in on us, through our eyes, ears, nose and skin, from our muscles and viscera and the countless feelings, thoughts and memories that are tending to surge up from below the threshold of consciousness."[10] This wakeful shower is normally enough to swamp out any parasensory information.

Although dream consciousness is a psi-favorable state, we must not jump to the conclusion that parasensory information can enter the mind only during a dream. It is quite possible, as psychologist Gardner Murphy argues, that such information may enter the mind of a person preoccupied with wakeful tasks, registering at some unconscious level. The information lies dormant while the brain busily processes the daily inputs of driving a car, transacting business, or making love; it emerges to consciousness only when the individual has shut down his mental works for REM sleep. An analogy can again be drawn with the child engrossed in a television program. His mother may ask him a question, and he may honestly not hear her at the moment. Yet, a few minutes later he may automatically blurt out the answer. The question registered in some unconscious level of the mind and had to fight its way through the information being processed from the television show before he became aware of it.

Professor Broad has postulated that "beneath the surface" we are constantly being bombarded by extrasensory information. If the mind were always aware of these inputs, however, it would be impossible to finish reading this sentence. Thus parasensory and sensory information seem to be in constant competition for the mind's attention. Dream consciousness is one mental plateau where parasensory information seems to win out.

Telepathically Induced Dreams

With the groundwork in dream mentation thus laid, in 1962, with grants from two private foundations, Dr. Ullman established the Menninger Dream Laboratory* at the Maimonides Medical Center. Two years later he was joined by an imaginative psychologist, Dr. Stanley Krippner. With the experimental procedures tightened so that no one could yell "Fraud!"—an all too frequent, but often justified, cry in psi research—the two men began an experimental odyssey which offered the first unequivocal proof that the average person can perceive thoughts telepathically.

The laboratory, which is housed in the basement wing of the center,

*The name was changed in 1973 to the Division of Parapsychology and Psychophysics.

is a series of rooms along a long corridor. At one end of the corridor is an acoustically shielded room with a comfortable bed, a chair, and wire leads running to an EEG in another room. Once a subject is sealed in the thick-walled room for the night, the only means of communicating with the experimenter is over an intercom. At the opposite end of the corridor, some fifty feet away, is a room for the agent who will attempt to transmit his or her thought to the sleeping subject. From the standpoint of occult folklore, the classic psi experiments conducted at Maimonides are of modest ambition. The scientists are not trying to conjure up spirits of the dead or prove the existence of the soul. Rather, they attempt to incorporate, time after time, bits of visual images viewed by one person into the dreams of another. The subjects in the experiments are not psychics but teachers, housewives, businessmen, and students.

One beauty of the experiments is their amazing simplicity. A subject reports to the dream laboratory at his or her normal sleep time. (Subjects are selected solely on the basis of their normally easy, lucid dream recall.) Ushered into the dream chamber and wired to an EEG which will detect REM periods, the subject is told before the experiment begins that when the graph shows that he or she is dreaming, the subject will be awakened by a voice over an intercom and asked to relate the contents of the dream. All conversations are tape recorded.

The agent, in a separate room, sits with a collection of sealed, opaque envelopes. Each coded envelope contains a post-card-sized reproduction of a well-known painting. On the night of the experiment a target picture is randomly chosen for the agent. After the subject and agent briefly meet one another for the first time, to establish some degree of rapport, the agent is escorted to the room at the other end of the corridor, given the sealed envelope, and asked to open it when he is alone. The agent is to look at the picture throughout the night, attempting all the while to transmit his thoughts to the sleeping subject. In the morning, tapes from the dream reports and the target picture are given to an outside panel of judges to determine a statistical degree of correspondence between them.

Of the several hundred dream experiments that Ullman and Krippner have conducted—and more are under way—space allows for only a few representative examples. But they more than make the point. A full series of studies appears in the Parapsychology Foundation monograph: "Dream Studies and Telepathy: An Experimental Approach." It also contains the statistical evaluation of the dreams, which I will omit here.

CASE I

The subject was a woman, call her Barbara, a young teacher from New York City who had no history of psychic dreams. She was fascinated by psychic phenomena, and volunteered for the study. The agent this particular night was Sol Feldstein, then a doctoral student in psychology at the City College of New York. Barbara and Sol had not met before the evening of the experiment. The randomly selected target picture was *Animals* by Tamayo. It depicts two large dogs with white flashing teeth standing over a piece of meat. In the background is a large black rock.

Feldstein, in his private room, concentrated on the details of the picture—its figures, forms, and colors. He tried to visualize Barbara's face, to imagine her sleeping in the dream chamber while he tried to project his thoughts down the corridor. He felt the picture, ran his fingers over it, tracing the outlines of the dogs. After the EEG showed that Barbara had been dreaming for several minutes, she was awakened over the intercom. Here, from the transcribed tapes, is an excerpt from her dream:

> I was at this banquet . . . and I was eating something like rib steak. And this friend of mine was there . . . and people were talking about how she wasn't very good to invite for dinner because she was very conscious of other people getting more to eat than she got, especially meat, because in Israel they don't have so much meat . . . That was the most important part of the dream, that dinner . . . Well, there was another friend of mine, also in this dream. Somebody that I teach with, and she was eyeing everybody to make sure that everybody wasn't getting more than she was too. And I was chewing a piece of . . . rib steak . . . She was not very nice to invite to eat because she was greedy.[11]

This somewhat humorous and revealing dream, by now well known among parapsychologists, never mentioned large dogs or a big black rock, but the central focus on eating meat and the emphasis on the greediness of Barbara's friends are unmistakable elements of the target picture. Although it is impossible to put the correspondences between the dream and the target information on a purely objective basis, the judges rated the chance of mere coincidence correspondence small.

What is most important to note in this, and in all other dream experiments conducted at Maimonides and elsewhere, is the manner in which telepathic information is fragmented and interwoven with the subject's personal experiences. Elements of a target picture seem to implant themselves in the subliminal mind like seeds that are watered and fed by the reservoir of past experiences into full-blown episodes. Here is another case to illustrate this point.

CASE II

The subject was a Ph.D. psychologist, William Erwin; the picture for the evening, Orozco's *Zapatistas,* which depicts a group of Mexican revolution-aries on horseback with clouds and mountains in the background. Here is an excerpt from Erwin's first dream of the evening:

> A storm. Rainstorm. It reminds me of traveling . . . approaching a rainstorm, thunderclouds, rainy . . . a very distant scene . . . For some reason, I get the feeling of memory now, of New Mexico when I lived there. There are a lot of mountains around New Mexico. Indians. Pueblos. Now my thoughts go to almost as though I were thinking of another civilization.[12]

The fact that Erwin once lived in New Mexico may well have facili-tated the direct incorporation of the Mexican element of the picture into his dream. Perhaps, if he had never been in that part of the country, the telepathic information would have entered his dream in a less obvious way. The war element of the painting did not enter the first dream episode, but it clearly worked its way into a later dream that same evening. Excerpt:

> For some reason, I begin to think of . . . was it Lucky Strikes? I remember about the time during the war when they changed the color of their pack . . . and their slogan was, "Lucky Strikes has gone to war."[13]

Again, elements of the target picture surfaced in the dream in direct relation to the dreamer and his past experiences. Such a subtle blending of telepathic information with subconscious memory indicates that many of our seemingly bizarre or uninterpretable dreams may be telepathically trig-gered by the thoughts of a relative or friend. In both the above cases, the significant correspondences would have been missed entirely had the spe-cific targets not been known.

A critic of these experiments could argue, and many have, that the panel of judges, despite their attempted impartiality, are searching the dream reports for words or phrases which have some relationship to ele-ments of the target picture. And, given the fact that the human imagination can unwittingly be stretched quite far, perhaps some parallels between the dreams and the target are inadvertently manufactured rather than telepathically induced. (Unlikely, since judging is done on a blind basis—several possible targets are compared with the dream report.) And how can such an argument account for the numerous direct hits? Here is one representative example, taken from several dozen, that does not require a panel of judges to determine the degree of correspondence.

CASE III

The target picture was George Bellows' *Dempsey and Firpo,* a picture of two boxers, one in the ring and the other falling over the ropes toward the right corner of the picture into a crowded audience. In the first dream of the evening, a twenty-five-year-old male subject gave this report:

> Something about posts. Just posts standing up from the ground and nothing else. There is some kind of feeling of movement . . . Ah, something about Madison Square Garden and a boxing fight. An angular shape . . . an irregular shape coming down from the right. The angular right-hand shape of the picture is connected with Madison Square boxing fight. I had to go to pick up tickets to a boxing fight . . .[14]

It should be made clear, of course, that not all dream studies at Maimonides or at other laboratories have yielded statistically significant results. Such is the nature of psi phenomena. One day a subject will have a dream which bears striking correspondences to the target picture, perhaps even a direct hit. But just as one's mood and health fluctuate, so too does one's psychical receptiveness. The next day the same subject's psychical pool may be completely dry. Of course, this fact does not diminish the reality of telepathy; it only displays our present-day inability to willfully elicit this psychical facet of human personality.

In addition to the many experiments conducted under laboratory conditions, Ullman and Krippner have performed dream tests with less rigorous controls for the amusement and intellectual curiosity of friends. "You don't need expensive laboratory equipment," says Ullman, "to demonstrate the reality of telepathically induced dreams." All one needs is an interesting target picture and two people willing to play the roles of agent and percipient. Of course, it helps if the percipient usually experiences full, storylike dreams and has easy dream recall. On a cruise to Russia, Ullman organized a psi dream clinic with many of the interested passengers. Each evening before retiring the players paired off, and one member of the pair received a target picture from Ullman. That person then attempted to telepathically transmit the picture to the sleeping partner. One young man was so fascinated by the experiments that he set up dates for a series of further experiments with Ullman after the cruise had ended. "I kept a diary of my dreams," says Ullman, who served as percipient, "and on prearranged nights he would try to transmit the target." When Ullman arrived in Vienna on October 15, a letter was waiting for him. It contained the target picture for the night of the thirteenth, a picture from the Beatles' film *The Yellow Submarine*. The picture showed the "Boob" going down the hatch to fix the sub. Ullman opened his notebook. "My dream record for October thirteenth showed a dream about a colleague of mine taking me into a new submarine to explore the water's depths."[15]

Although such "home" experiments can be performed easily enough, Ullman emphasizes that the chances for success are considerably less than when EEG equipment is used. Without the equipment to detect REM periods, there is no way of knowing when the percipient is dreaming and should be awakened for a report. One must wait until morning and hope that the dream, if it occurred, is remembered.

The reality of telepathy in dreams is opening the eyes of many once-antagonistic scientists. Already it has resulted in the first government grants for psychical research. In the early 1970s, Maimonides Medical Center was awarded a two-year, $52,000 grant to continue its psi research. The money came from the National Institute for Mental Health, an agency primarily interested in exploring new and improved techniques for maintaining a high national level of mental health. How do the telepathically induced dream experiments relate to mental problems?

Although this question is just starting to be explored, one obvious suggestion, perhaps the most significant one, comes from the interesting way target material emerges in a person's dream. We know that free-association is an invaluable psychoanalytic tool. Toss the mind a sudden name of a person, place, or thing, and watch the telling responses it triggers. The use of telepathically induced dreams appears to offer an even better way to explore the unconscious mind. A specific target element, such as a meaningful symbol, word, or emotional scene, could be telepathically implanted in a patient's mind. Like a rolling ball of snow, the element gathers bits of information from unconscious memory to fashion a full-fledged dream. But this is not a dream of random, guesswork making, for the very core of the episode, the seed which gives the dream birth, is known. Thus, Ullman believes, dream analysis could begin on more solid ground. Barbara, the young New York teacher, for example, had a dream in which such target elements as greed, viciousness, and fear emerged as traits of two of her friends. Such associations could be quite useful in determining the suppressed feelings that she harbors toward her colleagues. Is there professional rivalry between them? Jealousy? A common lover? The deep-seated psi-induced dream is woven out of unguarded emotion and could suggest meaningful avenues for a psychiatrist to explore.

Another person who is telepathically fed Tamayo's *Animals* might construct a very different dream. A veteran just back from war, for example, might have a dream in which the target elements emerged in a scene of fighting, burning, and killing. The same dream nucleus of greed, viciousness, and fear fed to a mistreated child, on the other hand, might spawn a dream about sadistic parents.

Free-association plants a thought-provoking seed in the *conscious* mind and watches for automatic, telltale sprouts. Telepathy has the decided advantage that the seed is planted deep within the *unconscious* mind; what grows from it, of necessity, must have deeper significance.

EXTRANEOUS MESSAGES

Once we accept the observation that during REM sleep an individual is opened to parasensory information, a straightforward question arises. Why should it be the thoughts of the agent concentrating on the target that are received? Why not the thoughts of the experimenters working in the next room? Or for that matter, a stranger down the hall? Does the telepathic sense have some directionality? Some selectivity?

There is clear evidence that extraneous messages are often received during well-controlled laboratory experiments. One evening at Maimonides, an agent seated in his isolated room was attempting to transmit the scene of Van Gogh's *The Starry Night*. A young psychologist was handling the routine experimental duties of monitoring the EEG printout and tape recording the subject's dreams. During a lull in his chores at about 5:50 A.M., he picked up an issue of *Life* magazine and read two stories. One was on the current summer's fad, topless swimsuits, and the other was entitled "MacArthur's Reminiscences." The article on topless swimsuits contained several descriptive pictures and a photograph of a barebreasted Minoan goddess with a reference to early Egyptian culture. The MacArthur article contained a detailed description of the general's campaigns in the Pacific. At 6:50 A.M., the young experimenter, who had been engrossed in his reading, noticed that the subject, also a young male, was dreaming. He awakened the dreamer and, asking for a report, received a description that had nothing to do with the Van Gogh picture, not a single correspondence. This is what the dreamer reported:

> In a park, and we were talking about two busts—women's busts —busts of Cleopatra . . . And we were arguing about that . . . And a friend of mine was explaining to me that he wanted to go—that he had to go—on several travels, but it was . . . to the island of Gulliver, and people told him . . . "Oh, you will be terribly lonely . . . That island is so lonely and far away in the Pacific . . ."[16]

This type of informational interference, or extraneous pickup, points to a critical issue: the role of the experimenter in any experiment. Since the mid-1920s physicists have realized that the observer and what is being observed are inextricably related in the subatomic realm. This notion is mathematically expressed in Werner Heisenberg's celebrated Uncertainty Principle. Stated in general terms it says that any experimental probe, regardless of how carefully it is done, must to some extent disturb that thing which is being observed. In viewing the atoms of a substance through an electron microscope, for instance, light must be shown on the atoms; its reflection provides the image. But the small quanta of light bombarding the atoms actually disturb their natural behavior, so what one sees is not the original state of the atoms that one set out to view, but those atoms in subtle interaction with the probing tool. Heisenberg showed that a certain amount of ambiguity is always introduced into every experimental observation, ambiguity which can never be overcome. In atomic and subatomic realms, the effect of the experimenter on the experiment is readily comprehended, and often easily measured, for the probing tools are roughly the same size as the atoms being studied. But the fundamental truth embodied in the Uncertainty Principle has validity outside the microworld.

On a broader scale, psychologists have come to recognize the subtle, irreducible interplay between experimenter and subject. Mice that are stroked and fondled daily, for example, learn to execute a maze much faster than their cage mates who are never touched. Such unintentional interaction can be hazardous in any experiment, and it can be all the more misleading in psi research, where the effects under study are so subtle in themselves.

To make matters more complex, extraneous interactions in psi experiments do not have to originate from spatially close sources. In fact, telepathy seems to show a total disregard for distance. The effect does not decrease as the distance increases between percipient and agent; by the same token, stray information can enter the mind of an experimental subject from a person who is emotionally close but spatially distant.

During one dream experiment, a young woman had a dream in which she was in an automobile accident while crossing the Verazzano Bridge from Brooklyn to Staten Island. The details of the dream bore no correspondence with that evening's target picture, and the researchers scored the night a total failure. However, on returning home from the laboratory the next morning, the woman discovered that as her boyfriend had been crossing the same bridge on his motorcycle that night, one of his tires had blown out. He was not injured in the accident, but the mishap held up traffic on the bridge and frightened him quite badly. Apparently, it was enough of a scare to override the thoughts of the agent in the experiment.[17]

The psychical ties between individuals who are emotionally close can be so strong that they make poor experimental subjects when paired with strangers. During another experiment, the same young woman again experienced extraneous pickup. Awakened from REM activity, she reported a dream in which her elderly grandmother was sitting on the floor in a pool of blood. Once again, the details of the dream had no relation to the target picture for that evening. On returning home the following day, however, she learned that her grandmother had fallen during the night, cutting her head on the edge of a wall. She was found by a relative, bleeding from the gash on her forehead.[18]

It would seem that out of the variety of telepathic impressions impinging on a person during dream consciousness, each individual experiences those sensations most significant to himself or herself. This is not to say that we consciously choose one particular telepathic message over another in the sense that we can choose between vanilla and chocolate ice cream. But it does appear that at some unconscious depth a particular message, rather than another one, is interpreted as being important to the organism when measured against a stored file of information; once recognized and interpreted, the message is passed on to a level of awareness.

If the telepathic sense has some measure of selectivity, albeit beyond one's conscious control, what about directionality? Is it enough for an agent merely to think of the target, or must the agent attempt to direct his or her thoughts to a specific subject at a specified location?

To date, most experiments have shown that it is important for the agent to be aware of the identity and location of the percipient. This is why the agent and percipient are always introduced and chat for a while in psi-induced dream experiments before the tests begin. Dr. Krippner feels that this essential communication establishes an informational bridge, a sort of shared communications channel, which he says "lingers on after the parties have separated."

Although knowing the identity and location of a percipient is an important factor in telepathic transmission, success has been achieved when only one is known. (Whether the combined parameters are more potent than either taken separately has not been experimentally established. But common sense, if it can be called upon in psychical research, certainly suggests this is true.)

One of several experiments which suggests the directionality importance of psi, using only the factor of geographical location, also involves a novel twist in experimental procedure. The agent was not a single individual, but 2,000 young people attending a rock concert at the Capitol Theater in Port Chester, New York, a distance of forty-five miles from the dream laboratory. In the lab's dream chamber was one subject, Malcolm Bessent, an English sensitive with an impressive history of psychic events. A second subject, Felicia Parise, a hospital hematologist, was sleeping at her home in another part of Brooklyn. (Ms. Parise had already demonstrated a strong telepathic talent in previous dream experiments.) Bessent was to be awakened by the experimenter whenever he was dreaming, and Ms. Parise would be awakened for dream reports by phone calls timed to correspond to her well-known pattern of REM activity.

The experiment was conducted during six different rock concerts, with six different audiences. Each time a target picture was projected on the theater screen, and the audience was told they were to visualize the details of the picture and attempt to send it mentally to a male subject (they had not met Bessent) who was sleeping at the dream laboratory in Brooklyn. The 2,000 agents were not told that Ms. Parise also was part of the experiment. Her identity and location were kept secret.

One evening, the target was Scralian's painting *The Seven Spinal Chakras.* It depicts a man in a lotus position practicing yoga meditation. All seven "chakras" (alleged energy centers of the body centering around the spinal column) are vividly colored. The picture was projected on the theater screen for several minutes, and 2,000 people jointly concentrated on it.

Each phone call to Ms. Parise recorded her results—an evening of experimentally meaningless dreams. But Bessent's first dream was uncannily close to the target:

I was very interested in using natural energy . . . I was talking to this guy who said he'd invented a way of using solar energy and he showed me this box . . . to catch the light from the sun which was all we needed to generate and store the energy . . . I was discussing with this guy a number of other areas of communication and we were exchanging ideas on the whole thing. He was suspended in mid-air or something . . . I was thinking about rocket ships . . . I'm remembering a dream I had about an energy box and . . . a spinal column.[19]

No conclusions can be drawn from this experiment, isolated as it is, especially because of its new and unusual design. But the bulk of telepathy research does indicate that selectivity and directionality, two aspects characteristic of all information propagation phenomena, are also features of psychical transmission and reception.

In this way, slowly and in piecemeal fashion, the bits of the psychical puzzle are beginning to fit together, and psi-induced dream experiments have been a major contributing factor. Although Dr. Krippner would be among the first to say that the pieces still do not form a whole, comprehendible picture, he is not hesitant to speak of the implications of telepathy. In an interview with *Psychic* magazine, Krippner spoke in terms somewhat more philosophical than those he uses in the laboratory: "It's my hunch that we'll eventually have to revise our image of man on the basis of telepathic evidence. At present, psychology views each person as an alienated man, cut off from his surroundings. He is basically alone. Telepathy may teach us that in the basic fabric of life everything and everyone is linked, that man is continuously enmeshed, that he is always an integral part of all life on the face of the earth."[20]

MULTISENSORY EXPERIENCES

The work at Maimonides is by no means the only psi-induced dream research. Ullman and Krippner's experiments of the mid-1960s excited psychical researchers throughout the world. Their experimental design is so beautifully simple and the high promise of success so enticing that dream experiments have been tried, and successfully duplicated, by other laboratories. Some innovative researchers have performed variations on the Maimonides setup, trying to devise procedures that increase the degree of success. Although not all variations have met with positive results, as must be expected, a few novel twists are extremely promising.

Hoping to strengthen the statistical evaluation of the experiment, some researchers have used simpler targets: circles, triangles, and superimposed geometrical figures. The less target detail, they reason, the easier it is to find unambiguous correspondences between a target and a dream report. But the dearth of emotional content in these figures has caused them to be poor targets. There is less chance for a subject to perceive information from a bland, emotionless target like a circle or square than from one that is richly colored and dynamic, one that the subject can relate to easily. Also, there is less chance for successful transmission if the agent is not deeply involved with the material he or she is attempting to transmit. A target that does not hold the agent's attention, one that is boring rather than exciting, is not likely to be telepathically transmitted. These facts have caused other researchers to *increase* the dynamic content of their targets. Some of the approaches have been ingenious.

In one highly successful variation, art prints were chosen for targets only if they combined emotional content, vivid colors, and archetypal themes. To these high informational targets were added a variety of multisensory material to fully involve the agent in the target theme. For example, when the target picture was *The Descent from the Cross* by Beckman, a painting of Christ being taken down from the cross, the multisensory materials included a wooden cross, a picture of Christ, thumbtacks, and a red ink pen. The agent was told to concentrate on the target print and also to tack the picture of Christ to the cross and color the wounds with the red pen.[21] Of course, every new variable added to an experiment also brings the potential for new problems. The agent in this particular experiment was Jewish. How that may have affected the results remains unknown.

At the University of Virginia, Dr. Calvin Hall has tried still another approach to engage the agent more fully in the theme he or she is to transmit telepathically. In Hall's experiments the agent pantomimes a randomly selected scene as the target material—activities such as exploring a cave, chopping wood, or cutting one's finger. He is told to think, feel, and believably act out the particular target experience. Hall also has conducted successful experiments in which some of the percipients did not know that information was being telepathically sent to them. In one study, only three out of six subjects knew that while they slept telepathic induction would be attempted. The unsuspecting trio thought they were participating in a sleep study. When all six people were awakened from REM periods and asked for dream reports, Hall found that in twenty-nine out of thirty-six cases direct elements from the pantomime situation were unmistakably contained in the reported dreams; this was true whether or not the subject knew in advance that psi induction would be attempted.[22] Thus, knowing that a message is going to be sent does not appear to enhance the probability of reception. The dreamer seems to be a passive receiver.

The new psychical research is still very young and many paths which promise rich rewards have not yet been investigated. One propitious area related to the dream experiments involves using an agent and percipient who are related emotionally, such as lovers, or by blood, such as a mother and child or a brother and sister. The strong emotional and physical ties might serve to greatly increase telepathic communications. The woman who dreamed of the accidents of her boyfriend and grandmother rather than the target picture is an example. Carrying this line of reasoning a step further, we can imagine a psi-induced dream experiment in which the agent and percipient are twins; still more ideal would be subjects who are identical twins, individuals who sprang from the same egg and sperm, and possess identical genetic blueprints. The physiological similarities between such doubles is so total that during dream consciousness one twin might be extraordinarily receptive to the telepathic transmissions of the other. Popular psi literature, and brain wave research to be cited later, strongly support this conjecture. If the first decade of dream experiments has yielded such impressive results using percipients and agents who are strangers, what success might some of these other combinations yield?

Dr. Krippner, who is now professor of psychology at Sonoma State College in California, laments the fact that more psi experimentation has not been done with young children. Anecdotal material suggests that children are exceptionally psychic. "One of the great needs in the field of parapsychology," says Krippner, "is to study the psychic potential of children and infants. There is reason to believe that the results would be very impressive." Besides the anecdotal evidence, Krippner is particularly excited by the fact that the younger the child, the more sleep time spent in REM cycles. A middle-aged adult spends about fifteen percent of the night's sleep in REM activity; a teen-ager spends about twenty percent; a three-year-old child, about thirty percent; a five-week-old infant, forty percent; a full-term newborn baby, fifty percent, and a premature baby, eighty percent. Logically it would seem, the more time spent in REM sleep, the greater the probability for paranormal happenings. Thus an agent–percipient team of a mother and her young child in a dream experiment might be an impressive combination—the mother possessing the ability to concentrate intensely on the target, and the child serving as the passive, closely linked receiver, falling into REM sleep for large segments of the night.

To carry this thinking a step further, it is believed that the brain of an unborn child idles constantly in REM sleep. Researchers feel that this electrical activity is related to the development of the sensory areas of the brain, especially binocular vision.

Since the brain during REM bursts is primed for the reception of parasensory information, the psychic potential of a fetus may be extraordinary. No one knows what psychical implications this fact holds, but Dr. Krippner has a theory. "It is quite possible," he says, "that while the child is physically forming in the uterus, it is in constant telepathic communications with the mother."[23]

If for a moment we let speculation run its course, we are led from the unvarying pattern of increasing REM activity with decreasing age to an interesting possibility. Extrapolating the phenomenon to its origin, it is possible that at the moment of conception, as the seed of consciousness is plucked from the primal pool, it is in full psychic communication with the entirety of nature. But gradually, as the cell cluster multiplies from embryo to fetus, as the infant is born and begins to grow to maturity, becoming his or her own person, establishing an ego, the psychic ties with nature may progressively fade. The notion is certainly not new; it has been held by Bergson, Jung, and the Eastern mystics, and is popular among many modern-day parapsychologists. What *is* new is that for the first time in history research is closing in on the possibility.

Telepathy for Everyone?

Are *you* psychic? What are the chances that *you* can experience paranormal phenomena?

Such questions are meaningful in light of the teachings of modern dream theory, for one of its unquestionable tenets is that all people dream, the sane and insane, the young and old. Does this mean that all humans are opened to parasensory information during dreaming?

Theoretically the answer is "yes," but in practice it is a big "maybe." We know that there is a considerable degree of variation in the subjective aspect of dreaming. A small number of people, even when they are awakened in the middle of a REM burst, cannot recall having a dream. They have a psychological barrier that prevents them from bringing information gleaned in the dream state back to wakefulness. The question we should ask is not—"Are all humans receptive to parasensory information during dream consciousness?" but—"What type of individual has full-blown dreams and easy, lucid dream recall?"

According to modern dream theory, dreaming is greatly facilitated in individuals who place a high value on the depth and spectrum of human feelings. Such people will normally be engaged in imaginative activities rather than rote, mechanical ones; they will be introspective, the thinkers, the creators. These people have rich and pregnant dreams, and "For these people," writes the eminent sleep researcher Dr. David Foulkes in *The Psychology of Sleep*, "dreaming may represent a fruitful resource, a means of augmenting the cognitive dimension of life."[24] On the other hand, the person who accepts without questioning, who acts rather than ponders, and who is content with the status quo, usually has a dream consciousness that plays a small to nonexistent role in his or her growth and development.

In a 1965 study, reported in the *Journal of Consulting Psychology*, standard creativity tests were administered to 105 college students who had faithfully kept dream diaries. Results showed that the students who scored highest on the creativity tests recorded the most imaginative, detailed, and storylike dreams. On the other hand, sparse dreams, devoid of rich detail and color, largely unimaginative, were found in the dream diaries of the low-scoring students. The study also suggested that art and music students remember their dreams much more frequently than science and engineering majors.

But this dream differentiation between personality types is not as clear-cut as it may sound. There are an exceptional number of individuals who never recall a dream spontaneously, yet if intentionally awakened during a REM flare, they relate the most cinematic experiences. Unfortunately, these individuals, who are highly primed for parasensory reception, never become aware of it. Such information may be lost forever to subconscious memory.

It is interesting to note that many nondreamers (i.e., "nonrecallers") have REM periods marked by more cortical brain activity and more rapid eye movement than do many dreamers. These nondreamers are actually having more vivid dreams than the dreamers. "But," says Foulkes, "it may be precisely because [their] psychophysiological state is more aroused and the associated content presumably more vivid or intimate, that [they are] motivated to forget their dreams."[25] This notion of forgetfulness due to embarrassment or fear is supported by the fact that nondreamers tend to score high on psychological tests which measure repression and inhibition. It has also been suggested by many psi researchers that the fear-associated inability to remember one's dreams may in some cases be caused by the paranormal content of the dream. It may forecast an accident, illness, or death which the dreamer does not wish to confront. Dr. Louisa E. Rhine, wife of J. B. Rhine, relates one such incident. A mother reported having the following dream:

> I dreamed I was bathing the children and left the bathroom a
> minute to run to the kitchen to get the towels, where I had placed

them in the oven to warm. While [I was] in the kitchen the children played a few minutes in the tub. When I got back to the bathroom I was horror-struck to find little Brad lying underwater at the bottom of the tub. I grabbed him, he was unconscious and his finger tips and lips were blue. I put him across my lap with his head down and started working feverishly over him. At this point, as dreams so often do, it faded.

On awakening the next morning the mother had no recollection of having dreamed at all. She saw her husband off to work and went about her morning chores. "At lunch time," she says, "I put a couple of towels in the oven to warm and then went on to the bathing of the babies. Before taking them from the tub I went into the kitchen to get the towels." Still the mother had no recollection of her horrifying dream; something in her psyche was holding it under the surface. She started tidying up the kitchen when she heard a sound. At that point the dream finally came back to her. "I flew into the bathroom," she says, "and found Brad exactly as I feared I might; he was lying absolutely still under the water. I had him out in a flash and even though I was filled with terror I noted the blueness of his lips and fingers."[26]

Fortunately, the child was revived through mouth-to-mouth resuscitation. But had the mother recalled the dream on awakening, or during the morning hours, the incident might have been prevented. How many significant dreams, perhaps psychical dreams, are lost due to suppressed dream recall?

There are many variables that affect dreaming and consequently influence one's psychic potential during dream mentation. The years of psi-induced dream experiments have revealed some of these. Dreams, for example, in which a person appears as a passive observer show more psi correspondences with target pictures than dreams in which the subject is an active participant.[27] Why this is true is not understood.

In the hundreds of tests conducted in psi-induced dreams a sex-dependent variable has also emerged. Although the correlation is weak, the best psi results have come from all-male percipient–agent teams. The next best performance occurs when the agent is female and the percipient male. And the least successful psychical combination is a team with women at both ends of the communications line. Just what this implies is still unclear.

Despite many unanswered questions on the nature and mechanism of psi, today one thing is quite clear—dream consciousness is a psychically pregnant state, and a potent tool for probing the paranormal nature of the human being. This being the case, is there anything the average person can do to increase his or her chances of experiencing parasensory information? Dr. Krippner, who has performed years of psi-induced dream experiments, feels there is. Here are his recommendations:

1. Each night before retiring tell yourself that you *will* recall your dreams. Place a pad and pencil next to the bed to reinforce the idea. These positive gestures may often be enough to trigger dream recall.

2. While drifting off to sleep, tell yourself that you will probably have four to seven periods of dream consciousness, and that dreaming is a common, healthy phenomenon, a bridge to the paranormal world.

3. Awaken gradually if possible. A gentle return to wakeful consciousness is better for dream recall than leaping quickly for the alarm.

4. Don't get out of bed immediately. Let your mind dwell on the first association which pops into it. Then try to encourage additional associations. You may find that a few words or images will suddenly spring into a full-blown episode.

5. Keep a notebook for recording your dream experiences. When a number of them have accumulated, see if they reveal any recurring theme, locale, or symbol. Remember that any thread of parasensory information—telepathic, clairvoyant, or precognitive—probably entered your dream woven in with past experiences.

6. Remember that since the REM periods increase in length toward morning, your longest and most detailed dreams come near the end of a full night's sleep.

7. A factor that has proven successful in increasing dream activity is the luxury of isolation. Days spent alone in a single room, writing, painting, or listening to music, lengthen and intensify that evening's dream consciousness, and thus enhance the probability for paranormal occurrences.[28]

2
Hypnosis and Psi

We must remember that what we see is not Nature, but Nature exposed to our method of questioning.

Werner Heisenberg

The Pliant Mind

A twenty-two-year-old man named John sits at the front of a brightly painted yellow room. The drapes at the windows lining the west side of the room have been partially drawn to mute the afternoon sunlight. John is not alone. Beside him stands a psychiatrist, an internationally known expert on hypnosis, and in front of him is a captive group of psychology graduate students who have come to witness a simple, striking demonstration. John, already in a deep hypnotic trance, does not see the graduate students, even though his eyes are open and directed at them. The instructor walks toward him and in a soft, reassuring voice, similar to the one he used minutes before to hypnotize John, tells him: "John, you are in a very deep, restful trance. Your whole body is soft and pliable. Rubbery. And your mind is calmer than it has ever been before. It is devoid of all thoughts. I want you to listen carefully to what I'm about to say." The students know what is coming; they've read about it. It is part of their studies in spatial perception under hypnosis, but all the same, this will be the first time they actually see it.

"John," the instructor continues, "you are beginning to lose the dimension of depth. Soon it will no longer exist for you. You will be in a planar world of length and width. There will be no depth." The effect of the suggestion is immediate. John's face contorts in horror, and his body begins to quiver. He lifts his feet from the floor as though it were red hot and pulls them up to his chest, wrapping his arms tightly around his legs. He is snugly locked in a fetal position with his head tucked between his knees. The students hurriedly take notes: *immediate and marked schizophreniform behavior, severe catatonic features, facial pallor. . . .* The instructor asks John, who is now a human knot, for a verbal description of what he's experiencing. With some difficulty it comes. *The ceiling is coming closer and closer. The walls are advancing inward. The room is the size of a broom closet and still shrinking.* The description sounds like a horror fantasy from an Edgar Allan Poe tale.

Then, in the same reassuring, monotone voice, the instructor reverses the suggestion. The dimension of depth is being restored. Slowly John begins to loosen up. The tenseness vanishes from his face. He raises his head fully, lowers his feet to the floor, and sits upright in the chair. Relaxed. Calm. He is back in three-dimensional space.[1]

There is nothing unique about this scene. The abolition of space is a canonical trance suggestion demonstrated in many advanced classes on hypnosis. It is not difficult to induce in a good hypnotic subject, and under competent hands it is innocuous enough. Yet demonstrations of spatial distortion, as well as those of time distortion, are profound phenomena which are helping to shed light on the possible mechanisms underlying psi perception. John's physical body existed in three-dimensional space, but for a time his mind did not. The shrinking room was *real* to John, and he reacted according to what he "perceived."

There is an all too easy tendency to dismiss John's experience as being only a figment of his imagination—a suggested and artificial idea; the room did not *really* shrink we say. But to harbor this attitude is to miss the very essence of the demonstration. For John, perceiving through hypnotic consciousness, the room truly did shrink. His experience of the moving walls and ceiling was as real to him as the stationary walls and ceiling were to the instructor and the students. To argue that John perceived only a subjective reality (as he did) is to ignore the fact that the instructor's reality is also subjective. John's world was not the same as the instructor's from the moment he surrendered wakeful consciousness. One standard definition of a good hypnotic subject makes this point clear: "A good hypnotic subject may be defined as a person who has the ability to give up voluntarily his usual reality-orientation to a considerable extent, and who can concurrently build up a new special orientation to reality which temporarily becomes the *only possible reality* for him in his phenomenal awareness."[2] (Italics added.) Given his new reality-orientation, the room *did* shrink for John.

To argue that John's subjective reality is not experimentally verifiable, whereas measuring devices can reassure the instructor that the walls and ceiling are stationary, is to miss the entire significance of altered states of consciousness. Physical measurements of the room might reassure the instructor that the walls and ceiling are stationary, but to John the measurements would be meaningless. Two people can debate a common issue when they share a common reality-orientation, but when they are entrenched in different realities, the issues lose their commonality.*

One salient feature of hypnosis in parapsychological research is that nothing seems impossible to a good hypnotic subject; that is, nothing is impossible because of preconceived constraints. The subject suspends ordinary disbelief, replacing wakeful logic and behaviorally learned constraints with whatever reality-orientation is suggested to him. And "out-of-the-world" psi phenomena, through appropriate depth of trance and suggestions, fall well within this new world. This is not to say that every hypnotized person spontaneously experiences telepathic or clairvoyant events; certainly not, or else parapsychology would have come of age years ago along with hypnosis. But with the careful construction of a new reality-orientation, one lacking the learned constraints of wakeful consciousness, modern research is showing that a person's parasenses have an excellent change of surfacing.

The psi potential of the pliant, amorphous mentation which becomes possible through hypnosis is not something that psi researchers have just recently stumbled on. In fact, trance states are as old as man's godly and demonic rituals and have been inextricably linked with paranormal phenomena since antiquity.

Through soothing incantations and droning tribal drums, witch doctors and shamans have shifted the psyches of entire tribes into altered states of consciousness. Such states, the primitives believed, were necessary to heal the sick and to receive divine revelations. The limitations of wakeful consciousness were clear to the most sophisticated ancients and intuitively oriented savages. Wakefulness had its place in activities such as hunting, governing, and building villages, but it was grossly inadequate for catching a "glimpse of the glory."

The modern history of hypnotic consciousness and its relation to paranormal events began during the latter part of the eighteenth century with Franz Anton Mesmer, the revolutionary Viennese physician, who noted several instances of psi phenomena occurring under hypnosis. Compelled

---

*For a superb discussion of the scientific method related to various phenomena of altered states of consciousness see Charles Tart, "States of Consciousness and State-Specific Sciences," *Science,* June 16, 1972, pp. 1203–1210.

to leave Vienna under the cold and eventually hostile shadow cast by his professional colleagues over what they called the "trickery" of Mesmer's hypnotic technique, he traveled to Paris. There he found not only refuge, but encouragement. To the delight of thousands, he gave demonstrations of "traveling clairvoyance"—a means by which a person obtains information of distant places and events by allegedly journeying in spirit to the locale. As Mesmer wrote of the hypnotic subject in his famous work on animal magnetism:* "Sometimes, through his inner sensibilities, the somnambulist can distinctly see the past and future."[3] This, he observed, was not true of all hypnotized subjects. In fact, it was rare, but it did happen.

Such clairvoyance happened most often and dramatically through one of Mesmer's stellar somnambulists, a peasant boy named Victor Race, who was able under hypnosis to diagnose illness with uncanny accuracy. As the story goes, in his trances, this largely unschooled boy, wholly ignorant of medical terminology, became an instant and fluent diagnostician. Bacterial infections, viruses and warts, eye dysfunctions and abdominal occlusions were laid open to him more clearly than they would have been in X-ray pictures—a technique which was not developed for another fifty years.

Nor was Mesmer alone. In England, hypnosis was a humane tool that preceded the discovery of anesthesia, and a few open-minded physicians of the day, most notably the surgeon James Esdaile, performed some 3,000 operations using it—including 300 major surgeries. They observed an impressive decline in the instances of postoperative infection, a stunning feat in a time when surgeons washed their hands after an operation rather than before it. Esadile believed that some mysterious aspect of hypnotism elevated a person's immunity. But despite the impressive medical accomplishments of a few physicians of the day, Mesmer was struck more by the psi manifestations which occurred in a trance. He often observed that his best hypnotic subjects would verbalize thoughts that he was thinking but had not expressed.

The phenomenon of parasensory communication between hypnotist and subject received special attention in 1823 from the French scientist A. J. F. Bertrand. Bertrand observed that the degree of telepathy under hypnosis depended strongly on the interpersonal relationship between the hypnotist and his subject, a fact that has been dramatically demonstrated by

*The words *hypnotism, mesmerism,* and *animal magnetism* are often used synonymously. The last two have the same meaning: the trance was induced by passing the hands over the body of the subject; no verbal suggestions were given.

several modern researchers. As Bertrand's records have it, on many occasions when he gave a specific verbal order to a subject, while he himself was thinking the exact opposite, the subject tensed, became confused and distressed, and remained that way until Bertrand made his verbal suggestion agree with his mental one. "Write your first name," Bertrand told one of his easily hypnotized subjects, all the while thinking of the man's last name. The subject squirmed in his seat and the pencil in his hand gyrated above the paper, but it would not touch down. The man's face tensed as though he were deliberating some life-or-death choice; a war raged between his hand and his mind. Only minutes later, when Bertrand told him the thought he actually harbored, did the subject relax, and immediately proceed to write his surname.

Hypnosis had its heyday during the mid-nineteenth century, and the investigation of paranormal phenomena in trance states flourished. One of the most authentic reports of that period, if any could be regarded as authentic by today's strict standards, was made by two eminent French physicians, Claude Richet and Pierre Janet. Their subject was a young girl named Leonie, who experienced clairvoyant perception while in a hypnotic trance. During one experiment, Leonie shocked Dr. Richet by informing him that his Paris laboratory, many miles away, was on fire. Indeed, the laboratory burned to the ground at the very time Richet and Janet were trying to calm their subject.

Hypnosis was fashionable then, and the literature of the period is so extensive that a recent summary by Eric J. Dingwall *(Abnormal Hypnotic Phenomena)* fills four thick volumes. Dr. Robert Van de Castle, a prominent psi researcher and University of Virginia psychologist, has classified the multitude of cases contained in Dingwall's scholarly work into four important categories: Transposition of Senses, Community of Sensation, Traveling Clairvoyance, and Hypnosis Induced at a Distance.[4] Since each heading is backed by modern-day experiments, they merit a closer look.

TRANSPOSITION OF SENSES

The phrase simply means an apparent interchange of two or more senses. For example, on hearing music a hypnotized subject might experience a visual display or a taste, or a bite into a fresh lemon might be "heard" by the hypnotized person as a loud bang. The psychic phenomenon of derma vision (Chapter 6), in which a person "sees" with his skin, is an ostensible manifestation of the transposition of senses.

COMMUNITY OF SENSATION

Here, for example, a hypnotist pricks his own finger with a pin and the hypnotized subject, eyes closed or in a different room, reacts to the pain. A nineteenth-century physician, Dr. J. Azam, supposedly had a male subject who could telepathically taste whatever Azam put into his own mouth. Azam discovered this quite by accident. One day, after having worked many weeks with the boy to achieve a deep trance, Azam bit into a tart green apple. The boy was across the room, his eyes were closed, and almost immediately his lips puckered and he wrinkled his nose. Azam experimented further, putting sweet and sour things into his own mouth, first while the boy's back was toward him, and later placing him in a separate room. But the boy could always identify the food Azam tasted; the hypnotic trance had forged a psychic link between hypnotist and subject. We need not accept Azam's century-old experiments though to tell us that hypnosis can psychically link hypnotist to subject, or, for that matter, one hypnotized person to another; several modern experiments, as we shall see, unequivocally make the point.

TRAVELING CLAIRVOYANCE

Here the hypnotized subject is instructed to travel psychically to some distant place and report on events taking place there. The case of Leonie is one example, and the section on Out-of-the-Body experiences in Chapter 5 offers some current views and recent experiments conducted in this area.

HYPNOSIS INDUCED AT A DISTANCE

Here, the hypnotist and the subject are out of each other's sight and hearing, yet the hypnotist induces a trance and gives hypnotic and posthypnotic suggestions to the subject. Dr. Richet and Dr. Janet, working with Leonie, supposedly succeeded in hypnotizing her at a distance in nineteen out of twenty-five attempts. Although Richet would stand in one room, many feet from the room in which Leonie was reclining, the very moment he willed her into a trance her eyes became glassy and her body musculature relaxed. With Janet observing Leonie, Richet was able to telepathically instruct her to raise and lower her arm, to have her write messages, and even to implant posthypnotic suggestions. Again, we need not accept the "old" experiments (which we have a tendency to disbelieve as though each passing year further tarnishes their credibility), for current research on hypnosis and psi quite nicely dusts many of the cobwebs off the old stories.

Fashions, by definition, eventually die, and as the twentieth century dawned, dark clouds had already begun to form around hypnosis as a research tools; its days of glory faded. One reason perhaps was the popularity of stage hypnotists; what legitimate scientists would consider as a serious laboratory procedure a technique employed by magicians on the theatrical stages of Europe and America? Another was the strong pronouncement Freud made against hypnosis as a psychoanalytical tool (a distaste which may have stemmed from his difficulty in inducing a trance state). Even in the parapsychological coterie, the highly psi-favorable hypnotic state was looked on by many with suspicion. This was due in part to the attitude held by the pioneer American parapsychologist, Dr. J. B. Rhine. Rhine felt that hypnosis was not a phenomenon of a different level of consciousness, but merely "a state of highly restricted consciousness to the point where attention is focused in a highly controlled fashion on a small area designated by the hypnotist."[5] This highly controlled attention, Rhine felt, was actually concentrated wakeful consciousness and therefore was even less conducive to psi events than the normal wakeful state.

In the cyclic pattern characteristic of fashions, locusts, and sunspots, hypnosis as a psychical tool has returned, and much of the present interest springs directly and unavoidably from the birth of the science of ASCs. If one is probing different mentations for their myriad prodigies, a state as priceless as hypnotic consciousness, with its easily induced and readily duplicated effects of space-time distortion and illogical logic, can hardly be overlooked. Stanley Krippner and Charles Honorton, a fellow Maimonides' parapsychologist, have surveyed the work of the last two decades in their paper "Hypnosis and ESP Performance: A Review of the Experimental Literature" and found the frontier glowing. Largely from work carried out in the 1960s, Krippner and Honorton have drawn three conclusions: (1) Hypnosis does enhance paranormal perception; they note: "Nine of the twelve studies involving direct comparison of ESP performance in hypnosis and the waking state yielded significant treatment differences. . . . This would appear to be a rather impressive level of replicability, particularly in view of the fact that seven independent investigators were involved." (2) Hypnosis affects the *magnitude* rather than the *direction* of ESP performance—that is, some hypnotic subjects score statistically significant negative results (called psi-missing). (3) The significant psi results derived from hypnosis are not merely the result of direct suggestions for success. (More on this point later.) Krippner and Honorton conclude their paper with the following comment: "While many problems of both methodological and interpretive importance remain to be resolved, it would appear that hypnosis provides one of the few presently available techniques for affecting the level of psi test performance."[6] This we shall now see.

Awakening The Parasenses

It was spring, 1970 and the morning activity at the Elmhurst Medical Center in Queens, New York, was busy, though not unusually so for a big city hospital. The night shift had just gone off duty, and a fresh, energetic team of doctors and nurses were beginning their rounds. Already several patients lay on stretchers waiting to be X-rayed; outpatients stood at the doors of the clinic which would open soon; several teams of nurses were readying the operating rooms for morning surgery. Amidst the excitement and confusion, however, something unusual was happening in the east end of the building. While other nurses checked patients' charts, took temperatures, and dispensed pills of every color and shape, one R. N., a twenty-three-year-old woman named Beth, sat motionless in a dimiy lit room. She had a detached look on her face, oblivious to the chaos in the halls, and her body was just slightly slumped forward. Beside her, Dr. Burton S. Glick was putting a silver fountain pen into the pocket of his white smock; he had just used the metallic object to hypnotize Beth.

"Your right arm is as light as a feather," said Glick to test her degree of suggestibility by arm levitation. "Imagine that a helium-filled balloon is tied around your wrist." Slowly Beth's right arm floated upward. When it returned, at Glick's suggestion, he told her that the arm was now as stiff as a piece of granite. Immediately catalepsy set in. Glick smiled. Beth was deeply hypnotized. Unlike the hypnosis scenario recounted earlier, Glick did not tell Beth that the dimension of depth had vanished or that time had stopped. Instead, he crossed the room to a large box, withdrew something, and brought it over to Beth. "I'm placing an envelope on your lap," he said in a soft, smooth voice. Actually it was two envelopes in a third, sealed, and opaque to the brightest bulb. Then, in a firm voice full of confidence, Glick launched the most unique event that had ever occurred at the medical center: "I want you to think as clearly and vividly as you can about the picture in the envelope that is resting on your lap. If you wish, you may hold the envelope in your hands. You will concentrate so hard on the picture that it will seem as though you are walking right into it. You will participate in whatever action is depicted. You will see everything very clearly because you will be part of it. When I count to three, you will start telling me all of your thoughts, fantasies, visions, associations, feelings, and moods concerning the picture."[7]

Beth was no psychic. She had never had even a single paranormal experience. But she did believe in such phenomena, and she was willing to be a subject in Glick's clairvoyance experiment. If anyone was a non-believer, it was Glick—or it *had been* Glick. As recently as a month prior to the experiment he would not have wasted his time with such nonsense, or jeopardized his reputation as a treating psychiatrist at Elmhurst and chief of psychiatric research at New York's Mount Sinai Hospital. Now last month's skeptic was asking a twenty-three-year-old nurse to walk mentally through a sealed succession of envelopes, merge with the picture inside, and take part in the action it depicted. Obviously, something had changed Glick's mind. The lightning bolt that had struck Glick and awakened his interest in psychical phenomena did not come from the sky; it sprang rather from a recent issue of the *American Journal of Psychiatry* in the form of a lengthy paper entitled "An Experimental Approach to Dreams and Telepathy." The paper was written by two men Glick had never heard of: Montague Ullman and Stanley Krippner. The snowball was rolling. Had the paper appeared somewhere else—in *Fate* or *The Occultist* or *Popular Witchcraft*—Glick certainly would never have seen it, or if through some strange set of circumstances he had, he would have laughed it off as the work of two colleagues who were themselves in need of psychiatric help. But here was the unlikely paper in a publication Glick had been reading since his days in medical school, a journal that he highly respected, one he had published in himself. "I was excited," he says today. "Their experimental approach was so simple, so foolproof, so thorough. And their results were so enticingly positive. I had to try it myself."[8]

Glick adopted many of the Maimonides group's procedures, using art prints sealed in opaque envelopes and randomly selected for test runs. But lacking the equipment to conduct dream studies as the Maimonides group had, Glick looked for a different approach. Wakeful consciousness, he read, was not a psi-favorable state. Dreaming was, but he lacked the necessary equipment. What about hypnosis, he wondered? External stimuli could easily be excluded and that would satisfy one of the prerequisites for psi. Not familiar with the current psi literature, Glick did not realize that a handful of successful hypnosis experiments had already been conducted, establishing hypnotic consciousness as a psi-favorable state. But he was quite familiar with hypnosis itself; he worked with it often, and from what psi material he had recently read, hypnosis seemed to fit the bill. To simplify his experiment one step further, he decided to eliminate the need for an agent by attempting to demonstrate clairvoyance rather than telepathy.

The print in the envelope that morning was *The Gulf Stream* by Winslow Homer; it had been randomly selected from a pool of twenty. It depicts a man stranded on a boat, suffering; his face is filled with pain as he tries to keep the craft from going under. When Glick finished his command to Beth—"When I count to three you will start telling me all of your thoughts, fantasies, visions, associations, feelings, and moods concerning the picture"—he stood there, not knowing what to expect. Beth could have remained silent or she could have uttered an infinite number of fantasies having nothing to do with the picture in the envelope. For a moment he had an image of himself as Svengali, trying to turn a tone-deaf Trilby into a brilliant singer. But Beth's words convinced him that he was no fool; indeed, they sent a cold rush of excitement and awe up his spine.

Here, transcribed directly from the tape recording of the session, is what Beth "saw":

> There's a figure—the figure in the foreground—a figure that's suffering—more than suffering—the figure is in great pain.
>
> It's a beautiful scene, though; the scene in the background is beautiful and the figure doesn't belong in that scene. Trees, and the colors—beautiful colors. The figure can't move; the figure can't see, can't see the—everything around him he can't see. It's a man.
>
> Everything is—the background is in perspective. It's just a beautiful scene, a scene of nature. It's very realistic but the figure is distorted. It's almost as though the figure is stretched out—on top of something; no, against something. Everything is going— everything is swirling around him, but nothing is really moving. I don't know if he's moving, swirling, spinning around. No. Everything around him is moving. He's standing still.
>
> Everything is sort of the same. Nothing's changed in the scene—but, now, he's changing. He thinks he's in pain but he's not. But he is suffering.*[9]

---

*Two impartial judges, both psychiatrists, using a modified Maimonides rating system, scored the correspondence between the picture and the subject's report seventy percent and eighty percent respectively.

Since that first morning Glick has conducted other experiments, some with Beth and some with a twenty-six-year-old recreational therapist at the hospital. As must be expected, the results have been mixed: some direct hits, a few partial successes, and some direct misses. Such is the frustrating flightiness of psi phenomena—or at least our present ability to elicit them. But Glick's overall results have been positive. "I don't know how to explain them," he admits. "I wouldn't even begin to try. But I'm now convinced that certain people in particular mental states do experience a substantial augmentation of their sensory apparatus. Some of our hits were unbelievably direct."[10]

In an experiment such as Glick's or the Maimonides dream experiments, it is not easy to subject the data to hard, cold statistical analysis. The subject is not guessing one card out of a deck of fifty-two, with a corresponding probability of one out of fifty-two associated with each guess. Such card or dice tests, conducted with a finite number of possible outcomes, lend themselves readily to standard mathematical procedures. But in Glick's experiment, there were not twenty or thirty or fifty-two different fantasies Beth could have reported; there were an infinite number of them, one differing from the other in the grossest to the minutest detail. Under such conditions there is no simple probabilistic measure of success or failure, hit or miss; correlation between a subject's report and the target picture must be done on an honest, albeit subjective, detail for detail, phrase for phrase, color for color comparison. Yet it is precisely *because* the odds against a particular fantasy's matching the target are, literally, infinity to one that a hit, when one does occur, is so meaningful. And when a few hits out of a dozen or so trials occur, the correlation is profound.

Glick has witnessed the profound, and he does not intend to stop experimenting now; the bite of the psi bug inflicts a lifelong fever. At the moment he is satisfied to reproduce his experiment, attempting at the same time to improve on the results by selecting subjects who are easily hypnotizable, and experimenting with psi scoring in relation to various depths of trance. Glick will not be working with psychics, but with normal individuals who have no psi history. His philosophy is simple: "If we're going to convince people of the reality of paranormal phenomena, we've got to start by winning over the average man. The gifted psychic already believes. And what better way to do it than by showing a nurse, a businessman, a housewife, or a secretary that under certain mental conditions he or she is psychic."[11]

The idea of working with average, psychically nongifted people is quite popular in the current wave of psi research. But it was not always so. In the past, psychically gifted individuals were sought out, recruited, enticed with money, promised overnight fame, or offered a stamp of authenticity (which understandably frightened off many). Today the pattern is different. For one thing there are more competent researchers, university laboratories, and private organizations engaged in psi research than even before. Experimenters need subjects, and, quite simply, there are not enough gifted psychics to go around. Every researcher cannot be fortunate enough to work with the likes of an Eileen Garrett.* And for one psychic to travel the psi circuit from one laboratory to another is not the answer. Being wired to monitoring devices, subjected to environment-altering stimuli, or awakened five or six times during a night's sleep is not only physically exhausting, it is a drain on one's psychical talents. Consequently, psi researchers have turned to the ordinary citizen as a subject. This pedestrian philosophy has already had some payoffs; a surprisingly large number of average individuals, subjected to the appropriate psi-favorable conditions, can pick up information parasensorily. One man who has seen this, perhaps more than anyone else, is Dr. Milan Ryzl.

A linguist proficient in English, Czech, German, Russian, French, and Dutch, Ryzl earned a doctorate in physics and chemistry from the University of Prague in 1952, and served for many years as a research biochemist at the Institute of Biology of the Czechoslovakian Academy of Sciences. He came to the United States from his native Czechoslovakia in 1967 and is currently a professor at San Diego State College in California.

From his earliest studies Ryzl had been fascinated by hypnosis. Its potential seemed limitless. The hypnotized mind does not demand that two plus two equal four. The sum can be four, but it can just as easily be five or ten or not even a number; it might be equated with a geometrical figure or a wild psychedelic image. And the hypnotized mind can do all this with no fussing, no rational unrest. This childlike willingness to add apples and oranges without a frown intrigued Ryzl.

For over a decade Ryzl has painstakingly worked with over five hundred normal individuals, attempting to arouse their parasenses through hypnosis. His approach to the problem is different from that of others. Dr. Glick, for instance, hypnotized Beth and suggested that she "see" through the envelope. She had received no prior conditioning in order to accomplish this feat, and consequently, she sometimes succeeded and sometimes failed.

*Mrs. Eileen Garrett died in 1971.

For some subjects, on-the-spot hypnotic suggestion is not strong enough to give them "X-ray" eyes; the cover on their human potential is not lifted high enough. Hypnotizing a subject and waiting to see if the parasenses open up has been the approach of many researchers but it is not Ryzl's. He *teaches* his subjects (perhaps "programs" would be more accurate) to develop a whole new reality-orientation through a structured five-step format in hypnosis. And the new reality-orientation is finely tailored to paranormal perception. In effect, Ryzl slowly develops in his subjects a new set of eyes to see things that wakeful learning has blinded them to.

Briefly stated, the five stages of Ryzl's program are (1) psychological preparation of the subject prior to hypnosis; (2) induction of deep hypnotic trance; (3) utilization of this level of consciousness to induce parasensory perception; (4) specific steps in reinforcing the emerging psi ability; and (5) reducing the subject's dependency on the hypnotist and on the formal hypnotic procedure.[12] It is of benefit to look closer at these steps and consider some illustrative examples where appropriate.

Phase one is the easiest in this program of pyramiding difficulty. If a person fears hypnosis, if he or she harbors some preconceived notion that hypnosis means relinquishing all free will to the whim of the hypnotist, psi training is halted before it begins. Thus, in phase one the subject is made to feel as comfortable with hypnosis intellectually, if not yet experientially, as the subject is with his or her nightly flow of dreams. Confidence is instilled, motivation established. Regardless of the hocus-pocus the person once thought surrounded hypnosis, he completes phase one of Ryzl's program with clear knowledge of hypnotic procedures, unafraid to enter a trance, and eager to embark on the next step.

In phase two some conventional clinical method is used to induce hypnosis, usually ocular fixation or verbal suggestion. Sessions are repeated again and again until the person can enter a trance quickly and deeply. And, contrary to popular belief, there are very few people who cannot, with proper and sufficiently intense instruction, achieve this state. After a long, satisfying trance is achieved, the real work, which has a faint scent of the program's final paranormal goal, begins. It focuses on developing in the person *real* tactile, auditory, and visual hallucinations. The subject must develop the ability to feel warm and cool breezes, to experience burning and tingling sensations, to hear the ringing of bells and music; all are planted in the subject through the suggestions of the hypnotist. Most important of these fantasies, the person must be able to *see* with his eyes closed, to experience brilliant colors, geometric shapes, and abstract figures, all with great ease, lucidity, and sharpness of detail. Of course, the aim in teaching the person to develop these sensations is to make him learn to accept the hallucinatory world as the real world, the only world.

The mastery of perfect fantasies is a prerequisite for the psi-induction procedures which follow. If the hallucinatory suggestion is a rose, for instance, the hypnotist will first tell the subject to "see" its soft crimson petals, its long green stem and jaggedly outlined leaves. Then "touch" it; feel its velvety texture and coolness; finally, "smell" its delicate fragrance. Once the rose is vivid and real to the subject, the hypnotist might run it through a spectrum of likely-to-bizarre hues—pink, tangerine, yellow, bright green, royal blue, black—making sure that each flower is real enough to grow in the subject's mental garden. The shocking blue flower, the ashen grey and kelly green ones, must become as real to the subject as the wakeful red American Beauty rose. If music is the mental suggestion, Beethoven's *Für Elise* say, the subject must learn to "hear" each simple note, feel its vibration. Then the tempo is altered—allegro, vivace, presto; the intensity is modulated from pianissimo to fortissimo. *Music becomes noise, and noise to the subject becomes music.* After weeks of such training, or months, the person has learned to temporarily live in a world of green blooms perched on pink stems, square circles, mellifluous noise, and two-and-two-are-five arithmetic. Then, into this bizarre but real world comes the paranormal phase of the training program.

Imagine that by now you have often visited this Alice-in-Wonderland level of consciousness. You are seated in a comfortable leather armchair. Anything can happen. Your eyes are closed, and your eyeballs are focused ahead and slightly upward as is customary in a hypnotic trance. A golden bracelet is placed in front of you on a clear piece of white paper. From out of the void you hear a soft voice saying: "Without opening your eyes I want you to look at the object I have placed in front of you. Look at it! I also want you to touch it *without lifting your hands from your lap.* Fondle it!" Your mind wants desperately to obey the suggestions, but where do you begin? How can you see without eyes, touch without hands? Here is a critical juncture. Where wakeful consciousness would waste no time in replying that the ordered task is flatly impossible, your new reality-orientation says, "Yes, I can do it." And eventually, as many of Ryzl's students can testify, it works. The mind augments or adds to its meager somatic senses, and parasensorily acquires visual and tactile information on the bracelet.

I do not mean to give the impression that this parasensory groping comes fast. It doesn't. Ryzl stresses that this third phase of the program is the most time-consuming. It often takes many weeks of three three-hour hypnotic sessions a week. The orders are repeated *ad infinitum.* They are varied and altered; the subject is constantly given encouragement. However, and one should not be surprised, occasionally there is an exception to the rule, such as the nineteen-year-old medical student who was able to "see" the target after only fifteen minutes, and then went on to name, clairvoy-antly and without a single error, a sequence of twenty-five images on cards. Under normal circumstances the student was in no way psychic, but through hypnotic consciousness he had formidable psi talents. Why he could do it so quickly is as much a mystery as how he actually obtained the parasensory information. For the average person, however, even after many hours of trying, the target object usually appears as a vague image, as though it were seen through a dense fog. Gradually the fog lifts and the object comes into focus. This process is illustrated by the case of one of Ryzl's subjects, Ms. J.K. The target was a pair of steel scissors, partly opened and with a dim luster. They were concealed behind an opaque screen.

For a long while J.K. said she saw nothing but blackness in motion. Gradually a series of rapidly changing pictures flashed through her mind like an accelerated motion picture. Ryzl relates what followed:

A metallic color with a dim luster then appeared—then an acute angle—and an obtuse angle—but she was unable to assemble color and angles correctly. Then the angles became more distinct. She noticed that there were two acute angles, with tips pointing toward each other. The metallic color fell into place along the two obtuse angles. It reminded her, she said, of two crossed pencils. Then she stated, "I said two crossed pencils, but I now have the impression of two things crossing each other . . . they are decid-edly not pencils. . . . The ends away from me are pointed . . . but those near me won't appear. I don't have it sharp enough yet. It strikes me as though two circles were projecting out of a thick fog . . . It is a pair of scissors."[13]

Here let us assume that as a subject you have been as successful in seeing the gold bracelet as J.K. was in perceiving the pair of scissors. Thus, you graduate from phase three of the program. But you are not yet a full-fledged psychic for three reasons: You occasionally hit on a target a few feet in front of you, but you can't perceive one located in another room; your answers contain too many errors; and your psi-favorable level of consciousness is dependent on another person, the hypnotist. Phase four is geared to remedy these shortcomings.

First, richer target objects containing several colors and details are used, for example, a Raggedy Ann doll. The target is not placed on a sheet of white paper in front of you, but in another room of the building. You are told the location, but you are also told to remain in your chair. Second, you are told not to make hasty judgments. If you see a slender, cylindrical image bearing red and white strips, you do not immediately say: "I think it's a candy cane." Rather, you hold onto the piecemeal facts and wait patiently for them to form a whole picture. There is a great temptation for the hypnotic mind to sum up the target prematurely in order to satisfy the suggestion of the hypnotist. But accuracy is more important than speed. The third part of phase four involves partially removing your dependency on the hypnotist for the depth and maintenance of trance. If you have difficulty perceiving a particular target, the hypnotist teaches you how to sink into a deeper trance on your own.

Finally in step five, the subject and the hypnotist get ready to part. By this time you have undergone hypnosis so often that you fall into a trance at a single word from the hypnotist. Now you are taught to enter your psi-favorable level of consciousness at will. When you sit back, relax, and close your eyes *with the intention* of entering a psi-favorable state, it spontaneously occurs. And what's more, you can regulate the depth of trance. Now you are a psychic. Or are you? Of course, the intention of Ryzl's training program is not to develop a generation of psychics or stage magicians. He wants to demonstrate that parasensory abilities are well within human reach, and that hypnosis is one way to grab at them. This he has done. But some people have grabbed and come up with fistfuls of psi, and others after enduring Ryzl's difficult program have come up empty handed. All subjects are not created equal.

In working with over five hundred normal persons, Ryzl has had a success rate of ten percent—some fifty individuals have developed their parasenses through tailored hypnosis. We might ask: Is that figure high or low? The answer depends on whom the question is put to—the psi critic, the psi enthusiast, or the psi researcher. For the critic, a ten percent rate of success is one-hundred percent too high. People are basically people as we understand them today, says the critic, and have little potential for significant future development. Of course, the critic is wrong. On the other hand, the psi enthusiast, on hearing the ten percent figure, releases a sigh of disappointment. "Damn," he says. "It's not an easy program to undertake, and there is no guarantee that I'll be in that ten percent, regardless of how diligent my efforts, how fervent my resolution." He is right. But the psi researcher, the most important of the three, smiles and says, "Ten percent is pretty good. But I'm sure we can do better."

Psi-Favorable Trances

Tell a good hypnotic subject in a trance that on awakening he must get out of his chair, cross the room, take from the second shelf Marcus Aurelius' *Meditations,* open it to page forty-one, and read verse forty-three, "Time is like a river . . .," and he'll do it every time. Afterwards, he won't be able to tell you why he did it. "I don't know," he will likely say. "It was more a *feeling* that made me do it, not a *thought.*"

Posthypnotic suggestions are common events in any good hypnotist's repertoire, yet witnessing them is always strangely fascinating. A person performs as a puppet when the hypnotist pulls a deeply planted string. Action occurs without conscious motivation, and free will is momentarily overshadowed. We watch like children who terrify themselves by viewing horror films; our fascination with posthypnotic suggestions comes from their horrific quality, their master–robot overtones. Yet a hypnotist's power over a subject is largely confined to the arena of the individual's personality structure. A loving mother, even in the deepest trance, cannot be forced to harm her children. Apparently the shift of consciousness to an altered state is never so complete that all wakeful behavior is left behind. A remnant anchors the mind to wakeful reality assuring that saints cannot be tranced into sinners, although, interestingly, the converse is often possible.

A person given a posthypnotic suggestion and then awakened from his or her trance appears thoroughly normal: awake, alert, perceiving real world events. The subject may walk and talk, read and play, eat and sleep —never suspecting or revealing to others that an action lies dormant in his or her mind. Considerable time may pass. But suddenly, thrown the right stimulus, the action must vent itself. For the next several seconds or minutes, however long the posthypnotic suggestion takes to execute, the person is functioning in a sort of behavioral daze. Some psi researchers have wondered: Can the parasenses awakened during a hypnotic trance be rekindled by a posthypnotic suggestion?

Kate* is a thirty-two-year-old Florida housewife and mother of two young children. She is a fine artist and an accomplished sculptor, and she

*The name is fictitious; the events are factual.

is luckier than most artists in that she owns her own gallery. Despite her considerable artistic sensibilities, however, Kate is not psychic. Even so, not long ago she performed as a gifted sensitive in a psi–hypnosis study conducted by hypnotist Lee Edward Levinson.[14]

It took several sessions before Levinson could lower Kate into a deep trance. One evening he felt she was finally ready for the crucial step. In the presence of two witnesses, a man and a woman, Levinson gave Kate the following command: "Immediately upon awakening you will leave the room. When I ask you to return to where I am seated, you will reenter the room and find an object I have hidden. As soon as you locate the object, you will bring it to me." She was then awakened and escorted out of the room by two assistants; Levinson and two others remained behind to hide something. Levinson asked the two for an object, either something personal or an article from around the room. The man offered the key to his apartment, and Levinson placed it high above one of the window sills in the room. But the hiding place did not satisfy the man. Either he thought it was too obvious and thus easy to find, or he did not trust Levinson, thinking the spot could have been preselected by Levinson and Kate. Instead, the man took the key from the sill, and scanned the room for a good hiding place. He found one. With some hesitation, he suggested that the key be placed in the brassiere of the woman observer present. When she agreed, the key was placed between her breasts. Kate then was escorted back into the room.

She had been fully awake now for a few minutes and out of hearing distance. Yet as soon as she stepped into the room in which the posthypnotic suggestion had been given, she was overcome by a strange feeling. She claimed that she "felt" there was something she had to retrieve from the other side of the room. After a moment's pause, she walked straight to the window sill. But now she became confused. She did not reach up to the ledge where the key had rested minutes ago. She almost looked as though she were straining to hear a faint voice. "Whatever it is you've hidden," she finally said, "I feel it was placed here first." She stopped as though another piece of information had just reached her and needed time to be digested. "But I don't feel," she continued, "that it is on this side of the room any longer."

With that Levinson softly but firmly asked her, "Can you tell what we have hidden and where the object is at this time?"

She saw no imagery, but she had a gut feeling. "It is small," she said, appearing to be fully awake and alert. "I *feel* that it is metallic." Quite naturally Levinson and his two witnesses were thinking of the key and its hiding place, so it is not clear whether Kate was receiving impressions telepathically or clairvoyantly. Either way, she suddenly parted her lips and gave a knowing smile. "It's a key," she said, walking over to the woman and pointing to her bosom. "They placed it inside there," she said smiling. "But I'm not going to retrieve it."

Kate had performed well. But once she found the key she was as nonpsychical as before the experiment began. Through suggestion under trance, her parasenses had been activated just long enough to accomplish the designated task. Under normal circumstances, a subject must wait for a trigger word from the hypnotist before a posthypnotic suggestion comes to life. But in the experiment with Kate, the stimulus words were thoughts never spoken. Also a subject must normally be in hearing range of the hypnotist to have the implanted suggestion activated. But one wonders what would have happened if Kate had not returned to the room that evening to find the hidden object, but instead had gone immediately home. Would Levinson's thoughts have nagged her while she prepared supper and put her children to bed? Would she have been able to sleep? This Levinson did not investigate. It remains a goal for future experimentation.

Levinson did, however, work with four other subjects besides Kate in the psi–hypnosis study. All were hand selected because they were excellent hypnotic subjects, and all demonstrated some psi talents through hypnosis. As with other researchers Levinson also had his share of failures. During the decade of the 1960s he worked with over one-hundred individuals, and not everyone who achieved a deep level of trance experienced a rallying of their psi senses. In fact, the numbers were relatively small. But those who did blossom, like Kate, convinced Levinson that hypnosis has an important role in psi research.*

Besides Levinson, Ryzl, and Glick, several other researchers are demonstrating that through hypnosis an average person can be made to perform as a gifted psychic. This brings up an interesting and theoretically important question: How similar, if at all, is a trance induced by hypnotic techniques to a self-imposed mediumistic trance? Are there any commonali-

---

*Just how awake a person is while executing a posthypnotic suggestion is open to debate. Ronald E. Shor writes: "A small percentage of well-trained hypnotic subjects can learn to reintegrate a generalized alertness to outer reality during deep hypnosis so that they have immediate and full availability of critical, waking standards of judgment and yet remain deeply hypnotized." ("Three Dimensions of Hypnotic Depth," *Altered States of Consciousness,* ed. Charles Tart.) There also may be some truth to the converse of Shor's statement, that is, the alert, awake individual, while executing a posthypnotic suggestion, may self-reintegrate a portion of his hypnotic trance. For a general reference see: T. X. Barber, *Hypnosis,* (New York: Van Nostrand Reinhold Co., 1969).

ties between the two levels of consciousness—aside from the fact that the end result of each is psychical performance? Mrs. Eileen Garrett, who could enter a mediumistic trance at will, offered a penetrating insight into how it differed (at least for her) from a hypnotic trance. Speaking of her self-induced mediumistic trance, she wrote: "It is withdrawal from the unconscious self into an area of the non-conscious self, where the objective mind can no longer invent nor predict activity. And yet, within this other mind, life is being worked out on a different level—a level not particularly identified with other, nor with the self as such, but a place within, an inner world where a battery of symbols takes over its own area of rhythm, sound and color."[15]

During a mediumistic trance Mrs. Garrett always felt "detachment . . . a sense of travel, of getting away from everything."

This contrasts sharply with what she experienced when placed under hypnotic trance. She said: "On the other hand, when placed under hypnosis by the physician, I am always peculiarly mentally alert. I am listening to what he tells me; at the same time, I am telling myself that I must be in contact with him on another level, so that I will be ready, anxious and willing to obey."[16] For Mrs. Garrett, hypnotic trance was not a relaxing, pleasant experience. Her feelings of being "mentally alert" agree with the fact that EEG studies of hypnotic subjects often show large amounts of wakeful beta brain-wave rhythms, and not the more restful alpha or deeply meditative theta waves which a mediumistic trance can produce. (Actually, a hypnotic subject's brainwave patterns depend on the nature of the suggestions provided by the hypnotist. But even suggestions of deep relaxation do not produce predominantly alpha and theta waves in all subjects.)

Implicit in Mrs. Garrett's statement is the notion that she felt subservient to the hypnotist. Whether this diminishes the psi-favorability of the hypnotic state is not known, but some researchers, Levinson among them, think the subservient feeling is undesirable. "It is not natural," he says. "Since it is man's nature to be a free individual and to think for himself, the relationship between hypnotist and subject does contain some negative aspects."[17] Despite this ostensible drawback, however, a hypnotic subject often performs psi tasks commendably. Kate, in another experiment, offers a lucid example of a subject "under the thumb" of the hypnotist, but still performing psychically.

Kate was once told that upon awakening she would telepathically receive an instruction to retrieve an object in the room and bring it to Levinson. When Levinson brought her out of a deep trance, Kate was very relaxed and alert. She remained in her chair and talked. But when Levinson began concentrating on the object he had selected, a flashlight on his desk, Kate grew quiet. Making no statement, she got up, walked across the room to the desk, picked up the flashlight, and brought it directly to Levinson. He observed that there was no hesitation in her actions; they were executed with confidence. But Levinson threw a curveball. He refused the flashlight, saying that he had not asked for it, and since it was daylight, obviously he had no need for it. Realizing that she was standing with an aluminum flashlight in her extended hand for no apparent reason, Kate turned, took it back across the room, and placed it on the desk. She still seemed fully awake, but definitely confused.

After she had sat calmly for a few minutes, engaged in conversation, Levinson again concentrated on the posthypnotic suggestion. Immediately she became tense. She got up, crossed the room, picked up the flashlight, and brought it to Levinson. Her actions were brisk as before and without hesitation. But again Levinson rebuffed her, asking why she thought he would want a flashlight. At this, Kate stood like a mute child, without an answer. Although the telepathic double-cross was definitely being received, it did not register consciously. Now Kate became irritable. She turned on her heel like a rejected child, crossed the room, and slammed the flashlight on the desk. When she returned to her chair, her anger and befuddlement were unmistakable.

Levinson's behavior toward Kate might seem cruel, but he was not teasing her, not the way a master might command his dog to fetch his slippers, and then when the animal brings them, reject them. Levinson's aim was to study two aspects of Kate's peculiar mental state: how often and how accurately his telepathic impression would be received, and whether the subliminal suggestion would eventually work its way to the surface of awareness by repeated refusal of the flashlight—perhaps through the friction of sheer frustration.

Kate was in the chair, tense and angry. She could not relax. For the third time Levinson directed his thoughts to retrieving the flashlight. Kate got up forcefully, marched across the room, grabbed the flashlight, and brought it to Levinson. Angrily she said, "I just can't seem to get away from this flashlight." At that point Levinson accepted the object, smiled, and replied, "That's because I have been directing you to bring it to me." Kate relaxed, and her parasenses, which had functioned so beautifully, submerged again.[18]

Altered states of consciousness give way to highly subjective events, as are our usual perceptions of the taste of vanilla pudding, the scent of carnations, or the color red. Thus, trances experienced by different people or one person at different times can vary greatly. Qualitative differences are hard to pin down, but quantitative distinctions are somewhat easier to make. Traditionally, hypnotic trances fall into four broad intensity classifications: light, medium, deep or somnambulistic, and plenary. The divisions are important in psi research because depth of trance seems to be correlated with parasensory performance.

In a light trance a person is hardly aware that he or she is hypnotized. The trance is usually marked by great relaxation and feelings of listlessness or lethargy. Lying on a couch, for example, the subject may feel able to get up and move about. And such activity is possible. But the person doesn't move because it seems to be too much trouble.

In a medium trance the subject still is not aware of being hypnotized, but the relaxation is deeper, and so is the lethargy. More standard hypnotic phenomena can be induced in the medium trance than in the light trance, such things as anesthesia of a hand, an arm, or a leg.

In a deep, or somnambulistic, trance all the standard hypnotic phenomena can be induced. The individual still has some degree of conscious awareness, but the subconscious mind is now nearer the surface. Thus the parasenses can be coaxed out into the light of day. Modern research is revealing a direct correlation between depth of trance and psi sensitivity. Kate was able to perform psychically only in a deep level of trance, and this is also true of Levinson's other subjects. "I have found," he writes, "that upon attaining a state of *deep* trance, the somnambulist often exhibits some natural telepathic and clairvoyant facilities without training and conditioning." He concludes that "only subjects able to enter the deepest stage of hypnosis were able to achieve noteworthy results."[19] This fact is not surprising from what we know of psi and its residence in the subliminal depths of the mind.

These trances, of course, can be induced by a variety of techniques: ocular fixation, tactile sensations, the rhythmic tick-tock of a metronome, or the monotone patter of the hypnotist. Although it may seem nice to have such latitude, this family of methods raises an important research question: Is one method better for achieving a psi-favorable trance than another, or are they all equivalent? It is an important question, one whose answer might explain why different psi researchers have experienced different degrees of success with hypnosis. Mesmer passed his hands over a subject. Burton Glick swung a metallic fountain pen in front of Beth's eyes. Milan Ryzl had his subjects fix their eyes on a stationary object and then talked them into a state of drowsiness. Lee Levinson used "mother-hypnosis" patter—a soft, gentle, persuasive method of inducing a trance. (The technique derives its name from the fact that it is strongly reminiscent of a mother rocking her child to sleep.)

The question of method was bandied about at the 1973 meeting of the Parapsychological Association in Charlottesville, Virginia. The discussion was sparked by a paper presented by psi investigator Donald Gibbons entitled "Hyperempiria"—a term Gibbons uses for a hypnotic induction procedure based on specific suggestions of increased awareness, mind expansion, and heightened alertness and sensitivity. Gibbons makes the point that since the experience of one's own awareness is a subjective phenomenon, the number of altered states of consciousness which may be brought about by means of suggestion is theoretically unlimited. Although there appears to be no way of getting around this dilemma of infinities, he feels that gazing at fountain pens or listening to ticking metronomes, mother-hypnosis patter, and various other suggestions of sleep and relaxation do not in themselves *prime* the subject for the desired psi-favorable state. A hyperempiric induction, he feels, does. Here is one example of such an induction which Gibbons presented at the Virginia meeting:

> Just make yourself comfortable, and close your eyes; and as you listen to my voice I am going to show you how to release your consciousness so that it may rise to a higher level than you have known previously. First of all, I would like you to picture yourself standing in front of a large wooden door, which is the door to a great cathedral. . . . If you accept each detail of the scene as I describe it, without trying to think critically, your imagination will be free to allow you to experience the situation just as if you were really there. . . . Just let yourself stand there a moment, gazing at the carved wooden panels of the door as you prepare to enter.

> . . . I'm going to count from one to ten, and at the count of one the doors will open and you will go inside, as I guide you into a higher state of awareness called hyperempiria. You will begin to experience very pleasant feelings of increased alertness and sensitivity as your consciousness commences to expand . . . Just let yourself be guided by my voice now, as I begin the count and your awareness begins to increase. . . .

> One. As the doors swing open and you enter the Cathedral, you first traverse a small area paved with stone, stopping at the

font if you desire, and then you pause before a second pair of doors which leads to the interior. . . . You are beginning to enter a higher level of consciousness now; for this Cathedral presents your mind with an image which is able to hold within it all of the vast reservoirs of strength and spiritual power contained within your own being, and within the Universe as well. . . . And as you enter, you will begin to feel all of these vast resources flowing into your own awareness. . . .

Two. As you pass through the second pair of doors and into the dimly-lit interior, you can hear the gentle tones of organ music floating upon the quiet air. . . . Let yourself breathe slowly and deeply now, as you inhale the faint aroma of incense, and your consciousness drifts higher. . . .

Three. Breathe slowly and deeply, and listen to the music and the chanting. . . . Feel it flowing through you, into the very core of your being. . . . Let your mind flow with it. . . . Just let the music merge with your awareness, and carry it along. . . . By the time I get to the count of ten, you will be holding within your consciousness an awareness of the entire Universe, and all its beauty. . . .

Four. You are entering into a higher level of consciousness now, one in which your ability to realize your full capacity for experience is greatly enhanced. . . . You are experiencing a pleasant exaltation in your ability to use your consciousness so much more effectively, as your awareness continues to expand, more and more. . . .

Five. Your perceptual abilities are becoming infinitely keener, as the music swells within you; yet you can still direct your attention as you would normally, to anything you wish. . . . It's such a pleasant feeling as your awareness expands more and more, multiplying itself over and over again. . . .

Six. It's a wonderful feeling of release and liberation which you are experiencing now, as all of your vast, untapped potentials become freed for their fullest possible functioning; and by the time I get to the count of ten your entire potential for experience will be fully realized. . . . Your perceptions of the world around you will take on new and deeper qualities, and they will contain a greater depth of reality than anything you have experienced previously.

Seven. Some distance away from you stands the high altar, bordered by banks of softly-glowing candles. As the music continues and your awareness continues to expand, you can feel yourself being drawn irresistibly towards it. . . . And as you begin to approach, the closer you get the more your awareness expands, and the more pleasant it becomes. . . .

Eight. As you feel your consciousness expanding more and more, you are experiencing an ever-growing sense of joy as all of your perceptual abilities are becoming tuned to their highest possible pitch. . . .

Nine. As you approach nearer and nearer, you feel your capacity for awareness and for experience becoming infinitely greater than it could possibly be in any other state. . . . In just a few seconds now, all of your perceptual abilities will be tuned to their highest possible pitch, and you will be able to concentrate infinitely better than you can in your everyday state of consciousness. . . .

Ten. Now, you are ready. All of the vast reserves within you have been freed for their fullest possible functioning. And while you remain within this state of hyperempiria, you will discern new and greater levels of reality, new realms of meaning, and new dimensions of experience, greater and more profound than anything you have encountered previously.

And now you will be provided with a series of experiences which you will find interesting and rewarding, and then you will be returned to your everyday state of awareness.[20]

To date no psi experiments have been conducted using hyperempiric induction. Whether it is more or less favorable than other techniques is open to question. It does have as its primary focus the expansion of awareness and shedding of wakeful reality; however, it also requires a subject to conjure images and sensations he has never before encountered. Anyone can visualize a white sandy beach drenched in summer sunshine with waves sounding on the shore, and be lulled into trance by such a familiar and relaxing scene; the necessity of hyperempiric induction to dwell on "levels of consciousness," "expanded awareness," "boundless potential," and "new dimensions" may be too alien and too staggering for most individuals to relate to. Only studies using hyperempiric induction will reveal its merits or shortcomings. For now, most researchers are sticking to proven conventional techniques to achieve deep, psi-favorable trances. Parapsychologist Charles Honorton at Maimonides is one of them.

If a hypnotic subject in a trance is told to dream, he will. Give the subject a simple suggestion—"You are attending a concert in a richly decorated hall"—and he will use it as a kernel to fashion a full-blown dream —orchestra, music, performers, audience, and dazzling crystal chandeliers. The dream is not exactly the same as a nocturnal one, for it lacks well-defined REM activity, but it is just as real to the hypnotized subject. Honorton has taken full advantage of the ease with which hypnotized subjects dream in order to perform an interesting psi study.

The study, conducted with the rigor characteristic of all the Maimonides work, involved sixty women subjects ranging in age from eighteen to fifty-three. The target pool was 145 postcard-size art prints similar to those used in the Maimonides telepathically induced dream experiments. However, the focus of Honorton's experiment was clairvoyance, not telepathy. Each print was carefully wrapped in three thicknesses of manila paper so that it was opaque even when viewed directly in front of a hundred-watt light bulb. Honorton divided the sixty subjects into two groups; one group was hypnotized and instructed to clairvoyantly *dream* about the target, and the other group, the control, was not hypnotized, and told merely to *daydream* about the target.

A subject sat in a comfortable reclining chair in a darkened room near a randomly selected target envelope. She was told by Honorton: "When I stop talking you're going to have a dream (or daydream for a control subject), a very vivid and realistic dream (daydream) about the target in the envelope. You will see it clearly, very clearly. It will be as though you are walking right into the picture, observing it from that standpoint, participating in it. . . . Your dream (daydream) will continue for five minutes, then you'll awaken (open your eyes) and report the dream (daydream)."

Honorton's experiment sounds similar to Burton Glick's, and it is. In fact, both studies occurred about the same time, though independently. The major difference between the two is that Glick worked primarily with two subjects, while Honorton's experiment involved thirty subjects and an additional thirty as a control. Glick could not get a feel for the importance of depth of trance with only two subjects, but Honorton could. What's more, working with a larger population Honorton witnessed a greater range of successes and failures. For this very reason, some of the successes were spectacular. A young New York City housewife who had no history of psi perception sat hypnotized in the chair near an envelope containing *The Adoration of the Shepherds* by El Greco. The picture depicts the Virgin Mary holding the infant Christ, with shepherds around the child and green leaves in the background. When Honorton awakened the woman from her dream, she reported: "The Virgin Mary. A statue and Jesus Christ. An old church with two pillars overgrown with grass by the church entrance. The Virgin Mary was holding Jesus as a baby."[21]

Honorton found that this type of brilliant success, though rare across the whole experimental population, was not that uncommon among the best hypnotic subjects. Another highly suggestible woman sat hypnotized near an envelope containing *The Anguish of Departure* by De Chirico. The picture conveys the sorrow associated with various types of final journeys. In the background a train is pulling out, and in the foreground two people are parting. There is also a bleak white building in the foreground and a tower beyond it. Here, the woman actually did "enter" the picture and fall under its mood of loneliness:

> A picture of a railroad overpass with a red light. My husband and I were standing and watching it. It was very nostalgic for him. We went into a garden and there was a wedding going on and we came in at the end. We mingled for a while and my husband said, "Let's go back to that overpass." It was very lonely and deserted. The yearnings of a child wanting to go to far-off places were evoked. The wedding was very gay and festive. A young couple going off to a new life. Then the feeling we had—wondering where the adventure was twenty-five or thirty-five years later. Not sad or tragic, but lonely.[22]

If a somnambulistic trance is a highly psi-favorable state, what about the deeper plenary trance? The plenary state is not easy to induce. It requires a great deal of time and patience, and is particularly draining on the hypnotist. Not all hypnotists can weave this peculiar spell. A man who could, and did so with impressive results, was the Swedish physician Oscar Wetterstrand. Wetterstrand's experiments, conducted before the turn of the century, concentrated on putting patients into a plenary trance lasting from several days to two weeks at a time. He reported that during these death-like trances virtually no food was eaten. The subject was in a state of suspended animation similar in many ways to deep yoga meditation where heart rate, respiration, and general metabolic processes slow to a crawl.

In recent years Leslie M. LeCron, a hypnotherapist, has worked with plenary trances, using two exceptional hypnotic subjects, both of whom have required more than three hours of continuous induction to reach a plenary depth. This length of time is dramatic when one realizes that the two subjects could achieve a somnambulistic trance in only two or three minutes. One subject, a young woman, remained in a plenary trance for thirty-six hours during which her rate of breathing fell from a normal eighteen breaths a minute to only three, and her pulse dropped from eighty beats a minute to forty-eight. "The plenary trance," says LeCron, "certainly calls for modern investigation, both therapeutically and as to the production of psychic abilities."[23] Among the many researchers who agree with him, however, only a scant few have had the fortitude to carry out the tedious research, which often involves weeks of many-hour sessions simply to induce a plenary state before controlled experiments can begin. If an experiment, for statistical purposes, is to involve many subjects and many controls, a single project could easily take a year.

Like LeCron, Robert Masters and his wife, Dr. Jean Houston, who head the Foundation for Mind Research, have had the hardiness to work in the plenary region. Masters first worked with a single subject, a high-school-educated woman in her mid-twenties. It took nearly a hundred hours of hypnotic training over a few months for the woman to enter a plenary depth. She was able to remain in this profound state for two-day periods at a time. Before her plenary training she had scored negatively on a whole battery of psi tests, but at a plenary depth Masters witnessed an awakening of the woman's parasenses. He tells of one example where she was given the randomly chosen name of a person unknown to her and asked to describe the person:

> She described a dark-haired woman, probably in her mid-thirties, crippled and largely confined to a wheel chair. She next described an impression of frequent rages, of someone striking out to smash things, someone throwing objects and cursing, during almost child-like temper tantrums. Finally, she imitated a growling, almost animal voice which, in fact, was an excellent imitation of the person named. All of the other impressions were core correct as well.[24]

Apparently the woman had scanned Masters' mind for information on the mystery person. Nor were her powers confined to telepathy; she was also clairvoyant. In another experiment she accurately described an event which took place in a shed on the laboratory grounds, an area she had not seen before. Masters recounts the incident:

> At first, she reported anxiety and pain and bewilderment, and stated: "I believe a kid was hurt." She then declared there was something wrong with the word "kid," which had seemed to her to mean a child. An image was forming where, at first, there had been only emotions and the word "kid." She then reported accurately that it was not a kid but a large goat, that the goat had been injured in the shed, that the goat had been badly cut and lost considerable blood.[25]

Masters found that the parasensory information in all cases was accompanied by strong emotions and vivid imagery. "The visual images," he says, "seen with the eyes closed, were images of action, as if she were looking at a filmed version of what she then described. In the case of the woman in the wheelchair, there were also auditory images, allowing excellent imitation of the voice." In describing another person, the young woman felt she actually entered that person's body as she saw it in her imagery. Masters soon learned that a researcher cannot keep a secret from his plenary subject. In her plenary trance, the young woman would often spontaneously reconstruct details of other experiments that were on Masters' mind, anticipate laboratory procedures, and provide highly personal bits of information about Masters himself—all things she had no sensory means of knowing. Since the time of the experiment, the woman has found that occasionally, through a self-induced trance, she can pick up parasensory impressions.

Masters has so far worked with about half a dozen individuals in plenary trances, and he has always observed some degree of paranormal perception. What is most significant about his work, he writes, "is the emergence of a repeatedly demonstrable telepathic capacity in the course of a human potentials training program which alters consciousness and makes available tools—especially imageries—which extraordinary functioning usually requires. These cases seem to offer good evidence that telepathy is a capacity of the average person, but is blocked by limitations on awareness and inhibition of specific mental tools."[26]

Masters is now venturing even deeper into the unknown reaches of the mind with subjects who might be able to remain in plenary trances for several weeks or even longer. How they will experience their environment and just how fully their parasenses will surface are two of the major questions the study will answer. Another is whether any deleterious effects spring from such extended periods of time in a plenary trance.

The Ego Surrenders

Jump from a thirty-story window. Before you hit the ground, something very pleasant will happen.

Fortunately, we do not have to take the leap to learn of the surprise, for enough people have done it and lived to tell of their experience. One highly publicized incident occurred during the first week of December, 1972, over Arizona. *Time* magazine gave this report:

> When both of his parachutes failed in a recent jump from a plane 3,300 feet above the Coolidge, Ariz., airport, Skydiver Bob Hall, 19, plummeted earthward and hit the ground at an estimated 60 m.p.h. Miraculously, he survived. A few days later, recovering from nothing more serious than a smashed nose and loosened teeth, he told reporters what the plunge had been like: "I screamed. I knew I was dead and that my life was ended. All my past life flashed before my eyes, it really did. I saw my mother's face, all the homes I've lived in, the military academy I attended, the faces of friends, everything."[27]

The "review of life" that Hall experienced and lived to tell about is typical of such close calls with death. It has been reported many times by people who have had, even for the briefest moment, one foot here and the other yonder. Not surprisingly, such individuals often report having psychical experiences. Dr. Russell Noyes, Jr., a psychiatrist at the University of Iowa, has made a lengthy study of sudden near-death cases. His unique subjects include individuals who were unconscious from near-drowning and were revived, fire victims who leaped from skyscrapers, some nearly successful suicides, mountain climbers who plummeted hundreds of feet and landed on a blanket of snow with only minor injuries, and survivors of airplane disasters and skydiving accidents such as Hall's. Out of this bag of miracles, Noyes has drawn a clear conclusion: What transpires just before the final curtain falls is a well-defined play in three acts.[28]

Act I Noyes calls "Resistance"; the mood is one of panic and desperation played out at a frenzied pace. The actor, alone on the stage, struggles to overcome the forces leading to inevitable death. The climber grabs for a rock or tree branch to break his fall; the exhausted swimmer looks frantically for a floating timber. Hall, in this phase, yanked again and again on the rip cord of his primary chute, then at the auxiliary one, and finally, in sheer panic, he reached around and attempted to tear open his backpack by hand. Of course, the real actor here in Act I is the ego, that ham of wakeful consciousness, determined to hang on, refusing to be upstaged by death. The obsession is to retain the present, the here-and-now in which the self thrives. But in such near-death encounters the ego is fighting a losing battle. And eventually, that "actor of actors" sees the fateful odds, makes a compromise, and Act II begins.

Noyes calls this act "Review of Life." When all chances for survival have been exhausted, the actor submits to a cavalcade of happy memories: family outings, a love affair or two, college days, and the tender times of childhood. All of these things and more roll by like an old home movie, all a little yellowed by age, but wrapped in the romantic quality of sunlight. Slightly out of focus, perhaps, but that is romantic too. The dominant mood of Act II is nostalgia; the scenes are warm and sweet and precious in their sudden propinquity. Since the ego can't have the present, it relives the past —anything to escape confrontation with death, an act in which it knows it plays no role.

Noyes calls the third phase "Transcendence." When the mind switches off its memory projector, the ego is silenced. It has been written out of the play, and a new character of consciousness enters, a character who values the spiritual above the corporeal. Since the physical body has become meaningless, smashing into the ground at sixty miles per hour is also meaningless, for wakeful life is no longer precious. The spirit has been freed from wakeful constraints, and it is able to soar above the physical plane. "Jump from a thirty-story window. Before you hit the ground, something very pleasant will happen." That something is Act III, Transcendence. Bob Hall found it exhilarating. Literary patron Caresse Crosby, who nearly drowned as a child, called it the high point of her life. "I saw the efforts to bring me back to life," she wrote, "and I tried not to come back. I was only seven, a carefree child, but that moment in all my life has never been equaled for pure happiness."[29]

Noyes refers to the transcendent mentation as a sort of threshold between life and death, "a mystical state of consciousness," because experientially it so closely parallels the reports of mystics. The experience is cosmic. Its verbal description defies even the most articulate tongues. This is clear in the writings of the great sixteenth-century Christian mystic Jacob

Boehme, who struggled to relate to others his ineffable encounters with transcendence. On one occasion he wrote:

> Who can express it?
>
> Or why and what do I write, whose tongue does but stammer like a child which is learning to speak? With what shall I compare it? Or to what shall I liken it? Shall I compare it with the love of this world? No, that is but a mere dark valley to it.
>
> O immense Greatness! I cannot compare it with any thing, but only with *resurrection from the dead;* there will the Love-Fire rise up again in us, and rekindle again our astringent, bitter, and cold, dark and dead powers, and embrace us most courteously and friendly. [Italics added.][30]

That transcendence should serve as a vehicle for psi perception should come as no surprise. It exhibits, in all of its various forms (Abraham Maslow enumerated thirty-five varieties, from the loss of self in sexual climax to the mystical fusion with the cosmos during intense meditation[31]), all the prerequisites for psi. As Maslow says, transcendence is a rising above "one's own skin and body and bloodstream"; it is the "loss of self-consciousness, of self-awareness and of self-observation." Herein, many parapsychologists see the ultimate explanation of paranormal phenomena. If the human mind can achieve such a freed state, one of seemingly infinite potential (with which scientists are just beginning to wrestle in a coordinated fashion), then psi phenomena seem not at all formidable. Dreaming, hypnosis, hyperaroused trances, some drug-induced states, conditions of sensory deprivation and bombardment—all ASCs which researchers are finding psi-favorable in varying degrees—have in some form or other the common denominator of transcendence—a "fusion, either with another person or with the whole cosmos or with anything in between."[32] What clearer statement can one ask as a principle underlying psi perception?

Dr. Karlis Osis is most interested in the transcendence that preludes death, not necessarily sudden accidental death, but the natural passing on. In his vast 1961 study, *Deathbed Observations by Physicians and Nurses,*[33] Osis demonstrated that death (or near-death) does not have to come suddenly to cause a transcendental shift in consciousness, sometimes with paranormal consequences. From 10,000 questionnaires sent out to doctors and nurses, Osis received detailed information on 35,540 dying patients, 3,500 of whom were verbally coherent up until the moment of death. Osis found, contrary to popular belief, that as death grows closer fear is not a dominant emotion. In fact, over 750 patients experienced "extreme elation" in the final moments before death. Hallucinations were frequent and very real. Over one third of all the patients saw visions of human forms, often of persons already deceased. Osis also found that during the shift of consciousness that heralds death there were a small number of cases of paranormal events—telepathic, clairvoyant, and precognitive in nature.

Transcendence and hypnosis, though different in themselves, share an important common feature: they are both mono-motivational states—conditions in which a single, powerful motive or preoccupation momentarily towers over all other sensations. The mono-motivational state of transcendence is brought on by a dynamically intense situation, one of ecstatic rapture or great fear. On the other hand, the mono-motivational state of hypnosis is produced at a low dynamic intensity. Peak excitement or fear results in the loss of wakeful consciousness by *intensifying* a particular situation above all competing ones; hypnosis achieves the same effect by *quieting* all situations except one until it is the only one. We can see the difference in terms of a camera with a zoom lens. Set the camera on one control and the scene to be photographed comes rushing in toward the film, growing ever larger in size. A small red berry on a tree explodes into a brilliant splash of color. Set another control, however, and the berry recedes toward infinity, growing smaller all the while, quietly pinpointing concentration.

One man who is looking into the psi-favorability of mono-motivational states is psychologist Dr. Kenneth Keeling of the University of Waterloo. When Keeling set out in 1971 to study psi perception through hypnosis, he was quite familiar with the related literature. But one thing bothered him: Almost all the past experiments involved one subject, the percipient, who is hypnotized, and an agent (often the hypnotist), who is in a wakeful state. If hypnotic consciousness is a psi-favorable state, reasoned Keeling, wouldn't it be better to place both sender and receiver in that state rather than just one of them? This he did.

Ms. Sender, a young housewife, was seated in a room, hypnotized, and given a randomly selected index card containing a single sentence theme. Keeling instructed her to read the sentence and use it as a nucleus on which to fashion a dream. She was told that down the hall, thirty feet away, another woman, also hypnotized, would try to have the same dream. Both women were excellent hypnotic subjects and believed strongly in the experiment. Using a stopwatch, Keeler allowed Ms. Sender and Ms. Receiver to dream exactly two minutes, at which time they were awakened from their trance states and asked to write down their dreams.

Keeling's suspicion that joint hypnosis might be better than the one-way variety paid off. When Ms. Sender's dream kernel was a scene of an automobile race on an open road, Ms. Receiver dreamed, in the same two minutes, that she "was a small puppy on an open road" who suddenly heard a "roaring noise." She turned around to see a steam roller inching up on her. Another dream suggestion, one of comedian Jackie Gleason slipping on a banana peel, prompted Ms. Receiver to dream of "picking bananas from a tree." Other subjects who were hypnotized and then paired also gave impressive results.[34] "With both subjects hypnotized," says Keeling, "the transference of dream material from sender to receiver is greatly facilitated. It would appear that this setup offers great promise for future research."[35] As we shall soon see, this approach, modified slightly but cleverly, has startling psi consequences.

Stanley Krippner laments the fact that more dream experiments have not been conducted with young children, and Keeling expresses the same sentiment about hypnosis. Although copious anecdotal material is to be found if one looks far and wide enough, there is disappointingly little solid research. Many researchers suspect that infants may be very open to parasensory information through hypnotic consciousness. Babies show a spontaneous and intense absorption with minute detail. Thus, they are often in a mono-motivational state that occurs easily. The reflection of light off a metallic object or a suspended trinket can absorb an infant's attention completely. The result is a trance. Adding to this desirable condition is the easy deterioration of a tired child's reality-oriented behavior. It clearly shows that infants have a loose grip on wakeful reality; the newly emerging ego is weak and keeps slipping off center stage. In fact, in very young infants, contact with the "real" world is more easily and frequently lost than it is maintained. As Keeling says, "The infant has no trouble letting go of wakeful consciousness, for he has yet to master hanging on."[36]

Where then is the infant's mind when it is not "here"? ask Keeling and Krippner. Where indeed! To say that it's nowhere is the lazy way out. We must ask: On what plane of consciousness does the prewakeful mind reside? What view of reality does it experience from down there—or up there? Psi researchers are now beginning to tackle these questions.

Forging Psi Bonds

Some experiments fall short of a researcher's goals. Others may nicely confirm his pet theory. Still others fall into a unique category—they not only support the theoretical predictions, but also reveal the theory to be only a corollary of a more general law of nature. These are the reputation-making gems which all scientists hope to stumble upon, but few in fact do.

A few years ago Dr. Charles Tart undertook a modest experiment, hoping to confirm a theory of his. Tart felt that somnambulistic and plenary trances could perhaps be easily achieved, even in individuals who were difficult to hypnotize, if instead of one person hypnotizing another, as is usually the case, each would take turns successively hypnotizing his part-ner. The idea rested on solid ground, for too often hypnosis is a one-way street; the subject is intensely attentive to the hypnotist, while the hypnotist may perform trance induction by rote—his thoughts on the golf course, the race track, or a more stimulating game. But with the mutual induction that Tart proposed, rapport between the two individuals would be two-way. What's more, each person's level of consciousness at any given moment would be entirely dependent on that of his or her partner. Innocently, Tart set out to test his theory. He got much more than he bargained for.[37]

Anne and Bill were the first set of partners. They were both graduate students in psychology at the University of California at Davis and were casually acquainted. They had volunteered for the experiment fully under-standing its goals, and each of them was proficient in hypnotic induction techniques. To prevent Anne and Bill from becoming locked into a mutual trance that might be unbreakable, Tart hypnotized each separately before the experiment, saying that throughout the test he would be able to make contact with them simply by resting his hand on their shoulders.

Bill hypnotized Anne first. He suggested that as she concentrated on her breathing she would see a blue vapor flowing in and out of her nostrils. After several minutes the imaginary fumes had carried Anne to a trance depth of twenty-seven.* Bill then used a standard counting technique to take Anne to a depth of forty. (After the session Anne reported the follow-ing experience during this induction stage: "I had a most unusual physical sensation of my body disintegrating—with great chunks folding off like thick bark on a tree. I was momentarily threatened, almost resisted . . . soon

---

*A hypnotic subject acquainted with a zero to fifty scale—no trance to deep trance—will automatically give a depth report on request. Under appropriate conditions the response is taken to be a good indication of the subject's depth of trance.

this feeling passed, after which my body was gone, and I felt like a *soul* or a big ball of *mind.*")

Bill then asked Anne to hypnotize him. She slowly opened her eyes; they looked heavy, glassy. She held up a finger and told Bill to focus on it while she talked about climbing down a deep manhole with him, saying that he would be deeply hypnotized by the time they reached the bottom. Soon Bill reported a depth of thirty-six. Tart wanted them to go into a deeper mutual trance. He placed his hand on Anne's shoulder and instructed her to have Bill deepen her trance and, as a safety measure, to remind Bill to respond to Tart's orders whenever he put his hand on Bill's shoulder. After about ten minutes Anne reported a depth of forty-three. The first intimation of the extent of the mental dependency between Anne and Bill came when Tart asked Bill for a depth reading. Although Anne had not yet worked on deepening his trance, Bill responded with a reading of forty-three—on his own he had gone to the same depth as Anne. Again Tart ordered a hypnotic volley, and shortly Anne and Bill both reported a trance depth of forty-seven, a very deep trance.

The experiment was running so smoothly that Tart wondered how much further it could go. But when he ordered Anne to deepen Bill's trance, she remained silent. Again he placed his hand on her shoulder and gave her the order. Again she didn't respond. Finally, after several alarming minutes, Tart was able to make contact with her. He asked her why she hadn't responded to his suggestion to deepen Bill's trance. "I did," she answered, explaining that she was walking Bill down a flight of stairs and deepening his trance with each step. Of course Tart asked her to do it aloud so that Bill could hear her and walk with her. To this she replied indignantly that Bill *was* with her; he *could* hear her. If this indeed were true, thought Tart, then Bill should be in a deeper trance. So he placed his hand on Bill's shoulder and asked for a depth report. At first it was difficult getting Bill to respond, but finally he answered with an astonishing reading of fifty-seven—ten points deeper than he had been before Anne's silent hypnotizing. Bill's body seemed totally inert and his breathing was faint, the symptoms of a plenary trance. Understandably excited, though somewhat alarmed and confused over what had happened, Tart decided to go no further that first day. He instructed Bill to dehypnotize Anne by getting her depth reading and counting backward to zero. When Anne awoke, she did the same to awaken Bill.

Two major themes emerged from this first session that Tart had not anticipated. First, Anne felt that she could communicate with Bill nonverbally, and in fact she had deepened his trance without uttering a word.

Second, it became apparent to Tart that both Anne and Bill strongly resented his intervention into their fantasy world. They viewed him as an outsider, and they wished to be left alone.

A second session soon followed the first. This time, while Anne was initially hypnotizing Bill, a fellow student, Carol, entered the room to witness the experiment. Anne told Bill, who was already at a depth of nine: "Carol is going to come in and sit down in the corner, but it will not bother you and you will not pay any attention to her." After several minutes of hypnotic volley Bill was at a depth of forty-three and Anne reported twenty-two. To deepen Anne's trance further, Bill began talking about an hallucinatory journey that he and Anne were on together. They were standing on the side of a mountain, in front of the entrance to a tunnel. They walked hand-in-hand down through the passage, Bill suggesting that with increasing depth they would *both* go into deeper trances. Soon Anne reported a depth of thirty-five.

At this point Tart noticed that Carol, who was sitting across the room, was hypnotized. (This is not an uncommon event. A good hypnotist can hypnotize several people simultaneously.) Tart watched Carol's facial expressions as Bill continued the fantasy trip deeper into the tunnel. It appeared to Tart that she was sharing Anne and Bill's experience. He placed his hand on Bill's shoulder and told him that Carol was hypnotized and coming along with them. To Tart's surprise, Bill firmly shook his head no. (Although there was no verbal rejection of Carol, during a separate post-session interview Carol stated that she never continued the journey with Anne and Bill because she "sensed" she was not wanted; she never heard nor saw Bill reject her.)

As Bill took Anne deeper into the tunnel his resentment increased at Tart's occasional intrusions. Either he would not respond to Tart's questions at all, or his retort was curt and hostile.

Tart, an innovative researcher, had an idea: If the tunnel were so real to Anne and Bill, could they bring some object out of it? He gave them an order: "I want you each to find some sort of object, like a rock or something, that you can bring back to this laboratory and look at here." The command was not well received. Bill, who had been difficult to communicate with, wasted no time now in speaking. Very sternly he said that anything found in the tunnel belonged there and could not be taken out. Bill was so vehement on the issue that Tart decided to work on Anne. He suggested that she locate a loose rock and bring it back to the laboratory. Anne wanted to very badly, but Bill sternly forbade her. In fact, he began forcefully leading her back out of the tunnel. In a loud voice Bill counted Anne out of her trance. Tart had never given Bill an order to do this! When Anne awoke, Tart asked her to dehypnotize Bill. Carol automatically awakened with Bill.

In the post-session interviews with the subjects several things became clear. The tunnel was absolutely real to all three subjects, and it was clearly Bill's property. He said later that he felt the tunnel had rules which restricted taking anything out of it. Carol's experience is of particular interest. She was near the mouth of the tunnel when she felt Bill reject her. Then she waited until Anne and Bill were deep inside before she followed them, always keeping far behind and out of sight. She had a strong desire to see the end of the tunnel but knew that Bill would not let her. When Tart suggested that the three of them find some objects and bring them back, Carol found a small picture of an unidentified person in a wooden frame. Every time Bill told Anne that she could not bring anything back, the picture would twist in Carol's hand with the face turning away from her. When Bill began forcing Anne out of the tunnel, Carol ran ahead of them to avoid being caught, and while she ran she dropped the picture.

Again, as during the first session, both Anne and Bill strongly resented Tart's entering their private world. They were both vehement on this issue. The strong rapport that they developed during mutual hypnotic consciousness seemed to last well beyond the session. "Following this second session," Tart says, "Anne and Bill developed an intense friendship, spending a great deal of time together. They felt extremely close to one another as a result of their shared experience." From casual classmates they had become inseparable friends. Bill would wait for Anne after class. He often had dinner with her, or they would take in a movie together. Although Anne and Bill clearly enjoyed their new relationship, others did not—especially Anne's husband and Bill's wife. "Their spouses," says Tart, "became very upset at the intense emotional relationship that developed between Anne and Bill. It began to cause some friction in their respective marriages." But the marital strife did not prevent a third session from occurring.*

---

*Anne's desire to know what was at the end of the tunnel persisted, as did Tart's. One day when Bill was not present, Tart hypnotized Anne and instructed her to find the tunnel and descend into it. Tart reports the incident: "She found herself running along the tunnel, hurrying to reach the end. . . . At the end of the tunnel she found a cave, blazing with brilliant white light, and occupied by an old man of angelic appearance. The room was filled with music from an unseen source. Anne repeatedly asked him what this experience meant. He ignored her at first, and finally said, very sternly, that he could not answer her question because Bill was not with her." Anne could learn nothing more.

After a short while in this session Anne and Bill had hypnotized each other to depths of forty-two and forty-eight respectively. As they spoke of their dreamlike fantasies, it became clear that they were together in their world, seeing and experiencing the same things. They climbed to a place they both described as Heaven. There was water in front of them—"it was like champagne, and had beautiful, huge bubbles in it." Anne heard a distant voice calling Bill, but he told her to ignore it. Bill claimed that this place also had rules of its own, and he did not want Anne to reveal them to anyone else, or to divulge the exact route by which they reached the heavenly place. They wandered around looking at brilliant, multicolored rocks and stones for some time. Suddenly Bill announced that it was time for them to leave. Later, he could not explain why they had to go. When Anne argued to remain, Bill immediately began counting backward from fifty, presumably her trance depth, to awaken her. Again, Tart had not ordered Bill to do this.

Later, Anne and Bill said that they both had felt disembodied, able to float through one another. At one point, when Bill had commanded Anne to give him her hand so that he could lead her out of their fantasy world, Anne reported that she had to "crawl back into my body, sort of. It was almost as if we were moving around with just heads. When Bill said give him my hand, I had to kind of conjure up a hand."

It also became clear that this passing through each other was accompanied by a sense of merging identities, which Tart describes as "a partial blending of themselves quite beyond the degree of contact human beings expect to share with others."

There seems little doubt that Anne and Bill communicated telepathically in their mutual trance. There were many times when they sat silently, not responding to Tart; yet when he finally contacted and questioned them, they reported that they had been engaged in conversation. In the post-session interviews Anne and Bill gave detailed accounts of their fantasies. When Tart compared the separate reports, he found that Anne and Bill had had many identical experiences, although there were no verbal exchanges of this information between them. Tart writes that Anne and Bill "felt they must have been communicating telepathically or that they had actually been 'in' the nonworldly locales they had experienced."

The telepathy extended beyond the laboratory sessions. When they were together, they found that each was anticipating the other's wishes. And even when they were apart, Bill would suddenly "know" what Anne was doing, or vice versa. Later, when they compared notes, they found that each had been correct about the other. The degree of rapport between Anne and Bill, and of strife between them and their respective spouses, grew to such an extent that they had to dissolve their friendship and abandon further hypnotic sessions. "They were not able to cope with the intense intimacy," says Tart.

Was the case of Anne and Bill an isolated incident? Not at all. A few months later Tart conducted the same experiment with two other individuals; again both were married to other parties. And again, he observed the same sequence of events: first a strong friendship developed; then the subjects resented Tart's intrusions into their shared world; and finally telepathic bonds were forged through the mutual trance. This experiment also grew too intense to be continued.

What fundamental secret had Tart stumbled upon? He had not set out to conduct a psi experiment; it just turned out that way. Now, in retrospect, he feels that he should have suspected the possibility of telepathic communications between persons apparently *sharing the same state of consciousness.* "ESP," he says, "is a function of the number of barriers we let down. As we begin to shed barriers, we automatically become more open to our environment; we perceive things differently. Let down enough barriers, and we can experience things telepathically. Mutual hypnosis, I believe, is one excellent technique for letting down barriers."

The subjects in Kenneth Keeling's telepathy experiments shed some barriers since they were hypnotized; both sender and receiver were in *similar* states of consciousness. In Tart's work, not only were Anne and Bill's mental states *similar,* each was *mutually dependent* on the other—a powerful blend.

If mutual hypnosis works so well with two people, what about with three or four? Imagine four people—A, B, C, and D—seated in a square. A hypnotizes B and instructs B to hypnotize A. One common bond has been formed. Then the experimenter, E, orders A to hypnotize C, and suggests that B further deepen C's trance. A triangular link is made. Now E orders A to hypnotize D, and then has B and C intensify D's trance. A square bond has been forged. The four people are dependently sharing a common level of consciousness. What type of friendships would result? What degrees of intimacy would be reached? What fluidity of telepathic impressions would occur? And—why stop at four people? Perhaps one might have a group of ten people seated in a circle weaving a spiderlike network of psi bonds, bonds stretching round the circle and crisscrossing it, lacing everyone together. Would this be a first-order approximation of Jung's "collective unconscious"?

The idea of extending mutual hypnosis to many individuals is not farfetched. In fact, Tart has mentally tinkered with the notion. But how would such an experiment change the people involved? How would it affect their private and public lives? Their marriages? Their family ties? The questions run on endlessly, and their central importance prevents mutual hypnosis research from proceeding recklessly.

There is no doubt that one day the technique will play a major role in psi research. But not yet. "Our culture," says Tart, "does not prepare people for such sudden, intense intimacy." Will it ever? Will we gradually learn to handle the extreme closeness that fluent telepathic ability could make a common daily experience? The question transcends the field of parapsychology and becomes an issue for all humankind.

3
Psychic Healing

If the head and body are to be well,
you must begin by curing the soul.

Plato, c. 300 B.C.

Laying-on of Hands

Scene 1: In a major Chicago hospital, a forty-one-year-old woman suffering from arthritis makes an unorthodox request. She asks that a psychic healer be called in to treat her gnarled hands and relieve the pain she has endured for the last few months. Since the crippling condition has failed to respond to medical treatment, her physician can see no harm in granting her request—so long as the incident receives no publicity. Although he does not believe in psychic healing, he feels that the woman might benefit psychologically from the experience. So, a tall, middle-aged man, with several years of healing experience, is brought to the patient's bedside. After a brief conversation, the healer closes his eyes and enters a mental state which he later describes as "immensely relaxed and open." After meditating for half an hour on the sick woman's hands, the healer leaves. The next morning the pain is considerably less, and the knotty lumps at the finger joints are much smaller. By week's end, the hands look normal and the once excruciating pain is only a vague memory.[1]

Scene 2: During the clamor and frenzy of a group healing session held in New York, a young man who has been unable to walk for five years is helped onto the auditorium stage. Several hundred people shout the name of Jesus while scores more kneel in fervent

78

prayer. This drama is part of the religious ritual beseeching Jesus to have mercy on the crippled man and all the others who are on the stage to be cured. The man, in his wheel chair, is placed in front of a famous psychic healer. She holds her hands over his legs, tilts her head back and rolls her eyes toward heaven. Suddenly, to the shouts from the audience, the man gets up from his wheel chair, shoves it aside, and walks off the stage wiping his moist eyes.[2]

Both of these scenes actually occurred during the winter of 1972. However, only one of them is an example of genuine psychic healing. In the case of the woman suffering from acute arthritis, X rays taken of her hands on the days following treatment revealed a steady and substantial decrease in the knotty calcium deposits on her bones. By week's end, the X rays showed not a trace of calcium overlay. In the second case, however, the man who so happily abandoned his wheel chair to walk home was badly in need of that chair only a week later.

The first instance is an example of genuine psychic healing, while the second is an example of hysterical suppression of symptoms. In any discussion of psychic healing it is important to differentiate between the two, although the distinction is not always easy to make. In genuine psychic healing the healer–patient interaction should bring about biochemical alterations in the root of the ailment, not merely an apparent alleviation of symptoms. If the healing treatment is for cancer, for example, there should be a manifest decrease in the proliferation of renegade cells. A mere absence of pain and improvement in the patient's general health, although desirable conditions in themselves, are not indications of healing authenticity.

Dr. Lawrence LeShan is a tall, aggressive, no-nonsense psychologist who has spent many years investigating psychic healing. His research has been worldwide, and he has interviewed healers and seen many apparently miraculous cures, as well as many that were sheer fakery. LeShan readily admits that many reported healing cases, perhaps as many as ninety percent, are not true examples of psychic healing. "Most of the cases," he says, "involve only a temporary suppression of symptoms, but unfortunately, through rash judgment, they are held up as examples of psychic healing." (Here, we are not considering the numerous cases of out-and-out fraud.) Lamentably, the instances of temporary, incomplete healing which are routinely passed off as genuine examples of laying-on of hands weaken the arguments for psychic healing. The legitimate reports get buried under mountains of sensational misnomers.

But what about the remaining ten percent of the cases? LeShan eagerly interjects, "They are *solid* instances of psychic healing. They are cases medically diagnosed as incurable, where the physician could do nothing more for the patient except perhaps give palliative treatment, and suddenly, after a healing session the pathological root of the problem is gone. Vanished." These are the cases that merit a closer look in hope of understanding the mechanism behind the laying-on of hands. And fortunately, within the last five years several reliable, well-documented experiments have been conducted with healers performing their feats on plants, mice, and human subjects. These experiments have taken much of the occult stigma out of psychic healing phenomenon and provide a partial answer to the central questions: What does a psychic healer do to a patient to bring about a cure? Is there a transfer of energy? Some known form of energy or waves that have eluded modern detection?

In attacking these questions LeShan has taken a different route from the physical scientists. He has gone out into the field and observed Eastern and Western healers firsthand. Studying their techniques and rituals, he found a tremendous and somewhat perplexing diversity in methodology. "Some healers sit facing east," he says. "But then others face north. Some remove all metal trinkets from their body. Yet another group wears copper jewelry. Many of them pray to Jesus," he continues, shaking his head, "but others pray to Brahma. Some sit on sheepskins, others on grass, and some don't sit at all." But if the healers he studied had one thing in common, it was that they all felt they did not perform the healing themselves; "a 'spirit' did it working through them." They felt they were merely passive agents, intermediaries between a higher intelligence and the sick.

In this last claim LeShan found what he was looking for—a common denominator running through the varied ritualistic practices. Facing east or north, sitting on sheepskins or grass, all the healers he studied slipped into altered states of consciousness in order to heal. This trance state is what they experientially felt as their contact with the healing "spirit," or force. Some referred to it as a trance, others as a hypnotic state, a dreamlike detachment from the external world, but in all cases the healer got the feeling of relinquishing his or her identity and volition. Undoubtedly, it is the extreme mental passivity characteristic of most ASCs which gives the healer the feeling that he or she is not the cause of the healing, but only the instrument of some external force.

The Healing Force

Recent studies of psychic healers that show a definite shift in the level of consciousness during healing still do not answer the question posed earlier: What is it about the healer–patient interaction that effects a cure?

Many parapsychologists feel that a healer in an ASC approaches a oneness with the patient. Experientially, this unification seems to be similar to the merging of a hypnotic subject with the environment once the subject has relinquished his or her superstructure. Linked in this common bond with the patient, the healer "mobilizes and aids the self-repair mechanism of the patient," according to LeShan, so that the patient essentially heals himself through the acceleration of his own bodily repair functions.

An analogy might make this point clearer. We know that any skill an individual possesses—reading, playing the piano, hitting a tennis ball—can always be improved. The human organism simply never functions at its maximum potential. Through more practice, more training, greater diligence, the level of performance of a task can be raised. But one area where this below-capacity functioning appears to be critically low, and an area in which we have surprisingly little control, is body self-repair. Certain facial warts, for example, can be cured by suggestion alone. In one study of children dotted with such warts, a brightly colored ink circle was drawn around each growth. Each child was told that as the colored circle faded the encircled wart would slowly vanish. And it did. But the success rate is high only with children, not with adults. Through the power of suggestion the child apparently mobilizes his or her internal bodily processes, unconsciously, to defeat the warts. But the average adult cannot activate the required self-repair mechanism. It is not that the task lies outside the potential of his body chemistry, for wart-plagued adults under hypnosis *can* vanquish the unsightly growths; it is simply that in the normal, wakeful state we have amazingly little control over our self-repair systems. Two other areas in which this is apparent are the common cold and general allergies, both of which can be fought by a well-functioning bodily repair system. But how many people have the required voluntary control to do this? Unfortunately, very few.

Surveying the various accomplishments of psychic healers adds further credence to the self-repair hypothesis. There are no known cases of healers regenerating a lost limb or initiating the growth of a missing eyeball, says LeShan. These feats are beyond the talents of the best healers; they are also beyond the human body's self-repair mechanism. Rather, healers bring about changes which depend on the patient's increased resistance to hosts, viruses, cancer—a general strengthening of the immunological system. All such changes are well within the body's ability for self-treatment.

Although a healer may rally a patient to cure himself, does the healer also transfer something *from* himself to the patient? Some form of energy? (The notions of self-repair and energy transfer need not be viewed as mutually exclusive; indeed, if anything, they are probably complementary.) There is considerable evidence to suggest that some energy flows between healer and patient. Dr. Thelma Moss, a medical psychologist at the Neuropsychiatric Institute in Los Angeles and a professor at UCLA, feels that there is an "energy flow" from the healer which initiates and augments the patient's self-repair system. She suspects that her research group, using a new lensless photographic technique called Kirlian photography, may have detected a hint of this exchange. Appropriately, Moss calls this force "psychic energy," and emphasizes that numerous cultures throughout history have reported its existence.

The ancient Egyptians called it *ka;* the Hindus and Yogis, *Prana;* the Hawaiians, *mana.* One term popular today among Russian parapsychologists is *bioplasma.* The Chinese name for this energy is *ch'i,* and it is supposedly the substance flowing throughout the body's acupuncture system. Many U.S. parapsychologists, inspired by the Russians, believe there is a connection between acupuncture and psychic healing. Ch'i energy was conceived by the ancient Chinese as coursing through meridians of the body in two forms, yin and yang. According to acupuncture teachings, when there is equal balance of the yin and yang forces nourishing an organ, a healthy condition prevails. However, any imbalance indicates a pathology, and the magnitude of the imbalance is correlated to the severity of the ailment. Although medical science has not yet detected ch'i energy, the success of acupuncture treatment can no longer be disputed.*

One cannot help being awed by the meridians on an acupuncture chart. The complex array of intertwining paths stretches to all extremities of the body over some very unorthodox routes. Although scientists the world over have sought desperately to detect the substance which is supposed to comprise these meridians, all attempts have failed. The body's blood, lymphatic, and nervous systems can be clearly seen by dissection, but no one has seen an acupuncture system. How did the ancient Chinese accurately chart the

---

*Although the Gate Theory, an opening and closing of nerve cell doors, currently is used in the West to explain the *modus operandi* of acupuncture, it has not been proven and does not rule out the existence of a yet undetected body energy system as Chinese theory teaches.

intricate meridians 5,000 years ago? If trial and error were their approach, they would still be drawing up the charts today, for the combinatorial richness of the problem is astronomical. Dr. LeShan suggests an answer: "The ancient chartings look like the work of a psychic healer." In fact, many healers today claim that they can sense the acupuncture meridians and the points for needle insertion by slowly passing their hands over a person's body. Is this how the charts were originally prepared? The premise is not without some experimental backing.

Dr. William Tiller, who is a physicist and chairman of the Department of Material Sciences at Stanford University, and Dr. Victor Adamenko, a Russian physicist, have independently found that acupuncture points can easily be detected with a simple instrument called a wheatstone bridge, which measures electrical resistance. An electrode is held in a person's hand and another one is systematically run over the person's body, following recommended acupuncture meridians. There is a large drop in resistance when an acupuncture site is encountered. Normally the body resistance between the two electrodes is on the order of one million ohms. However, when an acupuncture point is reached, the resistance drops by ninety-five percent to about 50,000 ohms.[3] Many parapsychologists feel that a good psychic healer, by passing his or her hands over a patient's body, can sense these large resistance changes.

Dr. Adamenko has gone a step further and related acupuncture directly to psychic healing. Adamenko inserted two needles into symmetrical acupuncture points on the right and left sides of a man with an infected leg and measured a resistance value (R). He then switched the needles around and measured the resistance in the opposite direction (R'). The values of R and R' were different, indicating a disturbance in that particular area of the body. Before a Russian healer treated the man, Adamenko performed the same two measurements on the healer and found no difference between R and R'. After a healing session, however, there was a noticeable difference between the measurements in both the patient and the healer; the patient's acupuncture circuit came into balance and the healer's went slightly out of balance.[4] Thus, it seems that the healer actually transferred a quantity of something to the patient. Since 1971, when Adamenko performed these experiments, Dr. Tiller has tried them and found the same results. Tiller says that there are many ways to stimulate acupuncture points —chemicals, manual massage, needles, electrified needles, and laser beams —but the undisputed best method is "the psychic energy (spiritual energy injection). This seems to be the best procedure for bringing about bodily balance."

That a shift in the level of consciousness plays a role in psychic healing is implied in some of Adamenko's work. In one experiment he monitored several acupuncture points in normal individuals before they were hypnotized. The values remained constant until each person began to fall into a trance. Then, Adamenko found, the people who were the best hypnotic subjects showed the greatest changes in reading at the monitored acupuncture points. In fact, the conductivity at the points more than doubled at the time of deepest trance. The few persons who were not hypnotizable showed no change in the needle readings.[5]

American scientists and reporters who have journeyed to China to witness operations performed under acupuncture anesthesia have been amazed that patients eat, drink, and talk during surgery. In 1966 James Reston, who is an editorial columnist and vice-president for *The New York Times,* observed such an operation at the Hun Shan Hospital in Shanghai. A young man was wheeled into the operating theater and transferred to a steel topped table. He was Chen Chien, a twenty-four-year-old factory worker suffering from an advanced case of tuberculosis that required removing his left lung and one rib. The surgeons deftly split open Chen's back, moved through the bone and muscle, severed and removed the lung and rib. While the gaping hole was still open, Chen Chien remarked that he was hungry. An attendant brought in some slices of orange and a beverage, both of which he finished off. But they had not been sterilized! During one of the most difficult and serious operations known to medicine, articles covered with bacteria were brought into the operating room. Reston wondered if the surgeons were fools to risk the man's life to satisfy his appetite.[6] But the case of Chen Chien is not unique. Quite often unsterilized articles are brought into operating rooms when acupuncture anesthesia is being used. Does the alleged ch'i energy activated through acupuncture ward off infection? Dr. Tiller feels it very well may. "It seems quite remarkable," he says, "that this absence of what we think of as the need for sterilization in the operating room does not lead to any problems. This may be because we are dealing here with another level of energy, and if we deal with these other levels of energy, then we can have energy effects that do not require the normal sterilization procedures."[7]

One well-known healer, Ethel DeLoach of New Jersey, who has been studied by scientists for the last five years, is convinced of the link between acupuncture and psychic healing. She has found that most of her patients report a "prickling sensation," a feeling of small needle points entering the skin, as she passes her hands over the troubled area.

Mrs. DeLoach is a cheerful woman in her fifties who found that she had healing powers rather late in life—about seven years ago. The realization of this ability first came when her daughter was severely kicked on the knee by a horse. No doctor was available, and the young girl was in terrible pain. In desperation, Ethel thought of a book that she had read recently— *Miracle Healers*—and decided that laying-on of hands was worth a try. To her amazement, she felt that her hands were "taken over" by an external agent, and the girl's pain quickly vanished. From that day forward Ethel DeLoach was convinced that she had paranormal healing talents.

She began reading all she could on psychic healing and practicing it whenever the opportunity arose. During the early years she had no personal theory about how her healing ability worked. Then, through a Japanese patient, she was introduced to acupuncture, and she found that using acupuncture charts improved her ability to heal. Today, whenever she heals, she follows the meridian lines and needle insertion points with her extended hands. During the last few years she has used this technique in the successful treatment of cancer in several New York City hospitals where she has been called in at a patient's request.[8]

In another case, a woman whom Ethel DeLoach refers to as Mrs. H wrote to the healer: "I want to see you as soon as possible. I have been going to a gynecologist who told me I have two lumps in my left breast. He wants me to go to the hospital as soon as possible to have my breast removed."

Three days later an attractive middle-aged woman arrived at Mrs. DeLoach's home. She was overweight and unhappy, and the two lumps on her breast were not her only ailment. The woman had badly ulcerated legs which had to be kept bandaged, one kidney had been removed several years before, a cataract operation three years before had left her with poor vision, and her hearing was rated at about thirty-three percent normal.

The woman reclined on the couch in Mrs. DeLoach's living room, and the healer began running her hands along certain acupuncture meridians. Several hours later, feeling very optimistic, the woman returned home. A month later Mrs. DeLoach received a letter: "As far as my breast is concerned, I feel wonderful. The breast has become soft now; before it was a little hard, but I haven't been back to the doctor since the last time. My hearing improvement is very slight, but my legs stopped hurting—they feel pretty good. Can you give me another treatment?"

A week later the woman returned, much changed in appearance. She had lost about ten pounds and seemed much happier and more cheerful. They went through another long healing session, and three weeks later another letter arrived. The woman had gone back to her doctor:

He examined both my breasts, and he had a funny expression on his face but did not say anything. He questioned me, not mentioning the breast, so I said I was anxious to hear about my breast. He said, "Oh, don't worry about it any more. It's so tiny that you don't have to have the operation." I was so happy that I told him you healed me. He was angry and said the lumps just dissolved.

Mrs. DeLoach's whole-body treatment had additional effects on Mrs. H. Three weeks later, on January twenty-second, Mrs. DeLoach received these words: "My legs are clearing up and have stopped draining. I am going to the eye doctor on Friday (28th)." That visit revealed that Mrs. H's vision had greatly improved. In fact, her right eye was tested at 20/20.[9]

Mrs. DeLoach feels strongly that acupuncture and psychic healing go hand in hand. "My technique," she says, "seems to be acupuncture without needles, magnetic passes over the meridian paths of the body, manipulation, and attention to the astral (spiritual) body as well."

Whether or not there is a direct relationship between the mechanism of acupuncture and that of psychic healing is still an open question; parapsychologists are widely split on the issue. Some feel that suggestive evidence exists for such a relationship, but others feel that the only feature acupuncture and psychic healing have in common is our ignorance about how each operates. As for psychic healing *per se,* it is clear from experiments that will be presented throughout the remainder of this chapter that there is a transfer of something, call it "psychic energy" for lack of a better name, from healer to patient, be the patient a wilting chrysanthemum, a wounded mouse, or a hospitalized human.

Kirlian Photography

Photographs of healers taken by a lensless, electrical process before, during, and after healing sessions suggest that something unusual may occur during psychic healing—to both the healer and the patient.

The process, called Kirlian photography, is named after two Soviet scientists, S. D. and V. Kirlian, who first demonstrated its operation in 1939. Although the Russians have been studying the process for over thirty years, parapsychologists in this country have just recently turned their attention to it.

The process is simple. The object to be photographed (in the case of a healer, the fingertip pad is usually used for convenience) is placed in direct contact with regular black-and-white or color film. An electrical discharge is sent through the back of the photographic plate to the object. When the film is conventionally developed, there is a brilliant halo surrounding the image. The color of this halo, its intensity, and its geometrical configuration vary markedly with the mental and physical attitude of the subject photographed. The photographed fingertip of an average person in good physical health and in a relaxed frame of mind, for example, has a corona that is typically pale to dark blue in color. If the finger pad of the same person is photographed while he or she is in a state of arousal, the corona is typically red and white, with fine spindles flaring radially outward.

Dr. Thelma Moss was one of the first American scientists performing psychical research to observe the Kirlian process during a trip to Russia in 1970. What she saw made a lasting impression. The Soviets claim to show through the Kirlian process that psychic healing involves a dynamic, detectable interchange of energy between healer and patient. On her return to the United States Moss and her co-worker Kendall Johnson built their own Kirlian device. It uses a low voltage (twelve volts), high frequency (3,000 hertz) spark to form the corona image on ordinary four by five Kodak film.

The researchers have observed an interesting effect when taking photographs of a healer before and after treating a patient. According to Moss, there is a definite, sizable increase in the width of the corona surrounding the fingertip of the patient and a corresponding decrease in the same parameters of the healer's halo. She has repeatedly observed this result. Of course, the question is obvious: Does this indicate a transfer of energy from the healer to the patient? Unfortunately, the answer is not so straightforward.

Professor Moss has photographed fingertips of two people with their hands almost touching and found two distinct results. "In some cases," she says, "the energy fields attract each other, and in other cases they push each other away—just like a magnet."[10] Moss is willing to speculate on this observation. "My guess is this is why some people like each other instinctively when shaking hands. You can call it good vibes and bad vibes."

Although the Kirlian process is new in this country, researchers are enthusiastic about its future as a tool in psychical research. Dr. Moss views it as "a laboratory tool, perhaps the equivalent of the EEG in its early stages of development."

EEG responses are correlated with certain electrical states of the brain and with corresponding mental attitudes; several researchers are attempting to establish the same type of correlations between the colors and configurations on Kirlian photographs and the mental and physical states of the person photographed.

At the University of Washington in Seattle, Richard Miller, a physicist and director of research in parapsychics, is interested in learning how alcohol consumption affects Kirlian photographs. Tests conducted on medical students at UCLA before and after their drinking seventeen ounces of straight bourbon showed a marked corona difference; afterward, the coronas surrounding their fingertips flared and brightened. This fact has led Miller to photograph feet instead of fingertips in his alcohol studies since one main acupuncture site located on the sole is supposed to bear a relationship to the bladder under stress. Volunteer subjects are given a six-pack of beer to consume, and at regular intervals Kirlian photographs are taken of the soles of their feet. The project, yet to be completed, is aimed at better understanding the numerous parameters which can influence the brilliant Kirlian pictures.[11]

Humans are not the only subjects for Kirlian pictures. A leaf freshly plucked from a tree and put flush against a Kirlian device produces an image of the leaf outlined with a glowing halo. Subsequent pictures of the same leaf taken over a period of several hours reveal an ever diminishing corona. Interestingly, once the leaf is dead no corona can be seen.[12] This effect has been observed by numerous independent researchers. Russian parapsychologists claim the same pattern of events occurs in a person nearing death. Dr. Tiller reported after a trip to Russia that it takes several days after death has been officially pronounced by a physician for the fingertips to lose their glow. "The self-emission of living things," says Tiller, "seems to be a direct measure of the life processes occurring within their system."

Several U.S. researchers traveling through Russia have been shown one effect that no one in this country has yet been able to duplicate (and there is much debate whether the phenomenon is genuine). It is called the "phantom leaf effect." If a freshly picked leaf has a chunk cut out of it before it is photographed, according to Russian researchers, the resulting Kirlian picture does not show the periphery of the cut leaf, but depicts the leaf in its entirety. Instead of a colorful center surrounded by a glowing halo as would be expected from a whole leaf, the uncut portion photographs normally with its characteristic corona, and the part that is physically missing photographs as a bright haze.[13] The phantom leaf phenomenon remains inexplicable, and suspiciously unrepeatable.

In photographing 500 finger pads of normal people, Moss and Johnson found that the blue corona varies in width from a sixteenth to a quarter of an inch. Moss feels this fact was foretold many years before the Kirlians developed their photographic process. She refers to a work entitled *Man and His Bodies* by the mystic Annie Besant, published in 1900:

> Every solid, liquid, and gaseous particle of the physical body is
> surrounded with an etheric envelop . . . in size it projects about
> one-fourth of an inch beyond the skin . . . In appearance, the
> etheric double is a pale violet-grey or blue-grey, faintly luminous
> and coarse or fine in texture, according as the dense physical body
> is coarse or fine. . . . Persons who have lost a limb by amputation
> sometimes complain that they can feel pain at the extremity
> . . . This is due to the fact that the etheric portion of the limb is
> not removed with the dense physical portion.[14]

"This last sentence," Moss and Johnson write, "vividly reminds us of the experiments reported by the Russians in relation to their 'phantom' leaves."[15] But a neurologist, of course, would explain an amputee's sensation of still possessing a limb as a conditioned nerve response.

E. Douglas Dean, an instructor at the Newark College of Engineering, has used Kirlian photography to obtain dramatic pictures of Ethel De-Loach. The equipment used by Dean is of Czechoslovakian design. It consists of a ten-inch by fifteen-inch copperplate table, insulated with plastic and varnish, and a high frequency wave of 50,000 hertz that is delivered to the photographic plate, which contains Kodachrome emulsion.

Even in a nonhealing state Mrs. DeLoach's fingertip pads reveal great color and flare. The massive blotches of vivid royal blue surrounding her fingertips stretch far beyond the normal limit of one-quarter inch Dr. Moss has measured in others. With Mrs. DeLoach's fingertip on the plate, Dean asks her to think that she is in the process of healing. When she is fully in the healing state, he takes another picture. The results can best be described as resembling the solar flare emanating from the surface of the sun. The corona is composed of long licking flames, hot yellow in color with red-orange tips. After the healing state passes, the corona greatly shrinks and darkens to blue. Dean says, "With the technique of Kirlian photography it appears that we are able to confirm that healing generates increased energy emanations. The evidence gets stronger and stronger every day."[16]

Some parapsychologists feel that the Kirlian process actually photographs the long-sought psychic energy. Some claim that the mysterious human aura which psychics throughout history have said surrounds all individuals and reveals aspects of their mental and physical well-being is in fact the corona captured on a Kirlian picture. It has even been suggested that the halos believed to crown the heads of Jesus, mystics, and saints were exceptionally intense fields which the Kirlian equipment can record in weaker form. These notions seem overeager; needless to say, experimental evidence does not confirm any of them. Perhaps it never will. Even so, there is valuable information in a Kirlian photograph. Unfortunately, no one is sure just how to decipher it and it does not help matters to find an increasing number of parapsychologists making claims of having photographed "psychic energy."

Professor Tiller has an optimistic, conservative opinion on the Kirlian process. "It is clear," he says, "that the Kirlian process is photographing some fundamental characteristics of living matter. But we must ask ourselves; what effects are caused by psychic variables, and what ones can be explained by simple physical considerations—things such as body sweat, skin oils, surface contamination, and the like?"

Tiller lists five physical variables that could easily influence a Kirlian photograph by changing its color and shape, and thus trigger a false interpretation:

1. A change in the skin's electrical potential. This could be caused by contamination from a foreign agent such as small metallic particles or just an increase in sweat or skin oil. The result could give rise to an increase in voltage, which in turn would increase the ionization of the air between the object being photographed and the photographic plate. These factors might produce variations in the size, intensity, and configuration of the corona.

2. A change in surface chemistry of the skin. Ionization of surface chemicals by the spark discharge could produce a variety of physical effects and generate radiations of many wavelengths; this would give rise to a spectrum of corona colors.

3. Topographical alterations of the skin. Fingertips, the objects most frequently photographed, have ridges, loops, and whorls. Each of these serves as a separate contact point with the photographic plate, and they might produce constructive (bright) and destructive (dark) interference patterns on the film.

4. Resonance. Since biological cells contain energy of their own, it is only reasonable that there should be some type of coupling between the electrochemical energy of the cells and the electric spark from the Kirlian device. Under certain conditions these resonances could affect the shape and density of the corona.

5. The pinch effect. A pinchlike force caused by the high density spark could cause the photographic film to buckle at the time of discharge, thus altering the geometry of the initial setup.[17]

Allegations that the Kirlian process photographs psychic energy can be made only when all other parameters have been well controlled. In the meantime, Kirlian photography must be used with interest and caution. But its future as an investigative research tool is already well assured. Kirlian photography, says Tiller, will one day be used for "an objective evaluation of the physiological state of the living organism, for diagnosis of body health or pathology, and for registration of the emotional state."

The Nun and the Psychic

Sister Justa Smith is a soft-spoken Franciscan nun who holds a doctorate in biochemistry and master's degrees in physical chemistry and mathematics. Like many modern nuns she does not wear the conventional religious habit, but her unconventionality does not end there. For the last several years Dr. Smith has been research director of the Human Dimensions Institute, a large complex which serves as the laboratory arm of Rosary Hill College in Buffalo, New York. Her experiments with psychic healers comprise some of the most cogent and provocative research done in this field. In her well-equipped biochemical laboratory, working in an area in which she is considered an expert—the effects of magnetic fields on enzymes—she has offered the first solid evidence that psychic healing involves a transfer of energy from healer to patient.

In the summer of 1967 Dr. Smith began a series of experiments with the renowned Hungarian healer, Colonel Oskar Estebany. Estebany, who is known throughout Europe for his laying-on of hands treatment, came to the United States to be studied by scientists, and he was at least as curious as the scientists, for he desperately wanted to know how his psychic powers worked. Could science provide any clue to the mechanisms underlying laying-on of hands?

Dr. Smith accepted the challange, and her line of attack was straightforward. If psychic healing works, she reasoned, it must induce fundamental changes in an organism at a biochemical level, an enzymatic level. The intricate workings of our body's cells are largely controlled by enzymes. "In essence," says Dr. Smith, "enzymes are the brains of the cells, instructing them on how they must behave to maintain healthy organs. Thus, from an enzymatic standpoint, disease or illness can be viewed as proceeding from a malfunctioning of the commanding enzymes." When an enzyme runs amuck, vital information necessary for proper cellular maintenance is deleted or distorted, and as is the case with any system given false or incomplete information, irregular behavior ensues. Dr. Smith reasoned that if enzyme failure is the root physical cause of disease, then any therapeutic effect brought on by psychic healing should be detectable at the enzyme level. This means that if laying-on of hands does involve a transfer of energy, whatever the nature of that energy, it should be detectable in the enzymatic reactions within the patient's body. Dr. Smith had done years of research on the enzyme trypsin, which is produced by the pancreas and is essential in maintaining the body's ability to combat diseased tissue, abscesses, and fistulas. Knowing how it reacts under magnetic fields, she decided trypsin would be the best enzyme to start with.

There remained only one problem in the experimental setup. If human subjects were used in the experiment, there would be no *absolute* means of separating healing effects induced by a transfer of energy from Mr. Estebany to a patient from that recovery due to purely psychological factors on the part of the patient. Perhaps, Dr. Smith reasoned, in the presence of a well-known healer, a patient's will to recover might be so powerful that the patient would heal himself. For the experiment to be a success, there had to be some way to relate any observed chemical alterations in the enzyme to the work of Mr. Estebany and not to the psyche of the patient. "I decided," says Dr. Smith, "to use the enzyme trypsin *in vitro* (outside the body).* This would give me an objective measure of Mr. Estebany's healing powers." Although Mr. Estebany had been successfully treating people for over twenty-five years, this was the first time his patients would be pyrex flasks filled with enzyme solutions. The question was: Could he increase the kinematic rates of reaction of the enzyme by laying-on of hands?

In the first series of tests, three glass flasks were filled with aliquots of trypsin in solution (concentration: 500 milligrams per milliliter, pH 3). The first flask was put to one side to serve as a control. The second flask was periodically exposed to a strong magnetic field of 8,000 to 13,000 gauss (the magnetic field of the earth is about one-half gauss). The third flask was treated by Estebany in much the way he normally treats patients, by laying-on of hands. He simply put his hands around the flask, leaving them there for a period of seventy-five minutes. Every fifteen minutes, Dr. Smith pipetted small quantities of the solution from each flask and placed them in a spectrophotometer to determine the rate of chemical reaction. (One of her earlier experiments using the hands of a nonhealer ruled out the possibility that the heat of Estebany's hands affected the solution.) The results, after several days of work, were more startling than Smith had hoped for.

The solution that served as the control showed essentially no chemical change, and the solution exposed to high magnetic fields showed the change that she had anticipated. However, the flask that had been treated by Mr.

---

*The trypsin used in the experiments was of a twice crystallized, salt-free variety known for its purity and purchased from a biochemical firm.

Estebany showed a very marked alteration. Its accelerated reaction was chemically identical, qualitatively and quantitatively, to the solution that had been subjected to strong magnetic fields.[18] This surprised Dr. Smith, for it meant that the *net effect* of Mr. Estebany's treatment was identical to that caused by magnetic fields. She was aware that researchers at the University of Illinois and at the Medical Research Foundation on Long Island have found that strong magnetic fields greatly enhance healing in laboratory animals. Did a correlation suggest itself? Is healing energy magnetic in nature?

Dr. Smith is the first to caution against leaping at this easy, attractive, but all too premature theory. "It is naive to say," she warns, "that just because two effects are the same they must have been brought about by the same mechanisms." This we know, for certainly a bullet to the heart and a hefty dose of strychnine cause death, but through entirely different mechanisms.

This point is worth pursuing, for although Mr. Estebany and the external magnetic field had identical effects on the trypsin solution, no magnetic detectors, even the most incredibly sensitive, have ever picked up so much as a trace of a magnetic field in the vicinity of a healer. That Mr. Estebany did something remarkable to the enzyme in solution is undeniable, but it seems equally clear that he did not achieve results by projecting a known type of energy into the flask. Perhaps an analogy might reinforce this point.

Imagine, for a moment, two electrically charged balls, one positive and one negative, with the positive ball suspended in the air some distance above the negative one on the ground. Now imagine that the positive ball is released and begins to fall downward. If we were only familiar with one physical law—that unlike charges attract—we would naively say that the ball in the air is plummeting downward because of the electrical attraction between it and the negative ball resting on the ground. However, this answer ignores the very real and substantial gravitational force between the airborne ball and the earth. In reality, the upper ball is falling toward the lower ball under the influence of two distinctly different types of energy: electrical and gravitational. (And the gravitational force is almost wholly responsible for the motion.) All of this is to suggest that perhaps an *unknown* form of energy, call it psychic energy, is the dominant force in psychic healing, although other *known* energies might play a vital but less important role.

All pioneering research generates excitement, some of it adverse. And the fact that a Roman Catholic nun was "dabbling in the occult" upset some people. Dr. Smith readily relates such an incident. One day an irate woman who had learned of the nun's healing experiments telephoned the laboratory. "Does the Church know what you are doing?" the woman demanded.

"Just what do you have in mind?" Sister Justa gently replied.

"This healing business that you are working with," said the woman, seeing heresy in the research. After a long pause, Dr. Smith answered, "Now who was the first person we know who used the laying-on of hands?"

This silenced the woman, for what could be more appropriate than a religious dedicated to understanding healing powers which date back many centuries?

Dr. Smith's research did not stop with the revelation that Mr. Estebany could speed up enzyme reactions in solution. There was another, bigger question, which loomed in her mind. Mr. Estebany had affected whole, healthy enzyme chains, but could he repair enzymes that had been deliberately damaged? Such a test would more closely examine Estebany's ability to repair body malfunctions.

Ultraviolet light is exceptionally damaging to the enzyme trypsin. The small quanta of light, when shown on trypsin molecules, act like bullets chaotically rupturing energy bonds between adjacent clusters of atoms. If Mr. Estebany could repair such molecular damage, actually reunite broken bonds, then there could be no doubt that energy is indeed transferred during the laying-on of hands. This was to be his next task.

Under the same experimental conditions as before, a flask of trypsin solution was exposed to ultraviolet light (wavelength 2,537 angstroms) and its structure greatly damaged. Mr. Estebany held his hands above the sides of the flask containing the ruptured molecules, and every fifteen minutes Dr. Smith pipetted out small quantities of the solution and studied them in a spectrophotometer. Somewhat astonished and noticeably elated, Dr. Smith found what she was looking for. The entropy of the solution significantly decreased during Mr. Estebany's treatment, and remained at that level, thus indicating a reorganization—i.e. repair—of damaged molecules. Mr. Estebany could indeed repair the damaged trypsin molecules! Here was an experiment which drew a clear line between genuine psychic healing and healing effects caused purely by a patient's desire to recover. More than encouraged by the results, Dr. Smith repeated the experiment with three other known healers, and each time she obtained statistically significant results.

But maintaining proper bodily health involves the action of many enzymes, not just trypsin. Besides infections, there are viruses, bacteria, and other hosts that regularly attack the body and must be warded off by the appropriate enzymatic system. Could a healer affect other enzymes? "It was in searching for an answer to this question," says Dr. Smith, "that it was decided to introduce other enzyme systems into this research—enzymes with totally different types of reactions."

Once again, she found an affirmative answer to her question. In some cases the healer (three different ones were used) *accelerated* the chemical activity of a particular enzyme. At other times the activity of a different enzyme was *slowed down*. But, the most amazing feature was that whether a particular reaction was *accelerated* or *decelerated*, the direction always corresponded to what would be, *in vivo*, a positive change in bodily health.[19] In one experiment with the enzyme nicotinamideadenine dinucleotide (NAD), for example, all the healers caused a deceleration of its chemical activity. "From a biochemical standpoint," says Smith, "a decrease in body production of NAD would have a positive effect on body healing." Hence, the healers always were able to affect the enzymatic reaction in whatever direction was in accord with improved body health, even though they had no prior knowledge of the favored direction—indeed, they never even knew what was in the flasks.

On Saturday, June 2, 1973, Dr. Smith presented her research at a conference entitled Psychic Healing: Myth into Science, which was held at Lincoln Center's Alice Tully Hall in New York City. The capacity crowd consisted of psychic researchers and psi enthusiasts, but most interestingly, about a third of the audience were physicians. Dr. Smith's presentation was direct and scientific, presented in slides depicting the analytical graphs and data from her series of healing experiments. If anything attests to the significance of her work, it is the enthusiastic response of this audience, especially the scientists and medical doctors present. Here, in her experiments, was solid evidence of healing effects, not frothy anecdotes, and everyone recognized it.

Dr. Smith emphasizes that her work is only a minor piece in the healing puzzle; the major questions are still unanswered. But the petite Franciscan nun is very optimistic. "When it comes to psychic healing," she says, "we should not be too distressed that there are so many unanswered questions; after all, we really don't know how aspirin works."

Rye Grass, Barley, and Mice

In 1966 Dr. H. H. Kleuter of the U.S. Department of Agriculture developed an accurate device for continuously measuring the growth rate of plants. The featherweight arm of the device, which rests lightly on a young seedling, is connected to a rotary transducer which in turn is connected to a strip chart recorder. As the plant grows, pushing up the light arm, the slow-running chart recorder provides a continuous record of growth. A year after the device had been successfully used by Department of Agriculture research scientists, Dr. Robert N. Miller, a chemical engineer and former professor at Georgia Tech, set out to use it in a psychical experiment. He wanted to know if two healers, Ambrose and Olga Worrall, could measurably affect the growth rate of plants. After considering many types of greens, Miller chose vigorous, hearty rye grass. But there was a novel twist to the experiment. The grass would be kept in Miller's Atlanta laboratory, and the two famous healers would operate out of their home in Baltimore, Maryland, some 600 miles away. The husband and wife team, each of whom has been practicing healing since 1915, were noted for their miraculous cures at a distance.

A few months before tests began, the Worralls visited Dr. Miller's laboratory in Atlanta to be briefed on the nature of the experiment. A time was decided upon for the test, the Worralls returned home, and Miller began to prepare the experiment.

He planted ten rye grass seeds in a clear plastic container about one-quarter inch beneath the soil. Each morning he faithfully watered them with exactly five millimeters of water. Once the sprouts were long enough, he carefully put them in contact with the arm of the measuring device, and the recorder was turned on. The young sprouts were growing. In a few days the growth rate had stabilized at 0.00625 inch per hour. Now, with the blades growing at a known rate the test could begin. On the morning of January 3, Miller watered the plants as usual, locked the laboratory door, and made certain that the temperature remained constant at seventy-two degrees. At eight P.M. that evening the plants were still stabilized. He then telephoned the Worralls and asked them to "hold the seedlings in their thoughts" beginning at precisely nine P.M. And then Miller sat back to wait out the evening.

Ambrose and Olga Worrall perform their healing feats in a manner quite different from Mr. Estebany. The Hungarian psychic favors laying-on of hands, but the Worralls, intensely religious people, sit with eyes closed and pray. As is common among most healers, they feel that they are only agents for some higher power. "I consider myself to be a channel or conductor for the healing current," said Ambrose in an interview with *Psychic* magazine, "not a generator of the power that heals. I have seen extraordinary results from its curative qualities, none of which I take credit for."[20] The Worralls prefer the term *spiritual healing* rather than psychic healing, for as Ambrose says, "We feel that this power comes from one source, and we call this source God."

On the morning of January 4, Dr. Miller went to the laboratory and carefully examined the strip chart recorder. He reports what he saw:

> All through the evening and until 9:00 P.M. the trace was a straight line with a slope which represented a growth rate of 0.00625 inch per hour. At exactly 9:00 P.M. the trace began to deviate upward and by 8:00 A.M. the next morning the grass was growing 0.0525 inch per hour, a growth rate increase of 840 percent.[21]

Thus, instead of growing the expected one-sixteenth of an inch during the intervening hours, the grass had sprouted more than half an inch. As Miller says, "there was no known physical variable which could have caused any large variation in the growth of the rye grass." The recorder ran for two more days. During that time the growth rate decreased, but did not fall back to the original rate.

As a physical scientist who has done considerable research in polymer chemistry and heat transfer fluids, written more than twenty scientific papers, and is listed in *American Men of Science,* Dr. Miller finds the results of his experiments interesting but patently disturbing. Mr. Estebany stood next to the trypsin-filled flasks. He treated them with his hands only a few inches from the damaged molecules. But the Worralls were over 600 miles away! Certainly no known physical energy generated within the human body can travel that far. Telepathy has no earthly respect for distance, and it appears that neither does the healing force. The evidence in terms of both phenomena is strong and, for physical scientists, very perplexing. Today we know of electric, magnetic, gravitational, and nuclear energies, but none of them can account for psychic healing. Again the question must be asked: Are we dealing with a new, yet undetected, form of energy? It appears we are, but to date, there is not a scrap of scientific evidence to suggest what it is.

In working with psychics who are eager to be scientifically studied, it can be both interesting and informative to hear their personal theories about how they believe their powers work. Ambrose Worrall theorizes on psychic healing:

> I believe it is a rearrangement of the micro particles of which all things are composed. The body isn't really what it appears to be —it is a system of little particles or points of energy separated

from each other by space, and held in place through an electrically balanced field.

And I believe that disease is a manifestation of these particles being out of the health orbit, that the healing power brings them back into the health orbit—back into a harmonious relationship.[22]

Who does this shuffling of particles from orbit to orbit? Ambrose and Olga Worrall will tell you it is God. A safe answer, if somewhat difficult to research.

One scientifically desirable factor in both Dr. Miller's experiment and those of Dr. Justa Smith is the objective detachment obtained by not using human beings. Even in physical experiments involving such unemotional subjects as oxidized metals, near-frictionless ball bearings, and viscous fluids, the number of variables to be controlled can be astronomical. With human subjects that figure runs *ad infinitum*. This fact has encouraged some researchers to confine their healing research to plants and animals. Yes, Miller's rye grass that shot up unexpectedly could conceivably have been influenced by some overlooked variable in the laboratory, but at least we can be sure the rye grass does not lie.

Neither do mice. At the Institute for Parapsychology in North Carolina, researchers Graham and Anita Watkins are studying the interaction between healers and laboratory mice. They use pairs of mice from the same litter, identical in size, sex, and age. The pair is rendered unconscious by placing them in containers filled with ten milliliters of standard USP ether. Then, each mouse from a pair is placed in a separate plastic (not metallic) pan. One mouse, the control, is kept in a distant room, while the tray containing the mate is placed on a table before a well-regarded healer.

Being of the same body weight, age, and sex, and having been administered the same quantity of ether, both litter mates should gain consciousness at about the same time. The Watkinses wanted to know if a psychic, through his admittedly ill-understood talent, could awaken a mouse placed before him significantly earlier than the anesthetized mate. They repeatedly performed the experiments using three different psychics, and obtained highly significant results. On the average, the mouse under the influence of the psychic awakened thirteen percent sooner than the control mouse. There is no physical or biological way to explain this. It was true even when a glass window separated the psychic from the mouse he was to awaken.[23] How did the psychics act as early alarms for the mice? The Watkinses, happy over their positive results, really have no idea. It appears that that question will only be answered once measuring equipment detects a wave of psychic energy, whatever that is, in transit.

Many psi researchers argue that psychic healing effects are not as unique as one might first suspect. Often, they say, the magnitude of one class of paranormal events casts a shadow over lesser happenings that are equally psychical in nature. Otto Rahn cites several clinical instances in which normal individuals undergoing some temporary mental or physical strain affect living matter around them. The influence can be beneficial or deleterious. In his book, *Invisible Radiations of Organisms,* Rahn tells of menstruating women whose mere presence has been known to wilt flowers, upset bacterial cultures, and influence the rising of yeast-filled dough. This, and other evidence Rahn presents, raises the possibility of an antihealing force, the very antithesis of psychic healing.[24]

Although psychical studies involving human subjects tend to be more dramatic than ones conducted with animals and plants, Dr. Bernard Grad, a physiologist at McGill University in Montreal, has amassed a weighty sum of evidence on the powers of healers. He repeatedly has shown that water, treated for several minutes by a healer and then used to nourish barley seeds, greatly accelerates their growth.[25] Grad's experiments with mice, in which a healer by laying-on of hands increases the healing of intentionally inflicted wounds, are now classic in the field.[26] Whatever the mechanism underlying the laying-on of hands, a phenomenon once regarded as purely a religious manifestation is emerging as an actual force as real as the cures it produces. At one time only the Bible was replete with cases of psychic healing. Today, scientific journals are running a close second. In this sense, psychic healing research is closing the gap between religion and science.

Prana and Human Hemoglobin

Pumpkin Hollow Farm is a small, picturesque resort tucked into the foothills of the Berkshire Hills. Its quiet atmosphere and relaxed pace were just the environment that Dr. Dolores Krieger of the Human Dimensions Institute was looking for to conduct her healing experiment. In the summer of 1971 Dr. Krieger moved onto the farm and took over the entire facilities for her therapeutic program. With her were eighteen adults and one young child, all medically diagnosed as ill. Although their ailments varied, each was on medication and in a doctor's care, and each was eager to be treated under the hands of Colonel Oskar Estebany.

Dr. Krieger, who is a colleague of Dr. Justa Smith, wanted to try a different experimental approach to healing. Dr. Smith's work involved the kinematic changes in enzyme reactions in solution; Krieger wondered if Mr. Estebany could induce changes in the blood hemoglobin of actual patients. Blood samples were to be drawn from the sick before and after healing sessions with the Hungarian. Mr. Estebany felt very much at home with these experiments because he was used to treating real patients instead of enzyme-filled flasks.

Blood hemoglobin is a remarkably complex and versatile compound. Dr. Krieger chose it as a healing index because of its functional similarity with prana, the Indian yogic healing energy. One of the meanings of prana is related to the in and out breaths of the physical body. In this aspect it is intimately associated with oxygen. If there was any validity to the age-old prana notion, Krieger reasoned, the best place in the body to search for changes in oxygen concentration would be in blood hemoglobin, since it serves as the vehicle of oxygen transport.

Dr. Krieger, long interested in Eastern medicine, also saw another similarity between prana and hemoglobin. Prana, according to yogic tradition, is composed of two antipodal currents, one positive and one negative. An imbalance in these antithetical forces is supposed to manifest itself in disease. (Interestingly, the yogic prana notion parallels the Chinese acupuncture theory of yin and yang.) Hemoglobin, as an iron-containing protein, also wears a two-faced mask. It is able to act in either a positive or negative sense (that is, as either an acid or a base) depending upon the function called for.

The *in vivo* study on the farm lasted for six days. Each day Mr. Estebany individually treated all nineteen patients. During the sessions he laid his hands over the particular body location he felt needed curing; the length of time was determined by his psychic sense. Some patients, whom Estebany felt were more seriously ill than others, were treated twice a day. To ensure that various medications did not affect the experiment, the sick patients were taken off all drugs during the six days of treatment. An additional and quite necessary experimental procedure was also taken—a control. Nine completely healthy patients moved into Pumpkin Hollow Farm, eating the same food as the sick and following the same daily routine.

At the end of the experiment the results were undeniable. The sick patients looked and felt better—all of which could be attributed to just the pleasant surroundings and a strong will to recover—but there were also highly significant changes in their hemoglobin values. "The findings of this experimental pilot study," writes Krieger, "were all in the predicted direction. Taken together they indicate impressive evidence that 'something happens' during active healing therapy by the laying on of hands . . . this 'something' is of a nature that can measurably affect human hemoglobin values and so demands further and intensive study . . ."[27]

Besides holding a Ph.D., Dolores Krieger is also a registered nurse, and she is acutely aware of the simple benefits derived from physically touching and soothing the sick (i.e., by an ordinary individual, not a proven healer). She has written of her belief clearly: "In the past, one of the universal acts of nursing practice has been concerned with the actual touching of the patient's body . . . Although it is generally acknowledged that 'something happens' when two persons touch, little is known of what actually does occur during this personalized interaction."[28] Above and beyond the psychological benefits of stroking the arms, legs, and brows of the sick, is there some energy transfer which occurs? Perhaps not of a magnitude sufficient to affect total recovery, as with a gifted healer, but some small parcel of exchange from an ordinary person may be helpful in healing. Dr. Krieger suspects it is. She observes that "in many parts of the world there has developed a practice of touching an ill person's body for the purpose of helping him back to health, and in some parts of the world the practice has become highly formalized."

At present, there are further and intensive healing studies underway at the Human Dimension Institute, McGill University, UCLA, Newark College of Engineering, and Stanford University. Healers *can* affect the growth rate of plants and enhance the wound healing time in mice. They *can* enrich human blood hemoglobin to establish better health. And with uncanny facility, they *can* influence enzymatic reactions in precisely the direction that corresponds to improved human health. The ultimate question still begs for an answer. How, in a physical sense, does laying-on of hands work? That answer, although still in the future, is within closer reach today than ever before.

4
Intimate Communications: Telepathy

The stuff of the world is mind stuff.

Sir Arthur Eddington

In the Family

Less than 100 years ago an American newspaper printed the following editorial:

> A man was arrested yesterday, charged with attempting to obtain money under false pretenses. He claimed he was promoting a device whereby one person could talk to another several miles away, by means of a small apparatus and some wire. Without doubt this man is a fraud and an unscrupulous trickster and must be taught that the American public is too smart to be the victim of this and similar schemes. Even if this insane idea worked it would have no practical value other than for circus sideshows.[1]

The man arrested was Alexander Graham Bell, and his "small apparatus and some wire" was the first telephone, a device that within a few years would revolutionize the very concept of communications.

Since the invention of the telephone in 1876, there have been only three other communications milestones—or what Marshall McLuhan would call "extensions of the human voice"—radio, television, and communications satellites. Many parapsychologists believe that we are due for another major communications breakthrough, and it does not require precognitive talent to forecast that it will be telepathy—controlled telepathy, the ability to

102

transmit thoughts at will over great distances with no more difficulty than speaking across a room. An impossible dream? Yes, but no more impossible than the telephone, radio, television, and satellites. No one is saying that volitional telepathy is around the corner, not in the seventies, perhaps not even in the eighties, but given the present experimental picture, it is out there somewhere.

The physical scientist frowns and shakes his head in protest. "Never," he says. "You're talking about two different things—apples and oranges. Radio and the rest all operate on electromagnetic waves, but telepathy is something else." From all the evidence telepathy does appear to be *something else*, and researchers are beginning to devise some ingenious means to detect that something, to identify its nature, and to pinpoint its source and mode of generation.

Of the three major forms of paranormal communications—telepathy (information from a human), clairvoyance (information from a concealed source), and precognition (information from the future)—telepathy is by far the easiest to accept intellectually because it is the one that least violates our Western notion of reality. The dream experiments of Drs. Ullman and Krippner and Dr. Tart's experiences with mutual hypnosis—all telepathic in nature—possess a basic simplicity and inherent logic that make one accept them with scarcely a frown. In fact, some of parapsychology's staunchest critics, who smirk at clairvoyance and stridently blast precognition, find telepathy easily within the realm of human possibilities. This is understandable, for telepathy *is* a natural extension of the myriad modes of human communications.

Too often we tend to think of information interchange solely in terms of the written and spoken word when, in actuality, we frequently resort to much subtler communication techniques. Body language is a prime example. Raising an arm, pointing a finger, or shifting body posture often conveys more information than a whole barrage of words. And the raised eyebrow or fixed stare can be deadly. Here we are reminded of the old adage: "Actions speak louder than words." But if telepathy does become a common mode of communications, the expression might become: "Thoughts speak louder than actions."

The subtle modes of communication we commonly employ, however, go much further than mere winks and side glances. Consider how heavily we depend upon smells, noises, and touches to convey information. Surely these are modes of communication. (Any woman who spends forty dollars for an ounce of perfume realizes this.) And beyond such nonwritten, nonverbal, noninnuendoed communications lie even more subtle techniques.

The "invisible" information that passes between lovers or between mother and child are clear examples of this, as are the anticipation of a desire, or the sensing of another's contentment, happiness, troubles, or anxieties. What is the line that divides these subtle, everyday interchanges from telepathy? The psi researcher argues that there is no well-defined line, that telepathy is the gradual and logical extension of a whole communications continuum.

Many of today's experiments indicate that at the intimate level of human communications telepathy is more operable than one might expect. In an outstanding experiment conducted in a Moscow obstetrics clinic, for example, mothers were kept in a remote wing of the building. It was impossible for a mother to hear the cries of her baby, and there was no way for her to know when a doctor was attending the infant. Yet, when a baby cried as a doctor took a blood specimen, its mother would show measurable signs of anxiety.[2] And the Soviet study documented numerous other clear-cut cases of mother–infant telepathy.

We know that the physical ties between a mother and her unborn baby are total. In the intimacy of the womb, the floating fetus is *one* with the mother. There is no aspect of the new life form which is independent. The mother's body chemistry, her diet, her habits of drinking and smoking, pill-taking and exercising—all mold the intrauterine child. Even the mother's temperament throughout pregnancy is subtly reflected in the baby's make-up. Beyond these obvious physical ties, say parapsychologists, are incontestable psychical ties. Bergson called it "the special sympathy between mother and child." Doctors have routinely observed this special sympathy, scientists are currently measuring it, and all mothers have experienced it.

Dr. Berthold Schwarz, a New Jersey psychiatrist and a former Fellow in Psychiatry at the Mayo Foundation, is among those who have a deep interest in parent–child telepathy. Over the last ten years he has documented more than 1,500 cases of this intimate form of communications. "Telepathy pulls no punches," says Schwarz. "It shows how a child cannot be fooled. He sees his parents and peers for what they are." According to Dr. Schwarz, most parent–child instances of telepathy go unnoticed because they occur in the context of everyday experiences and are not dramatic in their informational content. Schwarz and his wife Ardis did not want to overlook any possible telepathic interchanges in their own household. They therefore decided to undertake a careful study of the actions of their two children, Eric and Lisa. "With the passing of time," says Schwarz, "my wife and I became skilled in recognizing what really went on in the family in a nonverbal, subliminal, telepathic way."

What really went on became the nucleus of Schwarz's book, *Parent–Child Telepathy*. Here is an incident which occurred a week before Christmas:

> My intention of writing "First Class Mail" on an important letter that had to go out right away was completely frustrated because there was no red pen on my desk. My search for it was to no avail. My thoughts went, "Oh, I suppose Ardis took it for the Christmas cards and never returned it!" . . . At that moment Eric (age three) bounded downstairs and into my office. "Here, Daddy, is the red pen!"

As an isolated incident, of course, this experience means nothing. Coincidence, we say, and that is just the point Schwarz strives to emphasize. The incident, he says, could easily have been overlooked or interpreted as mere coincidence, but that would have masked its significance. For as Schwarz and his wife began to faithfully record such seemingly trivial experiences, they found that Eric anticipated their wishes quite often. One day Ardis, who was upstairs in her bedroom, decided to hang a certain picture on the kitchen wall where a calendaer was then hanging. She came downstairs with the picture and went into the kitchen to find Eric up on a chair, removing the calendar from the wall. When she asked him why he had done it at precisely that moment, he could give no answer.

Schwarz points out that each incident in itself was so minor that without a written record, one event would have been forgotten before the next occurred. On paper, as accumulated events, they strongly suggested that Eric had a telepathic sense when it came to reading his parents' thoughts. Schwarz's premise is precisely that held by Carl Jung: not all coincidence is an example of telepathy, but neither can all instances of telepathy be dismissed as coincidence. Schwarz writes: We are "immersed in a sea of telepathic suggestions. We are tossed and buffeted by the waves and what we often consider to be solely the products of our own independent judgment and jealous prerogatives can sometimes really be the result of subtly operating telepathic influences that can tie us together in bonds of a complex interdependency."[3]

The evidence for telepathy existing between twins is even more voluminous than parent–child cases. At the Jefferson Medical College in Philadelphia, Dr. Thomas Duane, Chief of Ophthalmology, and Dr. Thomas Behrendt have studied the brain-wave patterns of identical twins. Each member of a pair is placed in a different room, and both are wired to EEGs. Duane reported in *Science* that when one twin entered an alpha state, the brain-waves of the twin in the distant room automatically switched to the same mode. This brainwave sympathy occurred even when the twins were placed on separate floors of the building.[4] There was no specific telepathic message that one member of the pair sent the other; the synchronous pattern oc-curred quite naturally at an unconscious level. The researchers feel that twins may be predisposed to telepathy because of the strong similarities in their central nervous system and brain. Already genetic commonalities in twins are known to account for the simultaneous occurrence of wrinkles, gray hair, bald patches, tooth decay, and even the onset of cancer.[5]

Joan and Joy are identical twins. To them, Dr. Duane's discovery is especially meaningful. One fall, while Joan was on Cape Cod, her sister was across the continent in Olympia, Washington. On an October after-noon Joy was stricken with a severe kidney attack, and her husband rushed her to a local hospital. As she was being admitted, Joan was also entering a hospital three thousand miles away complaining of sharp back pains. But all the tests on Joan were negative, and she was released. She had suffered sympathy pains with her sister on the West coast.

Cases of pain-sharing between twins are numerous. In their book, *The Curious World of Twins,* psi investigators Vincent and Margaret Gaddis relate the full story of Joan and Joy along with many other cases of twin telepathy. With the evidence of spontaneous brainwave sympathy existing between twins, such anecdotes take on new light. Once they realized their unconscious telepathic sense, Joan and Joy decided to try an experiment when Joan was about to give birth. Joan writes:

> While I was in labor . . . we decided to try something we had heard during our studies of ESP . . . for her [Joy] to take some of the pain from me. I was in labor all night but slept most of the time. Around eight the next morning the baby was born. The nurse who was with me all night was amazed. She said I had been having pains which I didn't even know I was having. This proved to me that Joy had accomplished what she was trying to do. Besides I already had one child and knew the pains could have been a lot worse. When I talked to Joy later, she and my sister-in-law confirmed she was in quite a bit of pain and knew when I had Beth [for] her pains stopped.[6]

There is a well-known tale in parapsychological literature that is worth recounting here for the striking similarities it bears to the intense feelings of oneness observed under mutual hypnosis. In reading it, keep in mind Dr. Tart's experiments.

In Purlear, North Carolina, there lived two identical twins, Bobbie Jean and Betty Jo Eller. From the time of birth the two girls were inseparable, so much so that they never truly became individuals. Betty Jo was the shadow of her sister in thoughts, desires, and actions. Whenever Bobbie Jean was sick, so too was her sister.

Shortly after the girls' graduation from high school, their parents noticed that the personalities of Bobbie Jean and Betty Jo had begun to change. Bobbie began sitting for hours staring into space, refusing to talk to anyone. And as always happened, her sister followed the same bizarre pattern. As the girls, bound in their deep partnership, withdrew further from the outside world, they began to weep uncontrollably. Now they never left their room and severed all external communications. In January of 1961 Bobbie and Betty were committed to the Broughton State Mental Hospital in Morgantown and diagnosed as schizophrenics. For a full year the girls were kept on drugs and under intense psychiatric care. But no one could seem to penetrate their private world. In 1962 the doctors separated the sisters, placing them in different wings of the institution. They were to have no contact with one another.

One spring evening Bobbie had a catatonic seizure. Shortly after midnight, the head nurse found her dead. Aware of the strange affinity between the two girls, she feared the worst for Betty and telephoned her ward. Betty was found lying on the floor dead. Both girls were curled up in a fetal position on their right sides.

Dr. John C. Reece of the North Carolina Pathological Society performed autopsies and ruled out the possibility of suicide. Leaving the cause of death on their certificates blank, he said, "I found no demonstrable evidence of injury or disease that could cause death."

Death came from within their common psyche. "They were like two people with one brain," according to their family doctor. Over the years both girls had gradually retreated from the real world, and they left it together.[7] Here, of course, we are not dealing with unambiguous cases from controlled experiments. Eric, Joan and Joy, and the Eller sisters are anecdotes—genuine ones at best. But they are tales which stimulate research, and research, in turn, is lending credence to the tales.

In Tart's mutual hypnosis experiments, Anne and Bill developed a common tie between their psyches, a bond so strong that it could support telepathic communications. Tart sees no other way to explain the results he observed. In reaching this level of intimacy both Anne and Bill retreated from Tart's world into an existence all their own. The deeper they progressed, the more difficult it was for Tart to speak to them. In fact, several times their isolation was frightening. One can only surmise that Bobbie Jean and Betty Jo Eller were psychically linked in life as Anne and Bill were, only much deeper. Their isolation was so total in the consciousness they shared, so altered from wakefulness, that eventually no one in this world could communicate with them. Their physical bodies were here, but their psyches were elsewhere. Exactly where? On what level of consciousness, with what view of reality? Answering these questions is one of the ultimate goals of psychical research.

The most intimate type of communication a person can experience is a dialogue between that person's conscious mind and his or her unconscious mind—a rather difficult volitional feat admittedly. We know that the unconscious mind is there, brimming with precious files of information, records of everything our senses have ever accumulated. Some folders contain information so personal the knowledge would shatter us; others, however, hold papers on our creative and paranormal talents that would surely delight us. But how can an individual converse with this storehouse of information? Psychoanalytic techniques such as free association are crude. Dreaming, hypnosis, and sensory deprivation are fortuitous at best. Meditation also falls short. Colin Wilson describes this dilemma well: "We know, theoretically, that we possess a subconscious mind, yet as I sit here, in this room on a sunny morning, I am not in any way aware of it; I can't see it or feel it. It is like an arm upon which I have been lying in my sleep, and which has become completely dead and feelingless."[8] For most of us this is true, but an increasing body of evidence suggests that Konstantin Raudive, a Latvian psychologist, is an exception.

Not long ago Raudive made a startling discovery. He found that if he tuned a radio to a band of pure static, which is random "white noise," and made a tape recording of it, the crackling sounds contained distinct voices when the tape was played back. Later he found this also occurred if he spoke normally into a microphone and recorded his voice. The playback always contained soft extraneous voices, voices that spoke in many languages with peculiar cadences. Raudive says, "The sentence construction obeys rules that differ radically from those of ordinary speech and, although the voices seem to speak in the same way as we do, the anatomy of their speech apparatus must be different from our own." The voices are not just extraneous pickups from distant radio and television stations, for they often respond to Raudive's questions.

Many reputable scientists and electronics experts have analyzed the thousands of tapes that have been prepared. There is no question that the sounds are there—and often clearly understandable—only their source is open to doubt. Professor E. Douglas Dean of Newark College of Engineering feels that the Raudive phenomenon is real enough and that the explanation is simple and straightforward. Raudive, a firm believer in survival after death, thinks the voices are those of the dead—he confidently identifies some of them as Goethe, Hitler, and his own mother. Dean and the many scientists who have studied the phenomenon are convinced otherwise.

In order to solve the mystery of the voices, several scientists decided to tape Raudive's voice in March of 1971 in the acoustically controlled setting of a recording studio. Engineers installed special sound equipment to block out any chance of high- and low-frequency interference from radio and television stations; the best equipment available was used, with high quality magnetic tapes. Raudive was not allowed to touch so much as a dial; all he had to do was talk into a microphone. Another tape recorder synchronized to Raudive's monitored every sound in the studio. For eighteen minutes Raudive's voice was taped, and no one present heard any unusual sounds. But on playing the tape back, the scientists found there were over one-hundred voices on it; some so clear that they did not require amplification.[9]

How the voices got on the tape is a mystery, but there is one major clue as to their nature: the voices only speak the seven languages with which Raudive is familiar. With the possibility of fraud eliminated to the satisfaction of the scientists who conducted the tests, they offered one explanation for the phenomenon: the voices are actually Raudive's unconscious mind speaking and answering question he directs to it. As strange as this sounds, direct communications from the unconscious mind seem vastly more feasible than Raudive's theory of the voices. We know so little about the unconscious mind, and it is such a giant. If, in an ASC, human parasenses spring into action, who can say that Raudive's unconscious mind is not telepathically spilling itself onto tape?

Emotion-Laden Messages

Spontaneous cases of telepathy, such as the Anton Rubinstein incident which opened Chapter 1, most often concern emotion-laden messages—a severe accident, an illness, the death of a loved one. This is a belief that parapsychologists have held for many years. In his thought-provoking book, *The Roots of Coincidence,* Arthur Koestler writes, "Spontaneous paranormal experiences are always bound up with some self-transcending type of emotion."[10] The self-transcendent nature of the event is believed to be the crucial factor in spontaneously perceiving it. A telepathic impression enters some subliminal level of consciousness, and depending upon its emotional content, it may or may not bubble up to a level of awareness. The argument in parapsychological circles has always been that this sifting out of important from unimportant information displays a filter system at play somewhere in that hinterland between the conscious and unconscious mind.

Undoubtedly, our senses and parasenses are selectively fed by filters. Vision, for example, is highly selective to both the quality and quantity of radiation that impinges on the retina. The so-called visual portion of the electromagnetic spectrum is only a narrow sliver from an extremely broad, continuous band. And hearing, taste, touch, and smell are even more severely limited. If the sensory filters appear to be set at high thresholds, parapsychologists have long held that the parasensory filters are virtually without upper bounds. This is the argument used to account for the paucity of spontaneous psi cases among the general populace. Cascades of telepathic impressions may bombard the subliminal mind, but few make it through the conscious turnstile. Sir Cyril Burt, Emeritus Professor of Psychology at University College, London, picturesquely describes the filter situation: "As a rule," he says, "it would seem, the mind rejects ideas coming from another mind as the body rejects grafts coming from another body."[11]

There is mounting evidence, however, that the mind rejects fewer telepathic impressions than parapsychologists once thought was the case. If they were misled, it was because many telepathic messages, as present-day researchers are finding out, are of a simple, unsensational nature, such as Dr. Schwarz's incidences of parent–child telepathy. Other messages blend with elements from subconscious memory to emerge partially masked; the psi-induced dream experiments are a perfect example.

In one study, E. Douglas Dean demonstrated just how low the filters which hold back telepathic information are set. The basis of Dean's experiment was the fact that certain physiological body changes accompany the perception of any emotion-laden information. Dean used as the index of change the fluctuation in blood volume in body extremities. For the experiments, agent and percipient were placed in separate rooms. Before the test began they each submitted a list of names of persons emotionally close to them, such as mothers, wives, children. Neither knew the other's list. Dean put each name on an index card, and into this target pool, he added an additional set of names taken randomly from a telephone directory, names which were meaningless to both subjects.

The index finger of the percipient was connected to a plethysmograph —a device which measures fluctuations in blood volume by shining a light through the fingertip and measuring the amount that is continuously transmitted. In another room the agent randomly selected the names and concentrated on them one at a time while visualizing the percipient and his location, and attempting to transmit the name to the percipient.

The test showed that for certain names there was a statistically significant change in the percipient's blood volume, a change characteristic of a mild emotional reaction. These fluctuations occurred when the agent was thinking of a name that was emotionally meaningful to the percipient. When the agent thought of an unfamiliar name, there were only normal fluctuations.[12] The most important feature of the experiment was that the percipient was never *consciously* aware of the names that were transmitted. He did not make statements such as "I believe the name is Carol Jones." In fact, if the percipient had not been connected to the sensitive detection device, there would have been no way of knowing that the telepathic impressions were received. The names registered at a subliminal level of consciousness and caused a slight body reaction, but not enough to make the percipient aware of them.

Thus, our bodies may react in very subtle ways to the host of telepathic impressions that bombard us daily, even though we do not know it. It makes one wonder how often fluctuations in mood, temperament, and even body health are the result of positive or negative thoughts harbored by those close individuals we call friends.

Cosmic Blueprint

The sea sponge found in tropical waters is a round, soft, living creature. But the sponge is different from many other multicellular organisms in that it has no nervous system, no means of relaying communication impulses throughout its bulky mass. Because of this, it is a miracle of organization. If you take a living sponge, tear it apart, and work the pieces through a fine sieve until it is nothing but a soft, granular mass, an amazing thing happens.

The billions upon billions of cells find one another and reunite to form a whole sponge, like an organism rising from the dead. There is an apparent blueprint of life, external from the cells which comprise the sponge, that is not destroyed when the sponge is shredded; it is this master organizational plan which permits the cells to regroup.

Plants also lack a nervous system and show no communication of impulse from cell to cell—and yet, like the sponge, they too display communal action. One example is the sweet-smelling *Mimosa pudica.* Touch one leaf of the plant and it immediately folds up. Touch it strongly enough and the local response somehow broadcasts itself throughout the plant. Even though it lacks a nervous system, the whole plant seems to cringe. The biochemistry of the sponge and *Mimosa pudica* are well understood, but their unusual communications behavior is still a mystery. It almost seems extrasensory.

Clive Backster is a polygraph ("lie detector") expert and a highly controversial plant researcher. As one of the foremost authorities on the behavioral use of the lie detector, Backster was called before Congress in 1964 to testify on polygraph usage in government. At present, he is director of his own New York City school, which provides advanced training to law enforcement officers in the techniques of the polygraph.

On the morning of February, 2, 1966, Backster made an accidental discovery while doing some routine polygraph work at his school's offices near Times Square. When he took a break to water a plant, a novel idea struck him. He wondered if the polygraph could measure the rate at which water rose from the roots to the leaves.

In human beings, a polygraph measures three functions: rate of breathing, changes in blood pressure, and variations in the skin's electrical conductivity. This last function is commonly known as galvanic skin response (GSR) (Backster's prime area of expertise). He decided GSR would be the best measurement to make on the dracena plant he had just watered. So he fastened an electrode on either side of a leaf and watched the pen and ink recorder for variations in electrical activity which would indicate that water was arriving in the leaf.

But as he watched, nothing happened. Disappointed, he wondered how the leaf would respond to an extreme stimulus. So he immersed it in his cup of hot coffee. The tracing remained constant. Nothing.

Determined to get some measurable response from the plant, Backster decided to get a match and actually burn the cells of the leaf. But at the instant he made this decision, Backster reports a dramatic change in the tracing of the recorder: an abrupt jump, followed by prolonged upward sweeps. He had not moved; in fact, nothing in the room had changed. The only change was his thought to do harm to the leaf. Backster wondered; did the plant somehow sense his intention?

Months of testing began to remove every possibility of human error. All procedures were automated. Finally, experiments were conducted, not on one type of plant, but eventually on twenty-five different varieties. The results were as Backster suspected; through some mysterious means of perception the plants apparently responded to thoughts of harm and mutilation. Backster calls this reaction "primary perception," implying that it is a mode of communications more primitive and fundamental than human sensory perception. Before casting a critical eye at Backster's work, as hundreds of scientists have done, first examine another of his famous experiments.

In one test three philodendron plants were placed in separate rooms. Each was wired to a polygraph, and the room was sealed off. In another room a large pot of boiling water was prepared. An instrument was programmed to dump a quantity of live brine shrimp into the water at a randomly selected time. No one was in the rooms with the plants, and no one knew exactly when the shrimp would be boiled. Backster's previous experiments had convinced him that plants were responsive to human thoughts; now he wondered if there was some fundamental communication between all living things. Would the plants respond to the mass death of the shrimp?

In this first test, two sessions totaling seven runs were made. Five to seven seconds after the shrimp were dumped into the boiling water, the polygraphs on all three plants showed sudden, large bursts of activity.[13] Backster wondered, "Could it be that when cell life dies, it broadcasts a signal to other living cells?" Today, after seven years of experimentation he feels sure of the answer. "I would say whatever is abruptly killed must send out a message. A more orderly dying involves some preparation for death, and we've found that where this occurs there is little if any plant reaction."

Backster's experiments have met with severe criticism from the scientific community. Much of it has less to do with his laboratory procedures, which for the most part are controlled, than with the implications of his results. Plants do not have emotions. They cannot respond to human thoughts and animal cries of death. As the standard critic might say, "First you ask me to accept parasensory perception in humans. This is hard enough to swallow, but I'll admit the laboratory evidence is rather impressive. But now you want me to acknowledge that plants possess extrasensory perception. It's just too much to believe." Admittedly, many of Backster's experiments sound more like science fiction than scientific fact. Over the years that he has been conducting plant experiments many of his investigations have been described so frequently, embellished and dramatized by reporters and Backster's supporters, that today the stories bear little resemblance to the original work. The Backster investigations are related here, not because parapsychologists believe them wholeheartedly (many do not), but because of a fundamental truth in the premise of Backster's work. As Dr. LeShan says, "I don't buy all the details of Backster's work. Some of it seems outright preposterous. But there is definite validity to the objective of his investigations."

To reject flatly the core philosophy of Backster's work is to deny the possibility that plants in some way interact with humans. Such rejection would necessarily extend to the plant research of people like Dr. Miller and Dr. Bernard Grad. The Worralls seem to have affected the growth rate of rye grass, and Mr. Estebany has apparently influenced the germination of barley seeds; how far removed are these feats from Backster's observations? In terms of research philosophy they all stand side by side. Backster believes "that a communication capability exists among all living things," and his experiments, he feels, are detecting this subtle interchange.

Plants are not the only cooperative subjects in Clive Backster's laboratory. As of a year ago he began experimenting with eggs. The idea came on a whim. "I wondered what would happen if I hooked up an egg." Using a white hen's eggs, he connected the two polygraph electrodes to the shell. "I succeeded in obtaining," he says, "a nine-hour recording from one [egg] ... the chart showed what seemed to be a heartbeat. There was a frequency —about 160 to 170 beats per minute—appropriate for a chick embryo between three and four days along in incubation."[14] Detection of a heartbeat in a fertilized egg is not amazing, but this egg was not fertilized. There was no chance that it would develop into a chick. Unfortunately, although the experiment sounds easy to repeat, not all attempts have met with positive results; in fact, few have, indicating Backster is observing an artifact. But the undaunted Backster wonders if he is tapping into an "energy field blueprint" which provides a basic pattern about which matter coalesces to form organic structures, something similar, in essence, to the pattern which permits a shredded, sieved sponge to reassemble.

Writing on Backster's egg experiments, psi-writer John W. White offers some interesting philosophical speculation: "Does the 'idea' of an organism precede its material development? Perhaps this is evidence for what the Bible and Plato say: In the beginning was the Logos—the structuring principle or thought-form of the entity-to-be."[15]

Some of the happenings in Backster's laboratory contain elements of humor. One day a woman physiologist who specializes in plants visited the laboratory to view the research firsthand. "The plants had been reacting quite typically before she arrived," says Backster. "But while she was in the room all we were able to obtain was a straight line. It was downright embarrassing." (A flat response on a polygraph of a human indicates that the person has fainted.) Backster could not imagine why they were not responding to any stimuli. "One at a time," he says, "I hooked up five different plants and couldn't get anything but a straight line out of any of them." Before the woman left the laboratory, greatly disappointed, Backster asked her, "Just what is it you do with plants in your experiments? Do you hurt them in any way?"

The woman quite innocently responded, "I put them in an oven and roast them in order to get their dry weight for my data."[16]

This incident, as insubstantial as it is, relates to one of Backster's most controversial experiments. A "plant murderer" was arbitrarily selected from a group of six men. Backster did not know who the man was. Each man, in random order, walked into a room which housed two identical philodendrons. It was the task of one man to pull the leaves off one plant, break the stalks, and tear it from its soil. When the six men had finished their visits, one plant was on the floor, mangled and dying. The only witness to the gruesome event was the remaining philodendron.

Backster entered the room and connected the unharmed plant to a polygraph. Then, one by one the six men entered the room and walked up to the witness plant. When the murderer approached the plant, the arm of the polygraph recorder began to jump wildly according to Backster—a reaction that he says is the "electrical equivalent of a shriek."[17]

For every person who flatly refuses to believe Backster's work, in part or in whole, there is someone who has taken it to heart. Biologist Lyall Watson feels that Backster's research "raises awesome biological and moral questions; since thinking about it, I for one have had to give up mowing lawns altogether."[18] Watson adds that if Backster's work "were to be taken to its logical limits we would end up, like the community in Samuel Butler's *Erewhon,* eating nothing but cabbages that have been certified to have died a natural death." In a more serious vein Watson says, "The answer to the moral problem lies in treating all life with respect, and killing, with real reluctance, only that which is necessary for survival."

Much of Backster's plant research may one day be proven valid. Some of it has already been duplicated in other laboratories, especially by Robert Brier at the Institute for Parapsychology in North Carolina. If Backster's notions are correct, what about all those people who, for the love of animal life, have become vegetarians? This question is often put to Backster. He claims that many vegetarians on hearing of his work become frightfully upset. But the polygraph expert has a reassuring answer for them: "I don't see that our discoveries are any threat to vegetarians. It may be that a vegetable appreciates becoming part of a higher form of life rather than rotting on the ground."

Despite the mixed scientific reviews of Backster's research, the fact that some of his experiments have been duplicated elsewhere is turning many heads. Already, says Backster, more than 7,000 university, government, and industry-affiliated scientists have written to him requesting detailed information; at his last count, more than twenty universities and research centers are busily working to see if plants really do possess "primary perception."

Universal Oneness

It is all a rhythm,
from the shutting
door, to the window
opening,

the seasons, the sun's
light, the moon,
the oceans, the
growing of things
. . . .
The rhythm which projects
from itself continuity
bending all to its force
from window to door,
from ceiling to floor,
light at the opening,
dark at the closing.[19]

The notion of universal oneness (expressed above by Robert Creeley), one of the theoretical cornerstones of parapsychology, is certainly not new. In a physical sense, it goes back at least 2,500 years when the Greek physician Hippocrates wrote, "There is one common flow, one common breath, all things are in sympathy." Several Greek philosophers of that era were ambitious enough to suggest the essence of this oneness. Thales of Miletus, the first philosopher of Western civilization, argued that the common wave which ripples through all matter is water. "Water," he wrote, "existed before all existing things came to be, out of which all things came and into which all things return." At that time, it was not a bad guess, but others soon disagreed with him. Anaximenes claimed the universal substance was not water, but air; Xenophanes said it was earth; and for Heraclitus it was fire—thus the Grecian quadruplet: earth, air, fire, and water. It is not hyperbole to say that most of the myriad intellectual probings of mankind over the last 2,500 years have centered on finding a physical basis for universal oneness. And that goal is even more relevant today with the birth of modern psi research.

A giant step toward oneness came in the first decade of the 1900s. By the beginning of this century, the physical stuff of which the universe is composed had been condensed, after much reshuffling and substitution, from the Grecian quadruplet to two distinctly different constituents: a tangible one called *matter*, and a somewhat less tangible one called *energy*. All that possesses physical existence was thought to be composed of one of these fundamental entities. It was a great theoretical leap forward. And within the first decade of the century an amazing unification occurred. Einstein, by his celebrated formula $E = mc^2$, showed that matter and energy are one and the same thing. This deceptively simple equation says that matter and energy are merely two different manifestations of a single, more fundamental entity, which for lack of a better name is called "physical existence."

Einstein's discovery was a supreme boost for the argument of physical oneness—as his superb biographer Banesh Hoffmann says, it was a stab at "cosmic unity."[20] Once matter and energy were known to be related, the next question was: could one be converted to the other?

That was dramatically answered on December 2, 1942, when, largely through the efforts of physicist Enrico Fermi, the first sustained nuclear chain reaction was achieved, ushering in the Atomic Age. Why had it taken over twenty-five centuries to recognize this physical oneness? Sir Cyril Burt gives a lucid answer in his essay on "Psychology and Parapsychology":

Our tactile perceptions of the gravitational effects of mass (e.g., a grain of sand falling on the skin) requires a stimulus of at least 0.1 gram, say about 10^{20} ergs. . . . On the other hand, the eye in rod-vision is sensitive to less than 5 quanta of radiant energy, about 10^{-10} ergs or rather less. In detecting energy therefore man's perceptual apparatus is 10^{30} times more sensitive than it is in detecting mass. Had the perception of mass been as delicate as the perception of energy, the identity of the two would have seemed self-evident instead of paradoxical. When seeing light we should at the same time have *felt* the pressure of impact of the photons; and mass and energy would from the outset have been regarded as merely two different ways of perceiving the same thing. . . .[21]

Thus, were it not for the severe limitations of the human senses, Thales might have hit on the matter–energy equivalence instead of Einstein.

Perhaps it is just as well that our tactile sense is not as acute as our visual sense, else when we enter a dark room and flick on a light switch we would be bodily assaulted. But the fact that the human eye is a trillion trillion million times more sensitive in detecting energy than the sense of touch is in detecting mass is more than just an interesting calculation. It dramatically illustrates the arbitrary view of reality we experience because of the particular limitations of our senses. The foundations underlying paranormal phenomena, which are as unknown today as the equivalence of matter and energy was to the Greeks, are so because of that old problem —the limited senses. As William Blake observed:

> *This life's five windows of the soul*
> *Distort the heavens from pole to pole*
> *And teach us to believe a lie*
> *When we see with, not through, the eye.*[22]

Einstein's enormous breakthrough in equating matter and energy has encouraged many modern scientists to speculate on a similar equivalence between matter and mind, a much desired relationship in parapsychology. The eminent astronomer V. A. Firsoff has suggested an idea parallel to Einstein's. Without much elaboration, Firsoff has suggested that "mind is a universal entity or interaction of the same order as electricity or gravitation, and that there must exist a modulus of transformation, analogous to Einstein's famous equality $E = mc^2$, whereby 'mind stuff' could be equated with the other entities of the physical world."[23]

Firsoff's suggestion of an equivalence between mind and matter can be taken a step further. Assuming that the link—call it psychic energy— between mind and matter is one day discovered, this energy, taken with Einstein's correspondence between matter and energy, would unite the three concepts. Once the equivalence of mind, matter, and energy has been established, the next logical step is the interconversion of one entity into another. Hence, just as a physicist today can convert a material atom into pure energy, a paraphysicist tomorrow would be able to materialize a thought. Given the three-way equivalence, not only would a thought be convertible into matter, but thoughts could be converted into energy in order to perform such tasks as lifting a glass or fetching a book. The whole notion does not sound so ludicrous when we realize that there are already a few individuals today with proven psychokinetic powers who *can* move a glass or a book merely by thinking the thought.

One man looking for the link between matter and mind is IBM chemist Dr. Marcel Vogel, an expert in the structure of liquid crystals. Vogel was so taken by the plant research of Clive Backster that he felt compelled to try the tests himself. He did, and obtained many similar results. This encouraged him to go further than Backster, not just to observe that plants react to human thoughts, but to attempt to correlate specific plant poly-graph readings with specific types of thoughts. Vogel found, as he says, that "plants are very sensitive instruments for measuring the emotions of men."

Currently, assisted by a team of three medical doctors, he is attempting to correlate human mental disorders and the reactions they cause in plants. He has found, as have Thelma Moss and Kendall Johnson, that certain people *do* have "green thumbs"; their frame of mind is conducive to the health of plants. Content, optimistic, benevolent individuals, says Moss, have been found to influence plants in a positive way while distraught, frustrated, whining individuals, and people with certain psychiatric aberra-tions, can be as lethal to plants as feeding them water laced with arsenic. Johnson calls these people "brown thumb gardeners" and claims it is futile for them even to attempt gardening and decorating their rooms with plants, for no matter how sweetly they smile or how gently they speak to a fern —if they are so inclined—the plant discerns their true feelings.

Dr. Vogel and his team have experimented with putting a person with a diagnosed psychiatric problem into a room with a plant that is wired to a polygraph. The person lives and functions in the vicinity of the plant, and the plant's reactions are monitored. Vogel claims to be obtaining polygraph traces which he feels may one day be useful in diagnosing and treating various psychological problems. In effect, he is using plants to eavesdrop on human thoughts.[24]

Of course, to date, mind stuff itself has not been detected, let along equated to matter and converted. In fact, at times it looks as if in this quest we stand where Thales stood with his notion of water as the universal substance. One engaged in psi research is constantly reminded of the ancient epigram: "Though many a thing is unfathomable to mankind, nothing looms more ineffable than the mind of man." But, as elusive as mind stuff has been, the physical seat of the mind, the brain, is well within the arena of experimentation. Drs. Duane and Behrendt, we have seen, demonstrated the "oneness" or sympathy between the brains of identical twins—a remnant of the unity they once shared in the womb. And recently, Soviet parapsychologists have found proof of a harmony existing between psychics engaged in telepathy. By monitoring the brain-wave emanations and heart-beats of two psychics in telepathic contact, they observe that there is a synchronization between their heart activity and brain-wave patterns. This sympathy occurs even when the psychics are separated by great distances.[25] To parapsychologists, the physiological harmony between individuals in telepathic communications is a significant find. It suggests the possibility of training individuals, through biofeedback techniques, to synchronize parts of their physiology to enhance telepathic communications.

The quest to understand and to observe the oneness among all things —a sort of common denominator of existence—is no longer the goal only of philosophers. Today it is a primary objective of the scientists who are flocking to psychical research in increasing numbers. The very reality of psi phenomena, and the laboratory evidence now being uncovered, attest to the interdependencies among all things: telepathy (between man and man), clairvoyance and psychokinesis (between man and nature), and precognition (between man and the very fabric of time).

Dreaming is a pregnant psychical state of the mind. In the telepathically induced dream experiments conducted at Maimonides Medical Center, Brooklyn, a sleeping subject in an isolated room is wired to detect brainwave patterns and rapid eye movements. An agent in another room concentrates on a randomly selected target picture (here "The Thinker" amusingly wired to a small peg board) and the face of the sleeping subject, all the while trying to telepathically send the target information. When the experimenter sees that the subject has been dreaming for several minutes, he gently awakens her over an intercom and asks her to relate the details of her dream. In the morning an impartial panel of judges rate the correspondences between the subject's dream reports throughout the night and the target picture. See Chapter 1, "The Dream Scene."

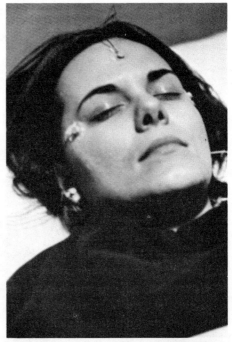

Tony Rollo, *Newsweek*

Kirlian photographs are made by passing an electrical spark through a photographic plate and then through the subject's fingertip. The coronas vary in size, shape and color according to the subject's psychophysical state.

patient

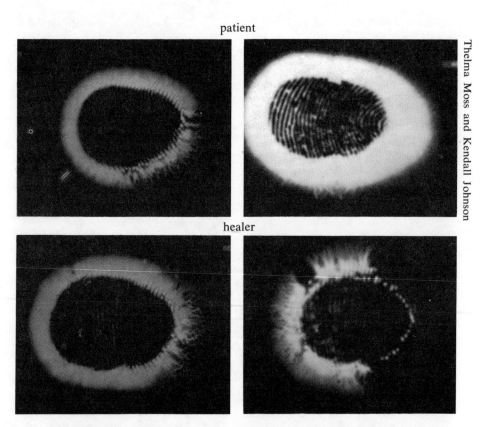

healer

Coronas of a kidney disease patient before (left) and after treatment by a psychic healer, and the corresponding coronas of the healer before (left) and after his ministrations. The broadening and brightening of the patient's corona, and the consequent dimination of the corona of the healer has been demonstrated by several independent researchers.

patient

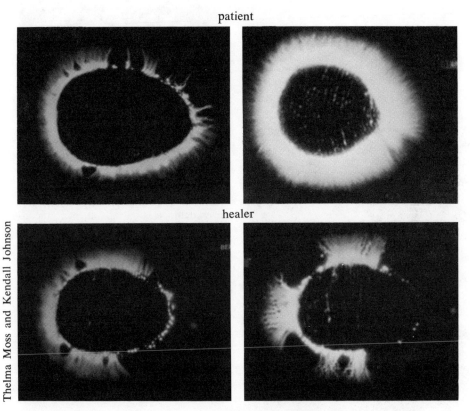

healer

The same healer as above works on another kidney disease patient. Patient's coronas before (left) and after laying-on of hands treatment, and those of the healer, before (left). The dramatic increase in the patient's corona and the reshaping and decrease in that of the healer's has lead many researchers to suspect that a form of energy passes from healer to patient during psychic healing. See Chapter 3, "Psychic Healing."

Dr. Justa Smith, director of research at the Human Dimensions Institute places a test tube containing damaged trypsin enzymes into a large electromagnet which exposes the sample to a magnetic field about 26,000 times stronger than that of the earth's. An identical sample of trypsin (which naturally occurs in the body) was treated by famous psychic healer Mr. Estebany. Repeated testing showed that Estebany favorably influenced the chemical rate of reaction in precisely the same way as did the strong magnetic field. See Chapter 3, "Psychic Healing."

Telepathic messages registering below the level of awareness can have subtle affects on a person's physiology. Using a plethysmograph, which measures fluctuation in blood volume of the fingers, Douglas Dean of the Newark College of Engineering demonstrated a subject's unconscious emotional response on having received a telepathic impression sent by an agent in another room. The peak on the graph shows a sharp change in the subject's blood volume just at the time the agent was telepathically sending an emotion-laden message. See Chapter 4, "Intimate Communications: Telepathy."

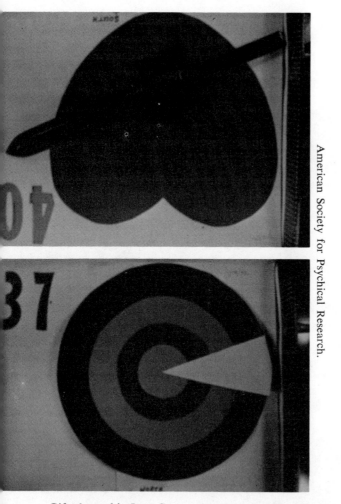

American Society for Psychical Research.

Gifted psychic Ingo Swann demonstrated his parasensory talents in producing sketches of target objects which were contained in boxes suspended from
the ceiling some seven feet above his head. The heart is red, the letter
opener black; Swann perceived the colors and shapes of the objects correctly. The concentric rings going from the center outward are blue, red,
green, and black. Swann perceived the correct shape of the target and all
four colors, with only the colors being out of sequence. He had eight
"hits" on eight different targets, and EEG monitoring showed a substantial
change in his brainwave output during the time of parasensory perception.
See Chapter 5, "The Twilight Mind."

Various altered states of consciousness yield different Kirlian photographs. The corona of a yoga in a normal wakeful state (top), and deep into meditation. For years researchers have known that meditation is accompanied by dramatic changes in such parameters as respiration, heart rate, lactate levels in the blood and EEG patterns. Kirlian photography offers another measure of change occurring from the meditative state. See Chapter 7, "The Mystic and Psi."

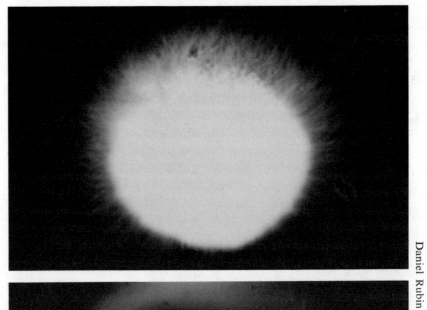

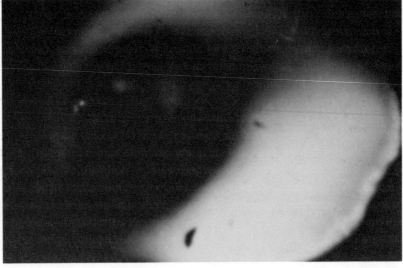

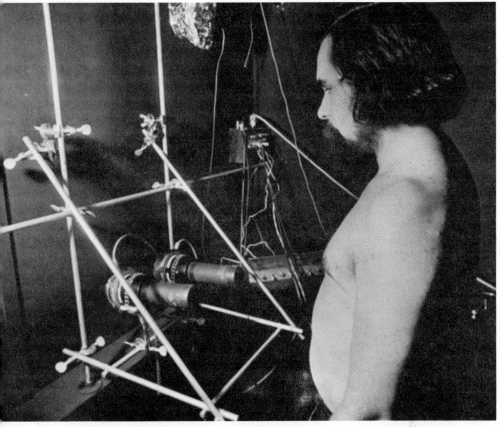

Tony Rollo, *Newsweek*

A visible aura radiating from the human body is detected by researchers in a specially designed lightproof room. For years scientists have known and experimented with the "invisible" electromagnetic radiations which naturally surround the body as a result of its various electrochemical processes. But it required highly sensitive light-detection equipment and a "black room" to demonstrate that the human body also radiates a faint *visible* glow. Scientists are studying the geometries, colors and pulsations of subjects' "halos," hoping to eventually use them as diagnostic tools in medicine. See Chapter 9, "Psychokinesis and Life Fields."

Dr. Gertrude Schmeidler of the City College of New York asks subjects to try and psychokinetically "heat" and "cool" sensitive temperature detectors (thermistors) that are sealed in insulated thermos bottles. Gifted psychic Ingo Swann has had repeated success in this experiment. See Chapter 9, "Psychokinesis and Life Fields."

5

The Twilight Mind

The universe begins to look more like a great thought than like a great machine.

Sir James Jeans

Automatic Writing

Federico Fellini, the famous Italian movie director, is probably the only man in the world who truly acts out his dreams. In the cutting room one bizzare incident after another is spliced together to produce a two-hour creation which came to Fellini in many nightly episodes. In *Satyricon* we are offered scenes of clowns and children laughing, the gaiety of a circus, while on the same stage a man's hand is hacked off with an ax. Nothing is simple, nothing singular; scenes are multithematic with a story of love and innocence in the foreground set against a backdrop of the grotesque and horrific. Scenes change abruptly, no rules of space and time logic obtain; characters are born, die, and are reborn; the future precedes the past, and the present is made unreal. Dreamlike as it is, a Fellini movie is not so much a nocturnal dream as a hypnagogic one—a dream born during the twilight time between wakefulness and sleep. Here, anything can happen—and usually does. For many individuals this transitional period is all but nonexistent, merely a thin threshold they quickly traverse. For others, however, it is a long corridor connecting the wakeful and slumber states, a hallway whose walls are lined with surrealistic fantasies, abstract imagery, and creative thoughts.

Anyone who has had a hypnagogic dream knows it is quite different from the nightly REM dream. It lacks both visual continuity and full-blown narrative quality—there is no continuum of actions and characters that form the quasi-logical and linear progression of events in space–time. The

129

brain is pulling away from wakeful realities, and the real world is spinning in the distance.

Researchers are learning that this twilight time of the mind, characterized especially by theta brain-wave rhythms,* is one of the most productive and provocative levels of consciousness. "It may be a period of enchantment," says Dr. Charles Tart, "with beautiful visions, sweet music, and insights into ourselves." The history of creative thought is replete with examples where hypnagogic consciousness has served as the wellspring for inspiration. Many great artists, in a variety of different fields, have turned to the period of drowsy reveries for original ideas. The practice of keeping a pencil and paper at bedside to jot down any momentary insight that came while traversing the twilight state was followed by such men as Tolstoy, Wagner, and Einstein, to name a few. But the same level of theta consciousness from which creativity springs also contains psi phenomena. The nonlinear, freeflow, transcendent nature of the state is ideal for psychical events. "The hypnagogic state," says Stanley Krippner, who has researched in that area, "seems to be significantly more conducive to paranormal events, and it may be the best place to look for psi in future experiments." One psychic event which seems to be rooted in the twilight mind is the phenomenon of automatic writing.

When she was sixteen years old, Stella Edwards developed a compulsion to write. It was more than a simple urge to sit down and compose poems and short stories; that is common enough and ordinarily a conscious process. But Stella's drive was unconscious and her symptoms frightening. When the compulsion seized her, she would become dazed and glassy-eyed, and her hand would pick up a pencil and automatically begin to fill page after page. She wrote of personal things: her family life in South Africa, school, and her eventual plans to marry and have children. After a few weeks the writing became an obsession, consuming much of her day and awakening her from sleep at night to grope in the dark for pencil and paper.

Her compulsion became more sharply defined. It was not her words that she put on paper, Stella claimed, but the thoughts of one Wouta Egelstein, a departed spirit who instructed her at all hours of the day and

*There are four major brainwave frequencies: beta, 30-13 cycles per second (normal wakefulness); alpha, 12-8 cps (passive alertness, light meditation); theta, 7-4 cps (deep meditation, believed to be related to creative mental activity); and delta, 3-1 cps (deep, nonREM sleep).

night to write. Wouta, whose name suddenly appeared one day in Stella's writings, said he had been a schoolboy who had recently died. Although he dictated much material for weeks on end, none of it was the least bit of help in building a coherent story of Wouta's life. In fact, from the evidence of Stella's communications, Wouta Egelstein was a pathological liar; he was constantly contradicting himself. One day he wrote that he had been hanged for killing his younger brother, but two days later he wrote a touching tale of how he had been sick and died of pneumonia.

Stella's parents were frightened. They did not believe their daughter actually was possessed, but her obsession had passed the bounds of safety. She was writing almost continuously to the neglect of school, her meals, and her sleep. She was put on tranquilizers by a psychiatrist, but that did not quiet Wouta; neither did shock treatment. Now Stella claimed that she could hear Wouta's voice ringing in her ears, not loud, but rather in the way one can hear words when reading a book. Soon Wouta began to touch her, and these tactile hallucinations came with increasing frequency. He would sit on her bed to dictate long speeches, and when he got up to leave Stella said she could see the wrinkled sheets and the impression of where he had been sitting.

Wouta never gave Stella any paranormal information, nothing at least that could be verified. Most of his talk was nonsense, and unquestionably he was nothing more than Stella's unleashed subliminal mind. In fact, the accepted view among parapsychologists today is that automatic writing is a pouring forth from the inner mind and has nothing to do with deceased persons, a belief which was once extremely popular. However, automatic writing can produce many unusual events. As quickly as Wouta Egelstein had appeared, he left—but not without naming a replacement, an American Indian named David Manala. David was more talented than Wouta. One day as Stella's father was reading the sentences she put on paper, he decided to experiment. He told her to ask David on what plane of consciousness he had died. Her left hand immediately wrote:

3rd plane

and drew a three-dimensional representation. Her father then told her to switch the pencil from her left to her right hand. She did (although she was left-handed), and he had her ask David the same question. This time the hand wrote:

 $\mathit{\unicode{0x0288}\unicode{0x026F}}$ ɓɭoυɢ   [sic]

The writing and the accompanying diagram were not only upside down, but written from right to left, perfect mirror images written quickly and in flawless penmanship.[1] Not an easy accomplishment. With her left hand she wrote as Stella Edwards, but with her right hand she could write as an enantiomorph of her self.

In his classic work *Human Personality* the psychologist F. W. H. Myers notes that it is not uncommon to find one stratum of the mind communicating with another, and in complex ways; usually one level denies knowledge of the other. Of automatic writing he says:

> . . . if these writings are shown to the primary personality he will absolutely repudiate their authorship—alleging not only that he has no recollection of writing them, but also that they contain allusions to facts which he never knew. Some of these messages, indeed, although their source is so perfectly well defined—although we know the very moment when the secondary personality which wrote them was called into existence—do certainly look more alien to the automatist in his normal state than many of the messages which claim to come from spirits of the lofty type. It is noticeable, moreover, that these manufactured personalities sometimes cling obstinately to their fictitious names, and refuse to admit that they are in reality only aspects or portions of the automatist himself.[2]

Stella Edwards wrote her material in the drowsy, twilight state of mind, a state highly conducive to psychical happenings. But after a frightening year for Stella and her parents, both Wouta Egelstein and David Manala had vanished without producing a scrap of evidential parasensory material. This is not always the case, for often, the automatic writing syndrome opens wide the doors to paranormal communications. Such is the recent case of Tina Johnson.

Tina is an automatist whose talents have been studied by scientists. She is not possessed by the syndrome to the frightening degree Stella was, although it sometimes creeps upon her unexpectedly. She may be in the kitchen cooking when suddenly an uncontainable urge ripples throughout her body, forcing her to grab pencil and paper. Other times she sits down at her desk, goes into a trance, and the pencil in her hand automatically begins to compose sentences. Her writing is not gibberish, nor a series of lies and contradictions as were Wouta Egelstein's dictations; often she writes telepathic impressions from distant friends, clairvoyant facts, or precognitive advice to herself or loved ones. Brainwave tests have shown that before Tina's writing begins, her EEG pattern consists of a normal desynchronized beta wave. But once she says, "Boy! They are really coming in strong now!" (a remark referring to the discarnate entities she believes motivate her writing), the patterns switch to rhythmic theta waves of unusually high amplitude, about 100 microvolts.[3] Dr. Krippner has found that Tina's intermittent reports on the strength of her spirit contacts quite accurately correlate with her percentage of theta waves. When she says, "They are beginning to leave now; it's difficult to hear them," sure enough, the theta waves have begun to fade out and beta rhythms are occurring. Tina described her experiential reaction this way for Krippner:

> When I do automatic writing, I simply relax my control over my conscious thoughts and let the thoughts from another source come into my brain and through my handwriting. It took a year before I was able to accomplish this. Other than a fraction of a second's warning, I am not aware until I am writing what I am going to write. It is as if the conscious brain only watches while it relinquishes control of my writing mechanisms. I am able to switch back and forth to my own conscious writing during the sessions in order to write down question for later reference. However, I am also able to ask the questions mentally and have them answered in writing.[4]

In clairvoyant experiments where she must perceive an image of a target picture in an envelope, Tina's spirit contacts do commendable reporting. In one instance, at the Maimonides laboratory, a target picture was *The Enigma of Arrival* by DeChirico, which depicts two people, one wearing blue and the other red. As Tina sat in front of reseachers holding the opaque envelope, electrodes connected to her skull, the following dialogue ensued in her voice:

Tina: Dear friends, are you there?
Spirits: Yes, we are.
Tina: I am holding an envelope with a picture inside. Can you see it?
Spirits: Yes. We can sense it.
Tina: What is the picture?

Spirits:	There is blue. A blue boy.
Tina:	What else do you see?
Spirits:	People . . .
Tina:	Are you certain?
Spirits:	We see a very young man in a blue suit. He is standing up.
Tina:	Do any of you see anything else?
Spirits:	No, we see the same thing. We are going to help you very much with this as we get used to this sort of testing.[5]

The trial was scored a hit. Besides the "spirits" promising to assist Tina even more once they got the knack of the clairvoyant experiments, they also express feelings. On the next test Tina told them, "We are trying the second of the experiments. You had a hit on the first one—the blue boy," to which they responded, "We are very excited and happy about it." But in another test where they did not score a hit, she reprimanded them; they answered sharply, "This is not the way to make us work. You are hurting us." Although Tina can perform clairvoyantly, an impressive feat for anyone, the dialogues at times get quite silly. After scoring two hits in succession, the spirits broke in to announce: "Now hear this! We are so glad for you. Wheeeee for all of us!" Krippner believes that Tina's spirits are what Myers calls "splinters of man's own split personality." Tina's opinion is that she is in contact with spirits, and that's that.

Although no one knows what initiates the automatic writing phenomenon, many individuals claim to have had success learning it by sitting in a comfortable chair, dimming the room lights, and holding a pad and pencil on their lap. "They try breathing exercises or meditation to achieve total relaxation," says Krippner—all to get the requisite drift into the twilight state. "With enough patience and determination," Krippner claims, "some individuals have found that their hand will automatically reach for the pencil and begin writing." The writing can range from poetic jabberwocky to profound psychoanalysis.

Because automatic writing seems to spring from the twilight level of consciousness, which also harbors creativity, it is not surprising to find the two phenomena often walk hand in hand. While experimentally undergoing LSD therapy, Dr. Thelma Moss began writing spontaneously. At first it frightened her, but then she realized that it was awakening the poetic aspect of her personality. She had never written poetry before, but now it was flowing forth. One of Moss's "automatic" poems describes the nature of "I":

> *There is nothing in the world*
> *More marvelous than I*
> *The living, breathing, miracle*
> * of I.*
> *The I of him, the I of thee,*
> *And, too, the I of me.*[6]

The prolific novelist Taylor Caldwell claims that many of her stories came to her in a twilight state, and literally forced her to put them on paper.[7] Another striking example is Mary Leader, the fledgling novelist. In February of 1973 she published her first novel, *Triad,* which sold well and was chosen by the Literary Guild as a monthly selection. But Ms. Leader had had no intention of writing a novel. She recounts the incident:

> The plot, which has a supernatural theme, came to me one unforgettable afternoon in 1971. I recall I was restless and strangely weary. I'd been watching television with half an eye and decided to take a nap.
>
> I settled myself in a contour chair and prepared to doze off —but I didn't sleep. Instead, I drifted into a peculiar state of consciousness, neither asleep nor awake. Then this—thing—began happening.
>
> I felt like I was in another world, a twilight world in which I wandered, as if in a forest. Never before had I felt like this. It was as though it were a film—the entire panorama of my novel reeled off before me, its theme, its plot, even details. . . .
>
> I don't remember how long I was gone, but when I broke out of it, it was all there. I had the whole plot . . .
>
> I was seized with a compulsion to write and write![8]

And she wrote and wrote and finished the novel in a few months. In a sense she feels the work is page after page of spillings from her subliminal self, a psychiatric report about the real Mary Leader that no team of psychoanalysts could extract. Psychoanalysis tries to coax information from the inner mind, but Krippner believes that automatic writing can be a window into the subliminal self. Myers says of it: "If once we can get a spy into the citadel of our own being, his rudest signalling will tell us more than the subtlest inferences from outside, of what is being planned and done within."[9]

Creativity and Psi

If we read the writings of history's greatest musicians, poets, and artists, it is clear that their masterpieces were not achieved by a conscious, step-by-step process. Rather, the work welled up in them, often *in toto*, knocking at the door of consciousness from some profound level of the mind. Mozart took pains to stress the fact that his musical compositions were not arrived at note by note or phrase by phrase, but came to him from an outside source as complete wholes—a sonata in all its developments, a symphony in full orchestration. "I do not have in my imagination," he wrote, "the parts successively, but I hear them, as it were, all at once."[10] The so-called pain of creation comes not in the joyous inspiration, but in the mundane process of transcribing the sudden mental imagery onto paper. A particularly vivid account of this is given by George Sand, Chopin's lover. She eloquently explains how, while composing the opus 28 Preludes in the spring of 1838, Chopin would return mesmerized from a solitary walk in the woods of Majorca, and then have to wrench himself from this twilight world to transcribe his musical visions onto paper:

> His [act of] creation was spontaneous, miraculous. He found it without seeking, without foreseeing it. It came on his piano, sudden, complete, sublime, or it sang in his head during a walk and he was in haste to let himself hear it by throwing it on to the instrument. But thereafter began the most distressing labour, at which I was never present . . . He shut himself into his room for days at a time, weeping, walking up and down, breaking his pens, repeating or changing a measure a hundred times, writing it down and scratching it out as often, and starting again the next day with a desperate and exacting perseverance.[11]

As with Mozart, Chopin was mystified by the source of his music; he felt sure that he did not create it. So too, the eighteenth-century poet William Blake, who believed that bursts of creativity came from beyond the mind of the creator. He expressed this belief in his final utterances as he lay dying. Although physically weak, he was working feverishly to record his last bits of poetry. His wife beseeched him to put aside the paper and pencil lest he unduly exhaust himself, but, he exclaimed of the poetry which poured forth, "It is not mine, it is not mine."

Whose is it? The eminent philosopher C. D. Broad has postulated that at a subliminal level of the mind all individuals are psychically connected:[12] painters, musicians, poets, scientists, businessmen, secretaries, and house-wives are linked through invisible bonds. The strength of a bond between one person and another is variable, says Broad, thus accounting in some measure for the natural affinity between certain individuals and spontane-ous hostility between others. We can imagine the bonds as Aristotle's "feelers"—long threads of varied thickness woven to form a humankind communications network. The idea is not unlike Jung's "collective uncon-scious." As Board's theory has it, the creative genius has such strong psychic ties with his fellow human beings that the artist pours into his masterpiece a blend of the yearnings, suffering, and joys of all people, making works like the *Choral Symphony, Hamlet,* and the *Mona Lisa* composites of human experiences, distilled, polished, and synthesized by creators who were inextricably bound to all other human beings. Is this not what is meant in saying that a work has universality? As Dr. Anthony Storr, an authority in creativity, says, "The great creators, because their tensions are of universal rather than personal import, can appeal to all of us . . ."[13]

We tend to imagine the genius as an introverted individual, shut off from others. Might that surface isolation, argues Broad, be nothing more than the result of a mind preoccupied by the psychic inputs of humankind? The act of transcendence in the creative process is not mere speculation. The artist *does* soar above the wakeful constraints of time and space, and the result is, as the great humanistic psychologist Abraham Maslow said, a "fusion between the person and his world."[14] Maslow notes that this "melting into one has been reported so often that it is an observable fact which we may now reasonably consider to be a *sine qua non* of creativity."

Camille Saint-Saëns, the great French composer, had an experience in which creativity and psi were intimately linked. He telepathically sensed the death of a close friend hundreds of miles away, and the tragic impression exploded in his mind into the mournful theme for the opening of his hauntingly beautiful *Requiem*. Saint-Saëns wrote of the experience in a letter dated January, 1871, to a friend, Camille Flammarion. It was during the last days of the Franco-Prussian War, and Saint-Saëns was celebrating gaily with some friends:

> . . . when suddenly I heard in my head a plaintive musical theme, of dolorous chords, which I have since used for commencement

of my *Requiem*, and I felt in my inmost being a presentiment of some misfortune. A profound anxiety unnerved me. That was the moment when Henri Regnault, to whom I was very much attached, was killed.[15]

Creativity is often defined as bringing forth something that had no prior existence; however, in discussing creativity with respect to psi a better definition might be: *bringing to wakeful consciousness patterns which had prior piecemeal existence only through dissociative states.* Although Freud denied the possibility of a relationship between creativity and psi, it was a favorite notion of his rebellious disciple Jung. For Jung the source of inspiration, and psi, lay jointly outside conscious volition. Freud viewed the nature of the creative process as a sublimation of frustrations; Jung saw it as a resolution of opposites—positive and negative, yin and yang, the material and the psychical aspects of humankind.

In his attempt to awaken the creative process in his patients, Jung turned to the ancient occult figure of the mandala—a circular form, replete with rich patterns, which expresses and symbolizes the union of opposites. The mandala, in the ancient text of the *I Ching*, represents the psychic energy ch'i, composed of the opposite forces of yin and yang; but the figure is universal and found in every primitive culture. As ancient theory teaches, meditation on a mandala draws on, and concentrates, psychic energy. It is no coincidence that Jung selected the mandala to arouse the creative drive. As he wrote: "The psychological machinery which transmutes energy is the symbol."[16] He would have his patients, one of whom was James Joyce, draw, redraw, and concentrate on mandalas to clear the dust from their temporarily blinded eyes. It is not known how often Joyce visited Jung or the exact content of their sessions. One can speculate, however, that Jung played a significant part in the novelist's sixteen-year labor *Finnegans Wake* —a novel, if it can be called that, which could never be taken as a product of the conscious mind.

All indications are that children possess a greater potential for paranormal communications than ego-encapsulated adults. Evidence presented earlier, especially the fact that infants spend a considerable amount of sleep time in REM dreaming, suggests that the younger the child, the greater his psychic potential. Interestingly, this hypothesis is further reinforced by the fact that the mandala—the king of psi symbology—is the earliest and most important figure a child draws. Commenting on this fact, and the extensive study which revealed it by Rhoda Kellog, the biologist Desmond Morris says:

The circling movement becomes a satisfying one and is purified and simplified until, at the age of three, the child is producing its first circles. Now that they are produced in a pure form, the circles look empty and the child begins to fill them up with spots and dashes. This gives rise to the idea of crossing out the circle and the child draws bold lines across it, this way and that. While all this has been going on the child has also learnt to make crosses and to combine crosses to make a star shape. When the circle is being crossed out, the star shape turns out to be a perfect fit and can be used to make a satisfyingly symmetrical pattern. This double cross inside a circle gives a basic aggregate of Mandala design. Kellog considers this to be the most important unit of prerepresentational drawing. Its occurrence is universal and frequent and it appears to be vital for the stages that are to follow.[17]

Are the infant and the genius in closer contact with the pool of psychic energy than the average person? Do their minds spend proportionately more time in a transcendental state beyond the four-dimensional space–time continuum? Is the difference that the genius can return to the "real" world and fashion in words, on canvas, and in clay what he has experienced, while the infant is helpless to share these encounters?

For the inquisitive mind, it is frustrating that psychical research and creativity theory are both in their early stages of development. The similarities between creativity and psi are trying to show us many profound things, and, like blind men, we are groping desperately for the light.

The Out-of-the-Body Experience

When Sylvan Muldoon was twelve years old he reported a frightening experience. He awakened during the night and found his body paralyzed. The catalepsy extended from head to toe, and apparently froze his vocal cords because he could not call for help. He lay there for several minutes, not in any pain, until the paralysis gave way to a floating sensation. Now, a body, identical to his own yet not his own, hovered above the bed. Suddenly he realized that his point of perspective was from the ceiling downward; he was looking down at his paralyzed body in bed. This moment of fear was followed by a jolt, a loud clang, and Muldoon sat up in a cold sweat, shaking uncontrollably.

It could have been nothing more than a nightmare, for what child has not experienced dreams of floating, but it continued to happen hundreds of

times over the next few years. Eventually Muldoon learned to control the
floating of his "etheric" or "astral" body. On one occasion he fell to sleep
thirsty only to find himself standing in the kitchen in the out-of-body state
trying to turn on the faucet. On another occasion he traveled in his "astral"
body to the house of relatives where his parents were visiting, and in the
morning dumbfounded them with specific details of the evening. During all
these years he had been a sickly boy confined to bed for long periods. But
when his constitution improved some years later, the uncanny ability to
travel out of his body waned and finally disappeared altogether. He lived
out the rest of his life in Darlington, Wisconsin, running a beauty shop, and
died in 1971. Hereward Carrington's 1929 biography of Sylvan Muldoon,
The Projection of the Astral Body, has become a classic on the subject. And
rightly so, for Muldoon, in his out-of-body flights, was able to bring back
accurate and detailed information from places he visited.

Through the 1930s, 1940s, and 1950s the out-of-the-body experience
(OOBE) was virtually ignored by parapsychologists. Many saw OOBEs
tangled with the messy and controversial issue of survival after death, and
after all, they were trying hard to establish a new science, not start a new
religion. Muldoon and others who had such experiences reported seeing a
silver cord connecting the physical and etheric bodies. Once "out," Muldoon could see it, slender and glistening, an infinitely elastic tether running
from the top of the head of his physical body to his floating double. Psychics
claimed it was the "thread of life," which once severed freed the etheric
body from its physical shell for eternity. OOBEs were so colored by religious overtones, that for many years parapsychologists pretended they did
not exist—a trick they had learned from establishment scientists. Up until
1960 the "word" on OOBEs was wholly anecdotal, tales collected now and
then, often years after an incident had occurred. The first attempt to give
some organization to the subject came from the eminent British researcher
Dr. Robert Crookall.

For over a decade now, Crookall has been diligently collecting reports
of over a thousand OOBEs. Unlike his predecessors, who read one case and
went on to the next, Crookall has analyzed the data searching for common
denominators that would reveal something about the nature of OOBEs. Up
until now he has offered four different analyses: (1) the six primary characteristics; (2) natural versus forced experiences; (3) psychics versus non-
psychics; and (4) confusion-vageness-confusion.[18]

In his first analysis Crookall found that shorn of their verbal fat the
anecdotes displayed six lean characteristics common to all: (1) the person
feels he or she is leaving the body through the top of his or her head; (2)

at the instant of separation of the etheric and physical bodies, the person momentarily blacks out; (3) before wandering, the etheric body hovers for some time over the physical shell; (4) when the etheric body returns from its travels to reenter, it goes through the hovering position again; (5) a blackout occurs at the moment of reintegration; and (6) rapid reentry jolts the physical body.

Crookall's study showed that there were no cases of people being unable to reunite their two bodies (or if there were, no one lived to report it). Regardless of how far the etheric body travels, the emotion of fear on the part of the person acts as a hook to yank the spirit back and merge it with the physical, says Crookall.

In his second analysis Crookall found a qualitative difference between OOBEs which occur naturally—through hypnagogic sleep, delirium, illness, and extreme lassitude—and those that were forced by the use of hypnosis, anesthetics, electric shock, and volition. The natural OOBEs tended to be more vivid and pleasant, much less frightening, and longer in duration. The person always felt able to go back to the body whenever he or she fancied.

In Crookall's third analysis he sorted out reports given by psychics and those from the average populace. Surprisingly, the OOBEs of psychics often resembled forced experiences while those of the average person had the characteristics of natural occurrences. Crookall could only conclude that most psychics experience OOBEs by willful projection. Of course, there are exceptions, and Mrs. Eileen Garrett was one. In a long-distance experiment the famous psychic claims to have projected herself from New York to Reykjavik, Iceland at a predetermined time and observed the actions of an experimenter, Dr. D. Svenson. In a semitrance state she reported exactly what Svenson was doing to another experimenter, Dr. Anita Muhl. She saw Svenson reading a book, and described the text, a bandage he had wrapped around his head, and the room. There was nothing forced about the experience for Mrs. Garrett, and reentry went smoothly. (Technically, Mrs. Garrett's experience is called "traveling clairvoyance," and not an OOBE. The difference, or lack of it, will be taken up later along with the nature of the whole phenomenon, and what is being done experimentally.)

Crookall's fourth analysis, published in the early 1970s, revealed that most OOBEs occur in three stages of awareness. Initially there is confusion on the part of the person as to what is happening. But once separation has taken place, he or she experiences a clearing of consciousness, often seeing things more sharply than ever. This crystal vision turns cloudy again on reentry.

Dr. Crookall's indefatigable efforts have done a great deal to rekindle interest in OOBEs. He has given organization to an area of parapsychology that once was scattered, and unification to data that once were piecemeal anecdotes. The weight of his evidence has caused researchers to sit up and take note, and to begin further investigation. Additional field studies, as interesting as they might be, can never constitute proof; the need was for controlled laboratory experiments. The first tests along this line were carried out in 1965 and 1966 by Dr. Charles Tart using the EEG facilities at the University of Virginia's Department of Parapsychology.

Tart's subject for the tests was a Virginia businessman, Robert Monroe, who began having OOBEs in 1958, and since has been "out" hundreds of times. Monroe is an analytical man of average intellectual training who realized the uniqueness of his experiences and has kept systematic, detailed notes. They comprise a wealth of curious information, some tales more credible than others, but all fascinating. If Monroe's experiences, published in 1971 under the title *Journeys Out of the Body,* were not backed by some laboratory experiments, they would fall in with the mountain of OOBE anecdotal material, but as they stand, in light of Tart's work, they take on fresh perspective. To get a feeling for Monroe's OOBEs, before turning to Tart's studies, here is an excerpt from his diary:

11/5/58 Afternoon
  The vibrations came quickly and easily, and were not at all uncomfortable. When they were strong, I tried to lift out of the physical with no result. Whatever thought or combination I tried, I remained confined right where I was. I then remembered the rotating trick, which operates just as if you are turning over in bed. I started to turn, and recognized that my physical was not "turning" with me. I moved slowly, and after a moment I was "face down," or in direct opposition to the placement of my physical body. The moment I reached this 180° position (out of phase, opposite polarity?), there was a hole. That's the only way to describe it. To my senses, it seemed to be a hole in a wall which was about two feet thick and stretched endlessly in all directions (in the vertical plane).
  The periphery of the hole was just precisely the shape of my physical body. I touched the wall, and it felt smooth and hard. The edges of the hole were relatively rough. (All this touching done with the non-physical hands.) Beyond—through the hole— was nothing but blackness. It was not the blackness of a dark

room, but a feeling of infinite distance and space, as if I were looking through a window into distant space . . .

I moved cautiously through the hole, holding onto its side, and poked my head through carefully. Nothing. Nothing but blackness. No people, nothing material. I ducked back in hurriedly because of the utter strangeness. I rotated back 180°, felt myself merge with the physical, and sat up. It was broad daylight, just as when I had left what seemed a few minutes before. Lapsed time: one hour, five minutes![19]

In August of 1966, Dr. Tart had eight sessions with Mr. Monroe in which brain waves, eye movements, and heart rate were electronically monitored while Monroe tried to travel out of his body and read a five digit number which was on a shelf in an adjacent room. Unfortunately, conditions were far from ideal. An army cot served as the bed and an ear electrode of the clip type clung to Monroe's ear lobe like a baby alligator. For the first seven nights nothing happened; Monroe could not get "out." The eighth night he experienced two brief OOBEs. In one trip he saw several people he did not recognize standing in an unfamiliar location; nothing verifiable. In the second brief OOBE he had great difficulty controlling himself; he could not enter the adjacent room to read the target number. His etheric body seem to drift of its own free will out of the laboratory and into a hallway of the building. On awakening three minutes later, Monroe said he had seen a woman, a laboratory technician, talking with a man. Tart checked the hall and found this to be true. Although neither OOBE enabled Monroe to read the target number, Tart found that during the three-minute experience Monroe's brain-wave patterns were those typical of dreaming with the accompanying REMs. His heartbeat was normal.[20]

In the summer of 1968 Tart had another opportunity to work with Monroe at UCLA under more comfortable conditions—a paste electrode was used rather than the alligator clip, and Monroe slept in a standard bed. Although Monroe was still unable to read the target numbers, he did produce verifiable information of things that happened in the courtyard behind the laboratory building. During the period Monroe was wandering out of his body, Tart observed definite physiological correlates. Monroe's blood pressure dropped, his eye movements increased, and his brainwave pattern switched to prolonged theta rhythms typical of the hypnagogic state.[21] "Such prolonged states," says Tart, "are not normally seen in the laboratory." At present Tart is attempting to work backward with Mr. Monroe, teaching him to produce theta rhythms through biofeedback training that may induce easy and more controllable OOBEs.

After Robert Monroe's first encounter with the hole in the OOBE reported earlier, he tried to duplicate the experience, and he did, several times. Nothing evidential ever happened, and the incidences may be nothing more than mere hallucinations. But Monroe has produced some evidential material during his OOBEs, and those times have shown unusual physiological correlates. Here are excerpts of his further encounters with the hole:

11/18/58 Night

The vibrations came in strong . . . Again, I thought to try to rotate. When I did, it worked and I rotated slowly into the 180° position. There was the wall and the hole and the blackness beyond. This time I was more cautious. Carefully, I reached a hand through into the blackness. I was astounded when a hand took mine and shook it! It felt like a human hand, normally warm to the touch. After the handshake, I withdrew my hand quickly . . .

12/27/58 Night

Upon setting up the vibrations, I again found the hole as expected. I gathered up courage, and slowly poked my head through the hole. The moment I did, I heard a voice say in utter excitement and surprise, "Come here quick! Look!" I could see no one . . . The other party didn't seem to be coming, so the voice called again, urgently and excitedly. The vibrations seemed to be weakening, so I pulled back out of the hole and rotated back into the physical without incident.

1/15/59 Afternoon

. . . I was a little nervous when I reached through with one hand. Then I mentally smiled and relaxed . . . a hand took mine and squeezed it, and I returned the grasp. I definitely sensed a feeling of friendliness from the other side.

1/25/59 Night

. . . I carefully reached into the hole. A hand again took mine and held it firmly . . . Then the hand passed mine over to a second hand. I slowly released the second hand and felt upward. There was definitely an arm attached to the hand, and a shoulder. I was about to explore more, when the vibrations seemed to soften, and I pulled my arm back and rotated to the physical.[22]

In addition to Dr. Tart's work with Robert Monroe, other OOBE research is being performed by Dr. Karlis Osis at the laboratories of the American Society for Psychical Research in New York City. Osis' star subject has been a forty-one-year-old psychic, Ingo Swann. Monroe produced evidential material, but not from the target; Swann, on the other hand, is a perfect subject who gives detailed information accompanied by definite physiological correlates.

In 1973 Swann was put through a battery of psi tests, first by physicists on the West Coast and then by psychologists in New York. In one OOBE experiment Swann sat in a long, narrow room. Electrodes pasted to his scalp connected him to an EEG which monitored his brainwave patterns. In the center of the room, suspended from the ceiling on a small platform about ten feet up from the floor, was the experimental target. It consisted of a red heart-shaped piece of paper mounted on a white surface and a black leather-sheathed letter opener, both in a thick cardboard box with the lid open. The only way to see into the box was to climb a ladder (which was not around) and look over the side. Swann's task was to draw a sketch of the contents of the box, which had been assembled earlier by a staff member who was not present during the experiment. As Swann sat in the chair, he was observed by scientists, and a television camera recorded his every move.

For many minutes Swann sat motionless, his eyes closed. Then he reached over, picked up paper and pencil and drew an asymmetric elliptical figure and a silhouette which closely resembled the letter opener. He labeled the drawings "red" and "black" respectively. Another time he identified a target of concentric colored bands—violet, red, green, and black—with a sector cut away. He saw the colors red, black, and green, and the cut-away piece; his only error was that the sequence of the colors on the target was out of order. In fact, during these tests Swann scored eight hits out of eight different targets with odds against chance of one in 40,000.[23]

Experientially Swann reported that he felt his spirit float to the ceiling, look into the box, then return to his body. That is his way of satisfying to himself how he "saw" the contents of the boxes. The researchers have no way to prove or disprove it, but they do have one objective fact: During the few minutes just before Swann drew each picture, the EEG recorded very definite alterations in his brainwave output and there was a twenty-percent loss in electrical activity.

At this point a long overdue question should be asked: What is the difference between OOBEs and clairvoyant perception? To avoid a lot of circular arguing and get directly to the point—no one has been able to find an absolute difference between the two. In an OOBE a person sees people and events at a distance and *feels* that he has traveled there. In clairvoyant perception a person also sees these things but *feels* he did so while sitting in one location. The net result in both cases is the same—the acquisition of parasensory information. The only difference is in the person's subjective interpretation of the experience.

Psi researchers are divided on the issue. Dr. Tart suspects that OOBEs and clairvoyant perception might be one and the same. Dr. Osis, on the other hand, feels they are not, although he is hard pressed to distinguish between the two. To say, as Osis and others do, that in OOBEs the entire personality of the individual travels to the distant location and not just his sense of vision, is to ignore the fact that that too is purely subjective sentiment on the part of the individual. Others argue that persons have sensed the presence of an individual undergoing an OOBE in the room with them; not only do they know that something etheric or spiritual is there, but they can also sometimes identify the person. This still does not prove, however, that a "double" of the person—an intact, separate entity—was present in the room. Who is to say that when a clairvoyant is perceiving a distant room the people in that room cannot sense being spied upon psychically—and at times even tell who is doing the looking?

Clairvoyant perception appears to involve the transcendence of space and thus there is no concept of distance-to-traverse for the percipient. The target and the percipient are in a sense superimposed—they are one. If the etheric body or spirit of an individual resides in this same hyperspace dimension, it too cannot appreciate our notion of distance. We are ascribing to a hyperdimensional entity a feeble measure called miles. Unless new facts are turned up, it appears that an absolute distinction between OOBEs and clairvoyant perception cannot be made.

Letting Go

The secret is to let go.

The phenomena of creativity, automatic writing, and OOBE demand temporarily loosening one's grip on the "real" world. Though it may work, sleep is not essential nor are hypnosis or mind-altering drugs—only the surrendering of wakeful realities: business transactions, household chores, conversations, petty preoccupations, and neuroses. It is not surprising to find that a large percentage of the Western population simply cannot let go. Our cultural trends have been directed toward a rigid, linear philosophy of "progress" and productivity which associates letting go with going insane.

Western man has worked so hard to emphasize "self" that each individual has become encrusted with his own self-esteem, thus locking himself out of the twilight world. Psychological studies of individuals who show none of the desirable fantasy material in the hypnagogic hall, who pass through it unaware, reveal them to have a "rigid, moralistic and repressive outlook on life."[24] In general, they cannot tolerate disharmonious ideas or peculiar logics; incongruous details must be dealt with immediately—either forced prematurely into a mold or discarded as irrelevant. This obsessive need to force immediate pattern and organization on all things strange, to make the new conform to the old, the fresh to the stale, nips the creative bud and blocks the parasenses.

For many years, Dr. Elmer Green, a psychologist of the Menninger Foundation, has been conducting research on the theta waves of fantasy. It is desirable at times to turn them on, and it is essential to be able to turn them off. Green believes that there is something to the age-old notion of a fine line separating genius from insanity. He feels that what the highly creative and the mentally disturbed individual have in common is high theta production, or in other words, a long hypnagogic hall. Psychotics may "lock in" on the eidetic imagery, says Green, and accept this hallucinatory world as their real world. Geniuses, on the other hand, merely dip into the reservoir of reveries for inspiration, then return to beta consciousness to execute their ideas. If this is true, it means that psychotics are more receptive to parasensory information than most normal, healthy individuals.

Dr. Harry Hermon, a New York psychiatrist, believes this is so, and is just beginning an experiment to test the hypothesis. Hermon feels that the imaginary voices and frightening suspicions that paranoid schizophrenics experience may actually be random telepathic pickups from the thoughts of persons around them. Hermon says that when a schizophrenic becomes frightened of a person entering a room and pulls away into a corner, the schizophrenic may be psychically sensing the aggressive and hostile side of that person, a side we all have. Thus, psychotics and schizophrenics could see beyond a friendly face into the inner personality of the smiling person, see things about the person that he or she does not know. Since telepathy knows no regard for barriers or distance, this inner vision would not be confined to perceiving the feelings of local persons. Hermon's theory suggests that the schizophrenic's fears might be due to telepathic pickup of global sentiments also—bad vibrations from a world more evil than good. By subjecting mentally disturbed persons who are gradually withdrawing from the "real" world to psi testing, Hermon hopes to demonstrate his theory. "It's a common expression in psychiatry," he says, "when speaking of the severely disturbed, to say they have 'withdrawn from reality.' I'd like to know where they go."[25]

So would others. Dr. Montague Ullman of Maimonides and the State University of New York also believes that there are strong ties between psi and the world of the withdrawn person. Ullman recently wrote: "Considering this challenge just within the field of psychiatry itself, it seems to me more and more apparent that any accommodation of paranormal data [into the field of science] will involve the elaboration of a radically different conceptual base for our understanding of psychopathological syndromes."[26] Ullman believes that certain psychiatric conditions might be conducive to specific psi phenomena. A schizophrenic is a future-oriented person. He lives in constant fear of what is about to happen to him; he feels threatened, which is a preoccupation with the future; he is afraid of change, to make a transition from the present condition to a future one. "The schizophrenic," writes Ullman, "is future-oriented in terms of his unrelenting vulnerability to unpredictable threats and assaults upon his isolation . . . Real time, in a sense, doesn't exist for the schizophrenic . . ." Ullman then speculates: "Does this mean that the schizophrenic is more prone to precognition than other psi phenomena?" This type of reasoning can be carried further.

During the depressed phase of manic-depressive psychosis, the psychotic is past-oriented. Past achievements so overshadow the present and future that his conversation is filled with such statements as: "I remember when . . . ," "At one time I use to . . . ," "Then things were fine . . . ," "The good old days . . . ." Ullman wonders if such a person, withdrawn from the present and obsessed with the past, might be open to retrocognition.

Just as certain mental syndromes might be correlated with a transcendence of time, Ullman feels space might also be overcome. In the manic phase of manic-depressive psychosis, the psychotic is concerned with his spatial environment and a desire to escape from it. There are problems at the office, problems at home, and the patient feels he must get away—not in time but in distance, putting space between the source of the problems and himself. "God, I've got to get away," the manic might be heard saying. "Anywhere, any distance. I just can't stay here." Ullman wonders if such a person might be open to telepathy and clairvoyance more than the average person, since both those phenomena occur in present time but transcend distance. "They are only theories," Ullman says. "I haven't done any systematic study, but over the years I have developed the clinical impression that certain people with psychopathological problems might make better ESP subjects than the average person."[27]

The secret is to let go, but not for good. The twilight state is a desirable mentation and not necessarily dangerous. Unfortunately most people turn off the lights at night, close their eyes, and suddenly go sound alseep. What happened to that beautiful gallery of untitled paintings? Even more perplexing are the times when a flash strikes passing through it, a solution to a problem that has eluded one for weeks. You say to yourself, "I must remember that in the morning." But come morning, all you can remember is that there is something you should remember. Since the hypnagogic state naturally leads to sleep, unless one is aroused from it there is little chance of remembering any information gleaned therein. Is there some way to overcome this? Is there some way to automatically awaken from a twilight dream to record its visions?

Researchers at the Menninger Foundation have devised a method. They use a mercury-switch ring which a subject wears on his finger. Lying down to sleep, the subject puts his arm in a vertical position balanced on the elbow. Once wakeful consciousness diminishes below a certain level, he loses muscle tonus and the forearm naturally begins to tilt. This closes the mercury switch and sounds a chime. The noise brings the subject back to a wakeful state so that he can verbalize the hypnagogic experiences into a tape recorder.[28] This procedure is repeated several times before the ring is removed and the subject is permitted to fall asleep.

But the mercury switch is not the only way to awaken from hypnagogic consciousness. Dr. Tart suggests merely lying flat on one's back and keeping one arm in a vertical position balanced on the elbow. You should be able to maintain the position with minimum effort. As you start to slip into hypnagogic consciousness, your arm will begin to tilt. Suddenly, muscle tonus will be lost, and the arm will fall to the bed. This is usually enough to awaken you. At this point though, you must make the effort of getting up and tape recording or writing down your experiences.[29] It takes practice.

Both the technique used at the Menninger Foundation and Tart's variation on it work. But from a research standpoint there still is a problem with hypnagogic consciousness—the natural brevity of the state. This is the primary reason so little psi laboratory work has been done in this ASC. Rather than awakening a subject time and time again to record brief experiences, as the Menninger Researchers do with their finger switch, it would be more desirable to extend the duration of one hypnagogic interval. Thomas Budzynski, a professor of psychology at the University of Colorado's Medical Center, has suggested how this might be done. The subject would be placed in a mild sensory-deprivation environment which would enhance entering the hypnagogic state. He or she would be wired to an EEG that would feed back an audible signal as a function of the EEG frequency. This way the subject would be made aware of the slowing of alpha and the gradual appearance of theta activity. The circuit would be designed so that as the theta frequency decreased toward the delta-sleep frequency, an artificial tone would be sounded. It would be just enough to stimulate the subject's cortical activity and move him or her back into the alpha-theta region. Thus, the feedback would be used to rock the subject back and forth between alpha and theta rhythms. With this extended period of hypnagogic consciousness, says Budzynski, psi experiments could be conducted. Perhaps so, but any rewards derived from such prolonged twilight periods, both in terms of creativity and enhanced paranormal talents, would have to be carefully weighed against possible deleterious effects. One goal of psi research is to make a person modestly paranormal, not psychotic.

6

Dialogues with Nature: Clairvoyance

We Are the Environment

One ancient goal of Eastern philosophy is to achieve a harmony between man and nature, to grow toward oneness. We will not be at peace with ourselves, teaches Hinduism, until we are in concert with our environment. But this has never been the way of the West. Western philosophy has viewed nature as our most ubiquitous and formidable opponent; nature exists "out there," not a part of us, but something to be conquered. For years the Western goal looked possible. But no longer. Slowly, often painfully, we have come to see the infinite number of bonds between ourselves and nature, bonds which make our parasenses seem more natural than supernatural. It is worth knowing of some of these discoveries because the subtlety and mystery they display make a phenomenon like clairvoyance—communication between humans and nature—seem more credible.

Everyone has noticed flickering warning lights on a highway, or the rapid flashes of a faulty movie projector. These might have caused no more than a vague uneasiness, quickly forgotten. But these patterned signals are not innocuous. Instead, they probe so deeply into the human brain that they can be deadly. Dr. Grey Walter, an authority in brain studies, has found that certain individuals react violently to lights flashed at about ten times a second, the frequency that corresponds to the brain's alpha rhythm. A person prone to epilepsy will immediately experience seizure. But epileptics are not the only people who have to avoid such flickering. Walters examined hundreds of individuals with no history of the disease and found that about one out of every twenty reacts in the same way. First comes dizziness, then brief moments of unconsciousness, then spasmodic jerking of the arms and legs *in rhythm* with the flickering light.[1] For such a person, driving down a tree-lined street on a sunny day could be fatal. If the trees were evenly spaced and the car cruising at the right speed, the sunlight flickering between the trees could induce a fit. Thus do we unwittingly interact with our environment.

Just as our eyes react strangely to dancing lights, so do our ears fall under the spell of inaudible sounds. Professor H. Gavraud, an engineering teacher, almost gave up an academic post because of such a silent phenomenon. Gavraud always became ill when he sat down in his office to work. No matter how healthy he felt when the day began, as soon as he spent a few minutes in the office he became nauseous and suffered headaches. Thinking that there must be something in the room that disturbed him, he tried to track it down with various physical and chemical detectors. All yielded negative results until the day he became faint and leaned against the office wall to find it vibrating at an extremely low frequency. Investigating, Gavraud found the source of the vibrations: an air-conditioning unit on the roof of the adjacent building. Its inaudible vibrations had penetrated his office enough to disrupt his normal body physiology.[2] Sounds do not have to be heard to be disturbing; another subtle interaction between people and their environment.

To go further, just as silent sound and intermittent light can unconsciously affect us, so too can invisible, pollution-free air. Air is filled with ions, particles the size of atoms with either positive or negative charges. Until recently few legitimate scientists paid much heed to ions, although many "popular scientists" insisted the particles influenced our disposition. Now the roles have changed. The legitimate men of science who study ions are making claims more extraordinary than the popularists have ever dreamed, and backing them up with proof.

One leader in the field, Dr. Albert Krueger, Professor Emeritus of bacteriology at the University of California, Berkeley, writes: "People traveling to work in polluted air, spending eight hours a day in offices or factories, and living their leisure hours in urban dwellings, inescapably breathe ion-depleted air for substantial portions of their lives. There is increasing evidence that this ion depletion leads to discomfort, enervation and lassitude, and loss of mental and physical efficiency. This syndrome appears to develop quite apart from the direct toxic effects of the usual atmospheric pollutants."[3]

The ratio of positive to negative ions in the air is normally 1.2 to 1. This ratio may change for a number of reasons: lightning, cosmic rays, general atmospheric conditions, pollutants, and dry indoor heat. It is the loss of negative ions which appears to bring about the deleterious effects. In one experiment Krueger found that patients suffering from burns who were kept in a room containing high concentrations of negative ions experienced significant reduction in pain and acceleration in healing. One Philadelphia hospital now has a special ion room for burn patients. Doctors have found that healing proceeds faster in the room, the person experiences less pain, and there is less scarring. Plants in the same room grow faster and are healthier. Negative ions also have been found to raise one's resistance to the common cold and infections, and to influence learning ability, food intake, and sexual activity. The charged particles, both positive and negative, induce histological changes in body tissue and affect the adrenal, pituitary, thyroid, and sex glands. Krueger's theory of ions is really quite broad. He believes that ion depletion could be a major cause for the seemingly unexplainable ups and downs in mood, appetite, and sex drive. Again, if he is right, we see a subtle interaction in the human–environment chain.

Our unconscious ability to experience sensory communications with nature does not end with flickering lights, silent sounds, and invisible air ions; the interactions go much deeper. The ancient Chinese knew that the moon affected the tides. They also thought that it influenced menstruation and caused mental disorders—a belief which later led to the word *lunacy.* With Newton's discovery of gravitation in the late 1600s scientists came to agree with the Chinese's first belief—the moon did governed the tides—but there they drew the line. The moon could not affect body physiology.

Recently, a well-publicized article stated that there is "the possibility of a heightened accident susceptibility for people during the phase [of the moon] similar to that in which they were born, and for the lunar phase which is 180 degrees away from that in which they were born." The quotation is not from an astrological guide, although it undeniably has that ring; it is from a forty-four page report by scientists at the Atomic Energy Commission (AEC) Sandia Facility in Albuquerque, New Mexico. In 1972 a pragmatic group of AEC physicists and engineers undertook a massive study, wading through twenty years of records of accidents that had occurred at the Sandia Facility, everything from fires and explosions to falls and turned ankles. The year, month, day, and time of each accident was fed into a computer, along with the birth dates of the people involved and information on the phases of the moon and sunspot activity over the twenty-year period. The study, entitled "Intriguing Accident Patterns Plotted Against a Background of Natural Environmental Features," suggests that many patterns of human behavior appear to fall under the influence of the moon and the sun. The data show that accidents tend to peak in cycles of the new moon in apogee—the point at which the moon is farthest from the earth. The sun also proved to be an influencing factor. Laboratory injuries were plotted against the twenty-seven-day cycle of disturbances in the earth's magnetic field due to the sun's rotation. Significantly more accidents were found to occur during the first seven days and the thirteenth, fourteenth, twentieth, and twenty-fifth days of each cycle, when the magnetic disturbances were most active. One of the most impressive correlations was between accidents and sunspot activity. (Every eleven-and-a-half years the sun erupts into immense nuclear storms spewing streams of plasma into space. The effect on earth can be considerable. An unexpected freak eruption in the summer of 1973 knocked out international communications for several hours and disrupted local telephone service, and, on August 7, the solar winds blew so strongly that the earth's rotation actually slowed, increasing the length of the day.)

The Sandia study found that accidents peaked sharply every eleven-and-a-half years. In 1968 and 1969, for example, when the normal sunspot activity reached a maximum, the accident rate was the highest in the past two decades. The Sandia study concluded that "natural environmental influences in conjunction and interacting with and on the individual create error, misjudgments, pressures, and situations leading to accidents." The interactions between humans and nature grow deeper with each new discovery. The Western notion of man living apart from nature, attempting to enslave it, has become ridiculous; and the line separating our senses from our parasenses has grown awfully tenuous.

Over the last few years it has become clear that the ancient Chinese were right on another point—the influence of the moon on menstruation. For many centuries it has been suspected that the menstrual cycle is related to the synodic lunar month which lasts twenty-nine and a half days, as a vestige from the time when primitive women slept outdoors in moonlight. But the proof came only a few years ago. Dr. Edmond Dewan, of the Rock Reproduction Clinic in Boston, was concerned about a woman who had a sixteen-year history of menstrual irregularities. Her period varied radically between twenty-three to forty-eight days, and no doctor had been able to stabilize it. Dewan decided to try a harmless experiment. If it failed she would be no worse off than she had been those sixteen years, but if it succeeded her period should lock into a twenty-nine-day cycle. He gave the woman a small electric light and asked that during the next four months she sleep with it at the foot of her bed, regulating the light exposure each night in accordance to a table he had calculated based on the waxing and waning of the moon. To the woman's amazement and delight, her period stabilized at exactly twenty-nine days.[4] Since that time hundreds of women with menstrual irregularities have been helped at the medical center by the same procedure. Researchers believe the pineal gland at the base of the brain detects the waxing and waning of the light and, through hormonal release, regulates the period.

If our senses fall so subtly under the influence of the moon and sun, the earth's global fields, and air ion concentration, how do these things affect our parasenses? There are several reported cases of men working around low-frequency electrical equipment who suddenly found themselves receiving telepathic impressions. This only happens in the vicinity of the equipment, never in other rooms or at home.* The first scientific evidence to support the cases came from Russian scientist Dr. L. L. Vasiliev, who claimed that ordinary individuals placed in electrically charged cages developed a strong telepathic sense.[5] The allegation, taken with the cases of the electrical workers, excited parapsychologists. Was this a simple means of awakening man's parasenses? One U.S. researcher to investigate Vasiliev's claim was a neurologist and electronics expert, Dr. Andrija Puharich.

Puharich designed an ingenious cage in which a subject would sit. The floor was made of thick spruce boards layered with copper screening. Over the screening was laid a rubber mat to prevent the eventual inhabitant from receiving electrical shock. The walls and ceiling were of tightly fused copper, and the entire cage was raised three inches off the floor by glass insulators. A wooden chair and a microphone were the only extraneous articles inside the seven-foot-square construction. Theoretically, such a room, called a Faraday Cage, is a kind of electrical vacuum that will prevent the entrance of all electrical signals from the outside world. Following Vasiliev's studies, Puharich wanted to explore two questions: Could a person so shielded detect changes in a surrounding field placed on the walls of the cage, and would the charged cage enhance psychic ability? The brave guinea pig was Mrs. Eileen Garrett, the renowned psychic.

In the first experiment the cage was randomly charged and discharged by an electric generator housed in a separate building. No one knew when the electrical conditions would abruptly alter, but they would be recorded by an electronic device along with Mrs. Garrett's verbal responses. As the current flashed on and off, the psychic's sensitivity to the environment

---

*Dr. W. Ross Adey, of the University of California, Los Angeles, Brain Research Institute has found that low-frequency electric fields actually can enhance and alter brainwave patterns in monkeys, cats, and chicks. Animals placed in ambient fields showed increased learning ability, delayed task performance, and altered moods. The frequency of the fields was below fifteen hertz.

amazed Dr. Puharich. Not only was she able to detect all of the subtle changes in the field, even though it resided on the outside of the cage, but she was also able to distinguish differences in the electrostatic field caused by electric irons, blenders, power saws, and even the discharging of car spark plugs.[6] Shielded from the shower of fields which normally bombard a person, Mrs. Garrett was able to pinpoint even the smallest electrical surge. Did this added sensitivity increase her psychic powers?

To study her clairvoyant ability, which was considerable to begin with, Harvard physicist Dr. Richard Wilson designed a crystal device that detected large cosmic-ray bursts from the ionosphere, several miles above the earth. The device was kept on a different floor of the building, and its output was marked on a recorder. Mrs. Garrett's task was to guess when each recorded cosmic burst occurred, a question that no one could give her the answers to in advance.

Puharich found, as he had expected, that with the Faraday Cage charged, her performance in discerning the recorded cosmic bursts was significantly greater. But, in addition, something quite unexpected happened; Mrs. Garrett was no ordinary subject. Sitting in the ideal environment of the cage, she was able to tell the researchers of events taking place in other parts of the building. Scenes would suddenly flash into her mind. Twenty-four minutes into one experiment she announced that researcher Robert Baker, who was in a different laboratory, was at that moment placing "a cylinder into the side of a boxlike machine." Mrs. Garrett had never been in that laboratory and was totally unfamiliar with its equipment. Puharich checked her claim and found that Baker had been placing a metal cylinder into a machine.

As if this performance were not enough, the caged psychic also saw things precognitively. At exactly twenty minutes and fifteen seconds into another experiment, Mrs. Garrett announced that an engineer in the control room down the hall was at that moment writing the figures 0, 2, 3, and 5, in that order. A checking of the records showed that the engineer had written the figure 23:50 at the time of a cosmic ray burst—but the writing occurred exactly three minutes and thirty-five seconds *after* Mrs. Garrett had announced it.[7]

Since Puharich's studies, further work has been done which relates subtle environmental factors to psychic ability. Dr. Edward Naumov, a Soviet physicist, says, "It's too early for final conclusions, but statistical evidence we're accumulating seems to be indicating that good receivers are often born when the sun is quiet; good senders, when there is sunspot activity."[8] The Soviets also claim that the most favorable time for psychokinesis is during the height of a magnetic storm on earth caused by nuclear explosions on the sun. So far, these theories remain to be confirmed by U.S. researchers.

Western society is just beginning to find that obvious sensory interactions are a poor measure of our position in nature. Through a better understanding of the action of electrical, magnetic, and gravitational forces on human beings, physical scientists are broadening our accepted modes of perception—and the results are leading right into psychical research. Never again can we claim to stand off, isolated from the rest of creation. The gap between the senses and the parasenses is slowly but surely closing.

Variations on the Senses

Synesthesia is a rare condition in which a person cannot hear sounds without seeing colors—every chord struck on a piano, for example, is accompanied by a vibrating splash of color; a symphony is a veritable light-show. In effect, the brain of a person afflicted with this psychedelic aberration possesses a built-in color organ. Alexander Scriabin, the great turn-of-the-century composer, is thought to have suffered from synesthesia —if "suffered" is the right word—and perhaps the condition had much to do with his brilliant and bizarre compositions, which are a fusion of sights and sounds, art and religion. A restless, mercurial man, Scriabin exclaimed, "I found light in music," and he peppered his scores with such instructions as "Luminously and more and more flashing." One of his colorful works, the Fifth Symphony, which Scriabin named *Prometheus: The Poem of Fire,* is meant to be played through a color organ. He gives the following color chart (abbreviated):[9]

Note	Frequency	Color
C	256	Red
C sharp	277	Violet
.	.	.
.	.	.
.	.	.
F sharp	383	Bright blue
G	405	Rosy orange
G sharp	426	Purple
A	477	Green
.	.	.
.	.	.
.	.	.

It is not known whether synesthesia caused Scriabin to turn toward mysticism, but it became a dominating factor in his life and his music. As he developed his "mystic chord"—C, F sharp, B flat, E, A, D—and worked out entire compositions based on it, his music began to ring with dissonance piled upon dissonance. The symphonic poem *Mysterium* was to be his magnum opus. Of it Scriabin wrote: "I shall not die. I shall suffocate in ecstasy after the *Mysterium.*" Unfortunately he died with all of the *Mysterium* still in his head.

Synesthesia mixes the aural and visual senses, but other variations are possible. In human subjects, LSD, MDA, THC, and a number of other mind-altering drugs commonly cause colors to create sounds, and sounds to stir odors. The phenomenon called derma vision, or eyeless sight, is a sensory mix between the visual and tactile senses. Derma vision is more profound than the others, for the skin of a person with eyeless sight becomes his or her eyes. Just as Scriabin could "see" colors through his ears, derma vision enables one to "see" colors through the skin. The person need not be blind to have this sense. When psi writers Sheila Ostrander and Lynn Schroeder returned from their tour of Soviet parapsychological laboratories, they brought back reports of individuals with the eyeless talent. Rosa Kuleshova, a peasant woman from Tagil with normal vision, was able to close her eyes and "see" colors with the third and fourth fingers of her right hand. At first Soviet parapsychologists suspected that Kuleshova was probably hypersensitive to the texture of dye. So they blindfolded her and put her behind a cardboard wall that was solid except for a hole that fit her hand. On the other side of the wall sheets of red, green, and yellow paper were placed under tracing paper, cellophane, and glass, but still Rosa was able to tell the colors. If she was not feeling the texture of dye, perhaps she was sensitive to minute differences in heat emitted from the colors, for each color radiates its own characteristic energy. Soviet neurologists decided to heat the sheets of "cool" colors—violets and blues—and to chill the sheets dyed with "warm" colors—red and orange. But Rosa's seeing fingers could not be fooled. She identified the colors perfectly every time. Later, as Rosa's uncanny parasenses grew, she was able to "read" arithmetic figures and written text with her fingers. The prestigious Biophysics Institute of the Soviet Academy of Sciences in Moscow invited Rosa to their laboratories. Day after day she was run through a battery of tests, experiments which permitted no chance of cheating. Rosa amazed the scientists not only by deciphering the colors of sheets of construction paper, but also by discriminating the colors of articles of clothing, book jackets, and flower petals.

Dr. Gregory Razran, chairman of the psychology department of

Queens College in New York, has examined Rosa, and he concurs fully with Soviet parapsychologists. "It is, after all," he says, "the kind of thing one automatically disbelieves. But there is no longer any doubt in my mind that this work is valid."[10] Excited by the possibility that science will eventually unravel the mysteries of derma vision, and use it to teach the blind to see, Razran says, "In all my years, I can't remember when anything has had me more excited than this prospect of opening up new doors of human perception. I can hardly sleep at night . . . To see without eyes—imagine what that can mean to a blind man!"

Rosa is not the only person with parasensory vision. Since discovering her, Soviet scientists have found a handful of others who can perform as Rosa does—although not so well—and they have had a margin of success in teaching young blind children to develop derma vision. This instruction begins by teaching a child first to tell the difference between two of the primary colors, red and blue. If he or she can successfully accomplish this after days or weeks of work, the child goes on to sorting out black and white checkers, then red and black playing cards. Eventually, a few children can discriminate among all the colors of the spectrum.

The children who have acquired derma vision claim that each color is accompanied by a characteristic tactile sensation. Ostrander and Schroeder report the following correlations: "Light blue is smoothest. You feel yellow as very slippery, but not quite as smooth. Red, green, and dark blue are sticky. You feel green as stickier than red, but not as coarse. Navy blue comes over as the stickiest, but yet harder than red and green. Orange is hard, very rough, and causes a braking feeling. Violet gives a greater braking effect that seems to slow the hand and feels even rougher."[11] One Soviet researcher, Dr. Iosif Goldberg, has found in teaching derma vision to the blind that those with damage to the eyeball or the optic nerve which transmits light stimuli to the brain can develop eyeless sight. However, Goldberg claims that people with damage to the visual layers of the cerebral cortex cannot acquire the talent. Thus, it appears that perception occurs in the visual portion of the brain, as one would expect, but the stimuli arrive through parasensory routes. Many researchers feel that derma vision is a parasensory talent as unique as clairvoyance—if not a direct manifestation of it.

In the United States, Dr. Thelma Moss has done some work with eyeless sight at the Center for Health Studies in Los Angeles.[12] In July of 1971 Dr. Moss received a phone call from a blind woman named Mary. One of Mary's friends had read about Rosa Kuleshova's eyeless sight and thought Mary should find out about it. Dr. Moss, who is known in the Los

Angeles area for her research into psychic phenomenon, was the likely person to contact. "In the first conversation," says Moss, "Mary said she did not know if she had any talent for skin vision but that she would like to serve as a guinea pig, if that were possible."

Mary had been born with cataracts. She recalls having seen colors in early childhood and being delighted by them, but soon glaucoma claimed the little vision she had. At eighteen, after many eye operations, she was pronounced totally blind. But her condition had not prevented her from getting an education. She had a masters degree in Russian, was a student of five languages, and worked as a typist-translator for the United Nations. Mary's determination impressed Moss. "With her background," says Moss, "it struck us forcibly in the laboratory that here was a determined woman who had surmounted grave handicaps, and who obviously would not give up easily." Mary had another desirable feature—an important one: since she was totally blind, no accusation of fraud could be brought against the research.

The experiments began that July, and since the work was new to both Dr. Moss and her subject, they had to improvise as they went along. The first day Mary arrived at the laboratory with her seeing-eye dog, Leah; she was noticeably excited by the prospect of developing a parasensory ability to see. Moss handed her ten pieces of construction paper, five black and five white, and asked her to divide them into two piles "using any kind of subjective impressions that her sense of touch could provide." Soon Mary realized that the task was not going to be easy, for after hours of work she could tell no difference between the black and white sheets. Somewhat discouraged, she went home. On her second visit Dr. Moss changed the experiment slightly. Instead of giving Mary all ten pieces at once, she handed her one at a time and asked for her impression of the color. Mary performed better that day, scoring slightly above chance results, but she had to admit that she felt it was due purely to lucky guessing. From there, Mary went on to make excellent progress, until, by the third week, she could discriminate between black and white with amazing accuracy. At this point, Dr. Moss confidently added a third color—red—and Mary immediately lost all derma vision ability.

Both women were nonplussed, but not discouraged. Months of further tedious testing passed. Different substances were tried: wool, silk, cardboard, plastic; first only in black and white, then slowly with red added, then green, up to five different colors. Moss found that although Mary could now learn two-color discrimination quickly with one type of material, the learning did not transfer to another substance. Each one required learning anew. And Mary's talent was sporadic; some days she performed brilliantly, while other days her fingers saw nothing.

By the end of the fourth month, though, Mary was up to five colors and several different materials, and she was going strong. In a series of experiments with 1,500 trials, Mary's score above chance results was five million to one. And she continued to rack up impressive statistics. "But," says Moss, "the glaring fact remained, despite the pretty statistics: Mary still did not know how she was making her choices and she still believed her success resulted from 'lucky guesses'."

Other UCLA psychologists offered different routes for Dr. Moss to explore. Mary was placed in a totally dark room, but this did not impede her. Light apparently played no role in her discrimination. Another psychologist suggested that unconscious telepathy might be Mary's means of discriminating colors; perhaps she was reading the minds of the researchers. That proved to be an interesting suggestion. Telepathy tests began in which Mary did not touch the colored papers but had to read the thoughts of an agent who handled the sheets one at a time. Surprisingly, now Mary claimed that she could "see" the colors in her mind, and in a series of over 500 trials Mary scored significantly better than chance: one-thousand to one. But there was a puzzle; her success in telepathically discerning the colors, though significant, never matched the phenomenal scores she achieved by touching the sheets. Was telepathy only part of the talent?

As a further puzzlement, Mary truly excelled in one material: nylon. Whether the color was red, white, black, or pale blue, Mary almost never missed. At a loss for any physical explanation, Moss feels that the fact that the nylon garments were women's silk panties might be an important factor. "It's possible that Mary's flair for drama and humor," says Moss, "has made the panties such a great success. She enjoys working with these 'sexy' stimuli in front of observers, and she enjoys the repartee which they evoke." For many years psi researchers have appreciated the need for targets with "dynamic content," targets which excite and involve the subject. The dream studies, of course, are a beautiful example of this. Perhaps Moss's belief is correct.

Despite Mary's success after almost a year of work, she could provide no clue concerning the origin of her gift. One young psychologist asked her, "Could you tell me the sensations you feel when you touch the purple?" Mary smiled. "I'll be happy to answer that question if, first, you will tell me what you see when you look at purple." Today, that is still her answer.

Mary's success, though encouraging, has come nowhere near Rosa's. Rosa could work for six hours a day, seven days a week; Mary tires after an hour. Rosa could discern colors with her fingers raised as high as twelve inches above a sheet; Mary's limit is two inches. Rosa could distinguish among every color in the rainbow and read newspaper print and figures as well; Mary sees only six colors. Rosa achieved her best results while concentrating on the task at hand; Mary scores highest when she is distracted by conversation in which she takes part. She touches the material almost casually now and then and suddenly interrupts her talk to give the color. Moss has found only one other person, a UCLA student who worked with Mary, who displays derma vision. The man, who has excellent sight, needed no training. One day, he simply demonstrated the talent, spontaneously and much to his own amazement. But, according to Moss, he is only a two-color discriminator whose fingers work brilliantly for about ten minutes and then go blind.

Derma vision is a remarkable parasensory talent, and a blind person with an earnest desire to see, and the great tactile acuity which seems to accompany loss of sight, is a prime subject for further research. But the road is long, hard, and often covered in fog as Moss and Mary have learned. There has been one great disappointment throughout the work with Mary; although she performs beautifully in the laboratory, she cannot take her talent home. Her personal world remains as colorless as ever. Neither Moss nor anyone else can explain why. Is there a psychological barrier which prevents her from seeing outside the laboratory? Rosa Kuleshova eventually lost her impressive talent. The excitement of becoming an instant celebrity, the pampering of scientists, and the adulation of millions transformed her over the years into a short-tempered, demanding woman. Eventually she suffered a nervous breakdown and was confined to a mental hospital. With her change in temperamant from a sweet, soft-spoken country worker to an irascible and disturbed prima donna, her parasensory talent drifted away.

Sensory Deprivation

Your body is immersed in a warm water bath from the neck down, resting lightly on a weightless nylon net. The temperature of the water is nearly that of your blood—93.6°. Wrapped in cotton and then in watertight plastic bags, your arms and legs are floating extended. They do not touch your body, and each finger is isolated from the next with soft wraps of cotton. The room is blackest black and acoustically shielded; the air is purified and odorless. There is nothing to see, nothing to hear, nothing to touch, smell, or taste. You have been in this environment for five hours. What are you experiencing?

This predicament is what you might find yourself in if you were a subject in a sensory-deprivation experiment. What could happen to you after five hours is frightening. First, let us go back to the first hour.* Time is passing slowly. The mind, hungering for information, any information, and not getting it, becomes introspective. You begin to evaluate your life and weigh future ambitions and goals. This is a pleasant period, one of planning and self-appraisal. Soon, though, you do not care about the future, or cannot imagine it. It is meaningless. Now you lazily call forth past experiences and select the ones you wish to relive. Happy times. But this too does not last long, for soon you cannot select; memories, pleasant and nightmarish, cascade into consciousness uncontrollably. The mind has lost its power to discriminate, or it does not care to. Without sensory fodder, wakeful consciousness cannot be maintained. Self slips away, and the mind simply cannot think of anything to think about. You cannot think. Soon the entire wakeful frame of reference has vanished, and with it, volition and ego. Blackness for awhile; then, meandering through uncharted terrain, you begin to hallucinate. First, simple visions. A brightening of the visual field and perhaps a few stray straight lines. Eventually these give way to geometrical figures, patterns, and superimpositions of figures. Colors enter and mix, growing to full-fledged hallucinations. Isolated objects appear. Arms of a chair, a cup with no saucer, the hands of a clock, all amidst a barrage of abstract paraphernalia. The mind is out of control, running rampant through fields of fantasy. So we say. The period of hallucination can last a long time. But it too eventually fades as though someone were gradually turning off the lights. Some people, having passed from wakefulness through various altered states, now slip into unconsciousness. Some experience parasensory events.

Let us go back an hour or two; the hallucinations are underway. At this point most discussions of sensory deprivation dwell on the nature and quality of the hallucinations. They are viewed as randomly pieced-together bits of information, as a collage pasted up from the unconscious mind, or gross magnifications of familiar details—a mountainous speck of dust, a globe-sized eye of a fly. But from a parapsychological standpoint a different

*What follows is a dramatization from actual sensory deprivation work reported in P. Kubzansky, "Sensory Deprivation," and S. Freedman, "Perceptual and Cognitive Changes in Sensory Deprivation," in *Sensory Deprivation* (Cambridge: Harvard University Press).

route might be taken. How is the sensory-deprived mind interacting with its environment? We might say it perceives nothing of the outside world since all sensory stimuli have been excluded. But this is a hasty answer.

The sensory-deprivation chamber is immersed in the geomagnetic sea which envelops the earth. It is bombarded by cosmic rays and a host of strange elementary particles—neutrinos, muons, gravitons—and swamped by the electromagnetic waves carrying radio and television programs. All these forms of energy impinge on the sensorially starved brain, depositing varying bits of energy. In Dr. Puharich's experiments with Eileen Garrett, the isolation provided by the Faraday Cage—although quite different from the water bath isolation—increased her sensitivity to the environment. Might the sensory-deprived person acquire an amazing hypersensitivity to the environment—aspects he or she normally is unaware of? In short, might not the hallucinations be due in part to faulty interpretation of unfamiliar stimuli?

We know that certain animals, birds, and fish navigate by sensing variations in the earth's geomagnetic field. In one experiment, clams taken from Florida waters and put in laboratory tanks in Evanston, Illinois, opened and closed in correlation not with their familiar Florida schedule, but with what tides would be in Evanston, if Evanston were an ocean. The clams sensed their exact global location by geomagnetic, and perhaps gravitational, parameters.[13] If other forms of life are sensitive to these subtle fields, might a sensory-deprived human, freed from all wakeful obligations, also perceive such aspects of the environment? If a congenitally blind person develops an acute sense of hearing and touch, what senses does the person in the water bath develop, being deprived of *all five* somatic senses? Parasenses?

For years, Dr. Woodburn Heron of McGill University has been conducting experiments in extreme sensory deprivation. Heron is interested in the psycho-physiological aspects that accompany it, not its parapsychological implications. But his experiments have turned up some things he was not looking for. Some of his subjects, after hours in a sensory-deprivation chamber, received telepathic impressions from distant associates; some clairvoyantly saw researchers in other rooms of the building.[14] Heron reports that the subjects were so impressed with the unexpected psychic twist in the experiment that many immediately headed for a library to read books on psychic phenomena. Some felt so confident with their unconscious performance in the laboratory that they tried telepathy experiments at home.

Some of the most interesting observations came from those people who felt the presence of another person in the deprivation chamber with them, even though the room was empty. One need not go to the extreme of ghosts or the spirits of the deceased to explain the feeling. Perhaps, in the state of sensory deprivation, the parasenses were strong enough to override the barriers of space and directly perceive the presence of the experimenter in the adjacent room.

Many parapsychologists feel that telepathy and clairvoyance will never be accounted for in terms of a physical radiation which passes unattenuated through walls. How can such an explanation account for perceiving the information on a picture card sealed in an opaque envelope, placed in a cardboard box which is then wrapped in black paper, enclosed in a vault, and, to top it off, located 1,000 miles away? Such perception *has* occurred. It seems more likely that in an ASC in which the parasenses spring into action, the enclosure properties of "inside" and "outside," and the notion of distance breakdown. They are transcended. The picture is not really in the envelope, the envelope is not really in the box, nor the box in the vault, nor the vault located 1,000 miles away—these relationships are only true for a wakeful mind perceiving a four-dimensional space–time frame. But existence must permeate into higher dimensions, dimensions independent of our concepts of distance and enclosure. The mind of the person in the sensory-deprivation chamber was apparently in such a dimension, and the walls and ceiling of the laboratory were no impediment to that person's powers of perception.

Psychic Footprints

On July 2, 1966, three young Chicago girls took a car trip to the dunes region of Indiana. The three—Renee Bruhl, Patricia Blough, and Ann Miller—did not return home at the appointed time. Police found Ms. Miller's car abandoned in the dunes park and filled with the girls' personal belongings. An extensive air, lake, and ground search was conducted, in case the girls had drowned or met with foul play, but it led to no clues of their disappearance. By mid-August the parents of the girls had almost abandoned hope of finding them alive.

At this point, the Chicago police did a most unusual thing—they called in Olof Jonsson, a Chicago psychic. It was not the first time Jonsson had worked with police in solving murders, kidnappings, and robberies—and for good reason. Jonsson has the psychic power of psychometry—the ability to hold a physical object in his hand and receive mental images of the person it belongs to. In his native Sweden, Jonsson had solved a brutal case of multiple murders simply by holding a sawed-off shotgun found at the scene of the thirteenth slaying. For months Swedish police had been able to find no clues while the psychopath ran loose killing and then robbing both men and women. When Jonsson held the gun in his hand, he went into a trance. As clear as a picture on a television screen, he saw the face of the man who had used the gun. It was a Swedish policeman, an officer named Hedin, who had himself been "investigating" the murders and carefully covering up clues.

In the present case, Chicago police gave Jonsson some articles belonging to the girls from the abandoned car. Holding the articles, in a trance he saw the girls; they were alive, but they looked quite different from photos he had been shown of them. Their hair had been cut short, restyled, and bleached a light blond. His clairvoyant talent further told him the girls were runaways living in Saugatuck, miles away. On August 27 the *Chicago Sun-Times* ran this article:

> . . . Jonsson . . . said he was sure the girls were in Saugatuck and that they had bleached their hair and changed hair styles.
>
> . . . Jonsson was urged by Mr. and Mrs. Joseph Slunecko, parents of Renee Bruhl, to go himself to Saugatuck. He did so on August 14, in company with the Sluneckos and an Indiana state trooper. . . .
>
> A waitress at the night club said that the night of July 30 . . . a customer called her attention to three girls sitting in a booth with a man. . . . The waitress went to the table and became convinced they were the girls whose pictures she had been shown, she said. In addition, she said, one of the girls addressed another as Pat. . . .
>
> The waitress noted that all three girls had bleached blond hair, cut short.
>
> At another night spot nearby, a doorman said he remembered checking the Illinois driver's license of a girl he said was named Ann Miller. . . .
>
> Park Superintendent Svetic said of the identification in the Michigan resort, "It is a creditable identification of all three."[15]

Psychometry is an ability which seems to combine bits of clairvoyance, telepathy, precognition, and retrocognition (seeing into the past). On holding a personal object, Olof Jonsson not only sees its owner in the present, but at times he receives information about the person's past or future. Speaking of his talent Jonsson says:

> I achieve the best results and the strongest impressions when I am in a half-trance, with my immediate surroundings completely shut out. When the impressions come streaming in, I feel as though I was actually fully present where the happenings related to the object took place. I may find myself in a strange city in the midst of strange people. I may hear songs, music, and foreign languages being spoken. Sometimes while psychometrizing an object, I may be transported . . . into the past and receive a true picture of the daily life and courses of events of an earlier time.[16]

Psychometry causes great confusion in parapsychological circles because it involves a combination of psychic talents, each in itself still a mystery. And the confusion runs deeper because psychometry is not a talent possessed by many psychics. Some who are adept at telepathy, clairvoyance, or precognition find they have no facility for psychometry. Even those who do have the talent differ in how it is used. Some can only operate using metallic objects belonging to the person they wish to conjure up. For others, it must be an object that the person has owned and handled for a long time. Olof Jonsson says:

> In my experience, it is more difficult to draw impressions from letters and written materials than from personal ornaments which have adorned the subject's body. Rings, brooches, necklaces, bracelets, and the like seem to have a special way of storing impressions from the wearer. The individual revelations received from such objects can, in an astonishing manner, be a mirror of the wearer's character and his involvement in past events. By holding a person's ring, pen, or watch in my hand, I have been able to make very accurate appraisals of character.[17]

Although cases of psychometry are well documented in police files in New York City, Baltimore, Chicago, and Los Angeles, its multifaceted nature and the real paucity of psychometrists have not made it what one would call a "hot" research subject. Parapsychologists would rather work with the "pure" forms of psychic phenomena in hopes of catching a glimmer of the light. A paranormal potpourri seems too complicated. However, one man, Dr. Charles Tart, has proposed a fascinating psychometry experiment.[18]

All material objects have *physical* properties—mass, color, density, form, and rigidity, among others. These are the intrinsic and extrinsic features which make an object what it is. Often the history of an object is reflected in the wear and tear of these properties. Colors fade and yellow from exposure to sunlight; sharp edges are smoothed and rounded through constant handling and use; curvature is altered by periodic heating and cooling. These subtle-to-gross alterations in an object's physical properties are routinely used by archeologists in inferring the history of an object, the people who developed it, their culture, habits, and various other traits. Dr. Tart has suggested that since conscious matter has both physical and psychical aspects, perhaps inanimate objects also have both sets of characteristics. Tart believes that an object's psychical potential might show wear and tear based on the people with which it comes in contact. Thus handling an object leaves not only physical marks and skin oil, but "psychic fingerprints" as well. Tart feels that a psychometrist might read these fingerprints much as a detective reads powdered fingerprints to zero in on the quarry.

In the proposed experiment, thirty identical objects, perhaps gold rings, would be divided into three equal groups. The first ten rings Tart would give to highly dynamic, outgoing individuals to wear at all times. Another ten would be given to bland, colorless individuals who live secluded lives; they too would have to wear the rings constantly. The remaining ten would be placed in a locked safe, away from contact with anyone for the duration of the experiment. At the end of some specified time, a few weeks perhaps, all the objects would be collected and a talented psychic would have to "read" them, sorting them into three different groups. If he or she successfully accomplished this, then the psychic would have to give physical descriptions, and any other relevant information he or she could discern, about the ring's wearer. Unfortunately, as simple as the experiment is, no one has tried it. When someone does, Olof Jonsson would make the perfect detective.

Russell Targ, a Stanford Research Institute physicist, does not work with psychometrists, but he has had some success in teaching ordinary individuals clairvoyant perception. A few years ago Targ designed a machine which he thought might be used to turn a person's lucky guesses into psychic bull's-eyes. The machine has four clear windows which randomly light up displaying 35mm color transparencies. The machine's choice for a particular trial, which no one can anticipate, is made and stored inside the device. The subject must clairvoyantly perceive what slide has just been stored and push the button of his or her choice. Then, and only then, does the stored transparency light up, telling the subject whether the guess was right or wrong. An important feature of the device is that it possesses a "pass" button. Thus, if the subject does not have a special feeling for a particular trial, he or she is not forced to make a decision. "The user," says Targ, "is spared making pure guesses and learns to differentiate between a genuine 'feeling' and a wild guess." Not everyone can learn to do it though. Targ has found, in fact, that relatively few people can actually develop clairvoyant ability. But those who do learn, learn well. In one experiment twelve people were selected at random; they had never displayed the least psychic talent. Each spent several hours with the machine. If a person made a wrong choice, the machine told him: "The feeling you had was not a clairvoyant one." However, if the person's choice was correct, the instant feedback was: "The feeling you had this time is perhaps a clairvoyant one." Targ found that, encouraged through this type of operant conditioning, one out of twelve was able to develop a psychic sense. As one successful young man practiced, his scores increased, indicating that learning was taking place. At the end of several days he was so proficient that he was running up odds against chance of over a billion to one.[19] There was no hint in the man's personality, background, or lifestyle that would account for his success—or for the failure of the eleven others. As Targ says, some people can learn and others cannot.

The Psychic and the Physicists

Uri Geller is a twenty-seven-year-old Israeli psychic with a broad smile, good looks, and the charisma of a stage performer—which he once was, and to a large extent, still is. As his supporters tell it, Geller is unequivocally the most gifted psychic of our time. Neither concrete walls nor the expanse of the Atlantic Ocean interfere with his reception of mental images, and his hands mysteriously bend forks, spoons, and knives (he has a definite penchant for kitchen utensils), wilt flowers, and erase information from magnetic tapes. One year after arriving in this country, Geller took his talents on parade. Viewers of the Jack Paar Show saw him bend a thick steel spike which Paar held in his hand; Geller merely rubbed it lightly between his thumb and index finger, and like heated plastic it bent in half. On the Mike Douglas and Merv Griffin shows, Geller performed telepathic and clairvoyant feats as well. But the Israeli's numerous public appearances during 1973 and 1974—on television and stage, in nightclubs, and in front of high-school and college audiences—have opened him to attacks from critics. Professional magicians claim Geller is an out-and-out fraud. They argue that a good magician could duplicate by legerdemain any feat Geller performs. Professional psychics, on the other hand, argue that paranormal abilities cannot be turned on and off in time with television cameras and audiences as Geller's seem to be. But despite Geller's mode of operation during public demonstrations, which, given the capriciousness of psychic abilities, might well be a combination of genuine parasensory talents backed up by a bag of magicians' tricks, it appears that Uri Geller does possess a real and sizable gift. During six weeks of rigorous tests at Stanford Research Institute in Menlo Park, California, scientists ran Geller through the laboratory wringer. He came out exhausted, but "validated authentic" (in certain areas).

As is true with most psychics, there is no clue in Geller's family background to suggest why he was born with such incredible talents. His mother, Manzy Freud, a distant relative of Sigmund Freud, and his father, Itzhaak Geller, a retired military officer, have no psychic ability. Yet from about the age of four young Uri was reading his mother's thoughts, telling her when she came home from playing cards with friends exactly how much she had won; and at seven he first realized his psychokinetic ability. He was in school in Tel Aviv when it occurred: "In class I noticed that my watch would show a different hour than what it really was, which began to happen fairly frequently. I complained to my mother about the wristwatch being broken; she examined it and said that it kept good time for her. But it continued to happen, so one day in class I took it off and held it in my hands, watching it very closely. I began to notice that the watch hands would change their positions almost instantaneously—very fast—like dematerializing from one hour to another."[20]

Geller claims he can still perform that feat with ease. In August of 1972, the noted Columbia University physicist Dr. Gerald Feinberg watched Geller pass his hand back and forth over the watch of Dr. Edgar Mitchell, the former astronaut. After only a few seconds, the hands of Mitchell's watch had moved ahead in time about an hour and a half. What amazed the theoretical physicist still more was that once the watch was placed back on the table the hands continued to advance. "I looked at it a couple of times in the next fifteen minutes," says the perplexed Feinberg. "Each time I looked at it, it had advanced by much more than the the time that had elapsed."[21]

At age twenty-three Uri Geller was giving stage shows throughout his native country, and by twenty-six, with over six hundred shows behind him, he was the major nightclub attraction in Israel. But a talent as unique as

Geller's was bound to attract scientific attention. In mid-1972 Dr. Andrija Puharich, who had observed Geller's performances for many months, convinced Uri to forego the adulation of the crowds for the scrutinizing eyes of a few scientists. Although the Israeli press claimed that Geller had to leave the country because he was exposed as a fraud—one article appeared stating that he used electrical devices, pliers, mirrors, and a bag of magician's tricks to accomplish his psychic feats—Geller vehemently denies that he left under a black cloud. "It is not true," he says, "that I left Israel in disgrace. That one article did make unfounded claims, but it did not stop the people from coming to see me. When I left, to be studied by scientists, about half the people believed the article and half did not. No one ever examined me or checked me."[22] Whatever the Israeli press claimed was soon eclipsed by the reaction of scientists in Germany and then in the United States. In Munich, at the world-famous Max Planck Institute, Geller amazed scientists by bending rings and spoons, rotating compass needles, and deforming objects merely by passing his hands over them. The Institute scientists were convinced of the verity of Geller's talents. Where, they wondered, did he get the energy required to perform such feats? A physicist, Dr. Friedbert Karger, said: "From the point of view of physics, for the moment, one cannot say anything regarding the energy he uses. One does know that the energy occurs only in connection with people."[23] In October of 1972 Geller finally arrived in the United States to be studied at Stanford Research Institute (SRI) by Dr. Harold Puthoff and Russell Targ, two laser physicists.

SRI is a giant think-tank in Menlo Park, California, a leading center for top military and private research in the sciences. It could afford no scandal. The board of directors knew that in studying Geller they were undertaking a controversial project, one that might damage their long-standing reputation for quality research. But they also realized that if Geller's paranormal abilities were genuine, it was the unquestioned duty of science to try to explain them. Furthermore, if the energy on which Geller's talents operate could be detected, it might go a long way in solving many of the mysteries of modern physics. SRI said: "We are well aware that this area of research is one of the most controversial topics in modern science, in part because of its history of charlatanism and fraud. However, we do not feel that controversy should deter us from what we believe is a legitimate subject for scientific inquiry . . . It should be explored without prejudice."[24] Needless to say, every conceivable precaution was taken in the experiments to eliminate the possibility of fraud. From day to day Geller had no idea what task he would be required to do next. Professional cameramen were brought in to film the experiments from a variety of angles. Highly respected scientists such as Dr. Wernher von Braun of NASA and Dr. Gerald Feinberg of Columbia were invited to watch Geller perform. He was searched thoroughly before each experiment, and he was never permitted to touch one piece of equipment. Many of the tests were "double blind," that is, no one, not even the researchers who planned the experiment, knew the outcome in advance. If Geller was a fraud, he was not going to get out of SRI with so much as an iota of credibility.

The experiments began in November of 1972. Into a small metal box, about the size used to hold three-by-five index cards, Dr. Puthoff placed a single die. The box was vigorously shaken and placed on a table. Geller had to look at the closed box (he was not permitted to touch it) and write down the number on the uppermost face of the die—a simple double-blind experiment in which no one could give Uri any answers. "Five," he said almost immediately, as though the die were in his hand; he was right. Eight different times the box was shaken, and eight times Geller gave the correct answer; the odds of that happening by chance are one in a million.[25] The experiment was repeated again and again, and Geller almost never missed. It is one thing to believe in clairvoyant perception and quite another to witness it. The scientists were amazed. How could anyone *see* through a metal box? Geller tried to be of help, explaining, "I put a screen in my mind, like a television screen. Even when I talk or listen, it is still there. When I am receiving something, the image appears there as a picture. I don't feel it; I actually see it." Geller says his "seeing" into the closed box feels no different to him than the normal visual process; he looks at the box and, as though it were not there, sees the die. He has been known to perform this clairvoyant feat twenty times in succession without a mistake—the odds against that are astronomical.

Like any talented person, Geller has his good and bad days. "If I am nervous or anxious," he says, "sometimes nothing happens. I draw a blank." He also has difficulty functioning if he feels his viewers are overly critical or harbor negative thoughts. But when he is excited and enthusiastic, and his viewers are warm and cheering, no one can hold him down.

A clue, a slight one, into Geller's powers came in the aluminum can experiment. One of ten small cylindrical cans was filled with a steel ball bearing by a laboratory assistant who was not involved with the experiments. She put the tops on all ten cans, randomly arranged them on a table, then left the room. After she left the researchers entered the room with Geller; he had no idea of what he was going to be asked to do. Dr. Puthoff pointed to the ten cans, told Uri one contained some object, and asked him to find it. Not only did Geller locate the correct can that time, by passing his hand about five inches above all ten cans and eliminating them one by one, but he repeated the feat twelve times without error, and with different objects.[26] The small hint into the nature of his powers came from the fact that nonconductive objects stumped him—paper and sugar cubes for exam-ple—but when a can contained water, a piece of metal, or a small magnet, he always found it. Even with the die-in-the-box experiment, Geller can perform much better if the box is of metal rather than wood. "It's a small clue," one scientist said, "but it's something."

How does Geller explain his paranormal ability? Where does he feel his powers originate? "I don't think the power is coming from me," he says humbly. "I believe it is a force channeled through me, one coming from extraterrestrial intelligence." Geller feels his ability is not a freak talent, but part of a master plan that he has been chosen to participate in to a greater degree than the average person. He believes in God, but he does not think a divine force is helping him bend forks and read dice. Although his per-sonal theory of a "super civilization" working through him sounds like something out of an Arthur Clarke or Isaac Asimov novel, at least the theory gives him peace of mind; the SRI physicists are still amazed.

"Why don't you go to Las Vegas and shoot craps?" is a question Geller often hears. And why doen't he? Well he has, and he learned that for some inexplicable reason neither telepathy nor clairvoyance nor psychokinesis keep him from losing his shirt. This is one paradox found in all psychics, especially healers, who, even if they are dying from cancer, cannot cure themselves.

Perhaps the most dramatic item in Geller's bag of talents is his demon-stration of "mind over matter," or psychokinesis. Instead of having him bend a kitchen utensil as laboratory proof of this power—a feat he usually performs once at every meal—the SRI scientists devised a different type of experiment using a precision laboratory scale. The scale generates an elec-trical voltage in proportion to the force applied to it. It is so sensitive that it can detect differences in weight of as little as one-thousandth of a gram. For the test, a weight of exactly one gram was placed on the balance, a glass bell jar was placed over it to eliminate air current, and a chart recorder continuously monitored the scale. In order to make sure that Geller would not shake the table and produce a false reading, the scientists did just that. They pounded on the table top, tapped the bell jar, and jumped up and down on the floor. Once all these variables had been tried, and their effects on the scale recorded, Geller was brought into the room.

He had to look at the scale without touching it and alter its reading, either, in effect, adding or subtracting weight. He stood motionless, with both hands several inches above the bell jar, gritting his teeth and frowning. It was plain that he was trying to muster as much energy as he could generate. The recording device showed that a force *was* being exerted on the scale, as though small weights were being added one by one. At his point of maximum concentration the force on the scale was one-hundred times larger than could be produced by striking the bell jar or the table top or by jumping on the floor.[27]

Where, wondered the physicists, did the energy come from that pushed down the pan of the scale? Geller feels certain he derives it from the people around him. "I have never been able to bend or break an object unless there is at least one or two other people in the room," he says. "When I am alone I don't seem to have this power. I feel that in some way I am taking energy from the people in the room." Geller is sure this is why he gives his most dramatic performances in front of audiences of two- or three-hundred people.

On March 9, 1973, researchers Puthoff and Targ presented the results of their six-week investigation of Geller at a physics colloquium at Columbia University. It was an eighty-year dream come true for psychical research. In front of an audience of science students and members of the Columbia Physics Department faculty, Puthoff and Targ discussed the experiments and showed a half-hour film. The colloquium stimulated excitement but no negative criticism, and made clear the fact that psychical research is no longer a taboo subject.

7

The Mystic and Psi

He heard the tiny spider as it spinned
and leaves of bamboo whisper in the wind
others only saw these things . . .
these small and all-important things.

Martin Buxbaum, *Whispers in the Wind*

First, Some Mystical Anecdotes

Once a year Hindus from all over the island of Ceylon gather to honor the god Kataragoma. The ritual begins with colorfully robed native women parading up and down in front of the temple carrying iron pots filled with burning coconut husks. The cherry red embers are laid in a pit about twenty feet long and six feet wide. Late in the evening giant hardwood logs are placed on top of the husks and set afire. The pit burns all night until it is a bed of hot nuggets. At sunrise, when the heat of the fire is so intense that it is difficult even to breath within a few yards of the pit, drums begin to roll, the golden doors of the temple swing open, and scores of Hindu priests solemnly walk down the steps, barefooted, and straight into the smoldering pit. Slowly and calmly they walk down the stretch and back, showing no sign of pain or discomfort.[1]

A trick? Not at all. Although the surface layer of charcoal can reach temperatures of 500 degrees centigrade, the priests perform this religious display with no chemicals or ancient concoctions coating their feet. The phenomenon has been witnessed and studied by dozens of scientists from all over the world.

Demonstrations of seemingly superhuman feats are comparatively common among Eastern religious adepts. One even more dramatic than fire walking is the immolation that some Zen monks undergo. Films taken of

175

these ordeals, triggered by a rash of politically motivated occurrences during the late 1960s, typically show a monk, doused with inflammable liquid, sitting upright, body ablaze, and yet, amazingly, his facial expression never once reveals an intimation of pain nor does his body twist and contort in agony. As real as the searing flames are to his physical body, his mind is on a plateau they do not reach. Such feats derive from deep mystic consciousness, a state of mind that Western science is currently attempting to understand in all its psychophysical aspects.

One of the early scientific tests took place on April 26, 1956, at the All-India Institute of Mental Health in Bangalore, India. It involved a frail forty-eight-year-old yogi, Shri Ihrishna Iyengar, who has been a practitioner of meditation throughout his adolescent and adult life, and who had consented to show scientists how he could survive under conditions that would be fatal to the average person.

On the laboratory grounds a large pit was excavated and Iyengar, dressed only in a loincloth, descended into the hole. Electrical instruments were wired to his body to monitor his vital functions, and the pit was covered with thick wooden planks and a heavy mound of soil. For hours a team of psychologists and physicians from the World Health Organization nervously watched the monitors. The recording needles showed that the yogi was alive, but just barely. His body, in the oxygen-starved pit, was in a state of suspended animation. When the dirt was shoveled off some ten hours later and the planks removed, Iyengar sat up and climbed out of the hole. An average person would have suffocated within two hours; the yogi was well-rested and refreshed from the experience. It had been a long afternoon nap.[2]

What impressed the scientists most were the data on the yogi's metabolism and his brainwave patterns during his ordeal. He had virtually turned off his body and brain, idling like a parked car, consuming little of his body energy. They wondered, but of course did not investigate, just how long a man could live—without water, without food—in that state of suspended animation. But this was not their only question, for the amazing feats of mystics extend well beyond fire walking and live burial. The whole realm of psi occurrences is open to them—a fact that should come as no surprise in lands where human physiology can be so masterfully controlled.

One geographical area where this is particularly true is Tibet. Throughout this cloud-enshrouded country, set against the snowy peaks of the Himalayas, itinerant shamans are well acquainted with psi events. Although it would be misleading to say that they have such experiences with everyday frequency (many of the casual anecdotes from the East are some-what exaggerated), they do regard psi as normal rather than paranormal. It is not freaks who experience psychical events, but the religiously enlight-ened. Those whom the West would call "magicians" are illuminati in the East. This positive attitude toward psi is highly significant, for with it the Tibetans view nothing as impossible. The fact that not every Tibetan can perform the dramatic feats displayed by high priests merely means that not everyone has mastered total control of mind and body.

Tibetans distinguish two categories of psychic phenomena, those un-consciously produced by one or several individuals, and those produced at will for specific purposes. In the latter case the doer is a person who has, through years of meditation, become master of his consciousness. In both cases psychic energy is the medium of transport, derived from a universal pool and directed like radio transmission to carry telepathic messages over the otherwise uncommunicable terrain. The Tibetans even believe that this life-giving energy can intentionally, or accidentally, animate an inanimate object.

One instance of this can be seen in the phenomenon of "self-killing." When a wicked person must be executed, a priest will shut himself in seclusion for a period of several months with a knife. During this time he concentrates his thoughts on the knife in front of him, endeavoring to impart to it the act of execution. The priest will spend all his waking hours visualizing the victim-to-be and attempting to animate the knife. When he feels that the knife is ready to perform its work, it is secretly placed in the home of the man who is to become its victim. As the Tibetans believe, the first time the man touches the knife it automatically forces his hand to drive the blade into his heart. An unlikely story we say, yet these self-killings are a frequent occurrence.[3] Western parapsychologists feel that the execution is accomplished by hypnosis at a distance. During the many months the priest spends directing his thoughts to the knife and the victim, he may be telepathically hypnotizing the victim to stab himself once he sees the knife. Explaining self-killings in terms of a sort of hypnosis at a distance is strongly suggested by modern laboratory studies in which subjects have been placed in deep trances by hypnotists who have telepathically transmitted the induc-tion procedures from a different room. Posthypnotic suggestions have also been transmitted under these conditions and perfectly executed after the subject is awakened.

In her book *Magic and Mystery in Tibet,* Alexandra David-Neel, a woman who has spent a lifetime studying Tibetan customs, relates a psychical incident which the Tibetans explain in terms of imparting life to an inanimate object, but which psi researchers feel is an obvious psychokinetic manifestation. As the story goes:

One day a trader was traveling along a road, and a strong wind blew off his hat. It was a soft felt hat with a fur boarder and fur ear flaps that could be turned down in cold weather. Tibetans believe that to pick up a hat which has fallen under such circumstances in the course of a journey will bring bad luck. The man yielded to the superstition and abandoned his hat. The wind tossed it around until the hat caught between thorny shrubs.

A few weeks later a man passing by the place where the hat was lodged noticed a peculiar form which seemed to him to be crouching among the thickets. It had an unusual appearance, and the man quickly passed on. On arriving at the next village he told the people that he had seen something strange squatting in the bushes. As time passed, other travelers to the village remarked on seeing a peculiar creature at the same spot.

By now the sun and rain had transformed the hat into an object of mysterious appearance indeed. Its color was a dirty yellow-brown, and the fur ear flaps, matted and projecting upward, looked like the ears of an uncommon animal. Villagers who had never seen the mysterious object began to warn travelers to avoid the particular road which was patrolled by a creature of demonic appearance.

Weeks went by and the weathered hat became the concern of the countryside, filling the villagers' daily thoughts and occupying their night-marish dreams. Someone had even seen the creature move from its lurching position; someone else had heard its shrill cries. Soon a party of men was formed to slay the demon, which now threatened villages for miles around. As the story goes, the brave group was cautiously approaching the hat when suddenly it leaped from the thickets and began chasing them through the woods. It pursued them for many yards before they escaped. Every man in the party attested to the actions of the creature. All had simultaneously witnessed its leap and subsequent chase.

Weeks later the weathered object was found and brought to the village. It was only a hat. How could it have chased the men? According to the village priest, the hat had for a while been animated by the constant thoughts of the villagers. Furthermore, their belief that the unknown object was a creature of evil sorts enabled it to take on such a life form.

Naturally, alternative and less extreme explanations can be ascribed to this story, assuming for the moment it is true. There are two possible alternatives. One is mass hypnosis. The group that had gone to slay the hat could have been so united by common fear as to induce a common ASC

—a type of trance so persuasive that when one person believed he saw the hat leap from the bushes, that impression was telepathically relayed to the others.

A second explanation, as mentioned, could be joint psychokinesis. United in their common fear and focusing their entire concentration on the object as they approached it, the group could have generated a joint unconscious effort in mind over matter. The psychic energy of the group could have lifted the object and conceivably attracted it toward them. For although we know virtually nothing about the nature of psychic energy, other energy forms do exhibit attractive and repulsive characteristics.

But regardless of the explanation, or for that matter the validity of the story in the first place, the significant fact is that here exists a whole nation of people who collectively believe that phenomena for which we have burned witches at the stake are not only possible, but available to any person who can master his or her own consciousness. This collective, positive belief in the virtually limitless potential of the mind is bound to result in a greater frequency of paranormal occurrences. We know that a major part of succeeding in any task is the positive belief of success. A person who approaches a particular project with a defeatist's attitude is almost guaranteed failure. Lamentably we in the West have culturally imposed severe restrictions on the potentials of the human mind. It can do this; it cannot do that. And, we can be sure that what we believe it cannot do, it will not do! This parochial attitude is not only operationally crippling, it is downright dehumanizing. Thus, the great impetus for the scientific community to study mystic consciousness is not only for overt paranormal manifestations *per se,* but also for the general collective attitude of millions of people who regard the supernatural as natural, the paranormal as normal.

The Mystic Mind

Within the last decade, the mind of the mystic has come under study by neurologists, logicians, philosophers, and parapsychologists who all but wallow in the delights of these well-tamed, dynamic models of pure human potential. Unlike the Western individual, who emphasizes the body, trains it, educates it, pushes it outward only to realize its severe physical limitations, the mystic is schooled in the infinite play of the mind. This the mystic trains through meditation, sharpens through an ascetic lifestyle, and expands outward and unbounded. "Americans," chides Walter B. Gibson in *The Key to Yoga,* "think of mental development as a form of growth; in the Orient it is regarded as a release from physical limitations."[4]

One of the chief routes to mystic consciousness is yoga. In Sanskrit the word means "union," which reveals the plot of the story—a union, a merging of an individual's spiritual being (mind) with the universal being (oneness). It must be understood from the outset that yoga is a *method* to bring about a metamorphosis of consciousness and not an ASC in itself. It is like the induction techniques of hypnosis, the swallowing of a tab of LSD, the sleep-lulling effects of soft music, and yet, it is unlike all these things. As we shall see, true mystic consciousness is a unique mentation, frightening in its scope and staggering in its grandeur.

A look at yogic theory reveals why the mystic frequently experiences psi. The mind *(chitta),* the centuries-old theory goes, is in a state of continual flux, being bombarded by a host of internal and external stimuli. What we call four-dimensional space–time perception, reason, memory, wakeful imagination, and sleep are all manifestations of this mental flux. But within reach of the numbed, overworked psyche, says yogic theory, is an independent, universal power *(sakti)* which cannot surface amidst the chaos. The essence of yoga, then, is the formulation of a psycho-physiological method to limit these worldly bombardments. Sound familiar? It should, for although the yogic theory is thousands of years old, its fundamental postulates are the foundation of the new science of ASC.

Basically, all the systems of yoga practiced in India fall into two categories: *Raja Yoga* (*Raja* means "king" in Sanskrit) and *Hatha* (forceful) *Yoga.* Both systems spring from two sacred books—the Vedas, the oldest written religious text in the world, and the Upanishads, the fountainhead of all philosophical systems and spiritual thought in India.

Hatha Yoga is primarily a physiological approach to mystic consciousness involving body exercises and breath control. The breathing exercises can be very strenuous. Their purpose, through abnormal manipulation of the chin, diaphragm, tongue, and other body parts, is to prevent expulsion or inhalation of air into the lungs in order to induce a state of suspended breathing. Many mystics stress the possible dangers of the Hatha system, and in India only those disciples who are prepared to face death undergo the extreme Hatha procedures.

On the other hand, Raja Yoga is primarily a psychological approach to mystic consciousness based on mental exercises and meditation. Although it is much less of a physical drain, it does require extreme mental stamina.

Both Hatha and Raja Yoga prescribe eight steps to attain mystic consciousness. It is in these steps that we can see the deliberate intention of transcendence, and the gradual attainment of psi-favorable conditions. The eight "limbs" of yoga are:

Yama: the abstension from all sorts of wicked thoughts and deeds. This is a preparatory step dealing with moral commandments of proper behavior.

Niyama: observance of daily religious practices focusing on purity, austerity, contentment, and the study of sacred scripture. This is a stage of social isolation, a severing of personal ties with people, places, and worldly things.

Asana: in this phase the student determines the most comfortable posture for him to assume during the long hours of work ahead.

Pranayama: the regulation and control of breathing and other physical exercises to help the individual achieve control over some of his physiological functions. Here perception by the somatic senses begins to diminish.

Pratyahara: subjugation of the senses to bring them within the control of the mind. This is a state of introspection where the psyche begins to dominate the activities of the body. Wakeful consciousness is rapidly slipping away.

Dharana: a state of intense concentration where control is finally obtained over the fluctuations of the psyche. All external stimuli are quieted.

Dhyana: the yoga attempts to hold his pinpoint concentration for longer and longer periods of time. His world superstructure is lost.

Samadhi: this is a standstill state in which the mind becomes one with the object of concentration (often a mandala), the attainment of ecstatic contemplation of a new reality. Passivity is the keynote.[5]

The effects of rigorous yogic training on the mind were dramatically demonstrated in 1961 by three Indian researchers, B. K. Anand, G. S. Chhina, and Baldev Singh. The brainwave patterns of yogis were studied before, during, and after Samadhi meditation. In order to test the belief that in Samadhi all external stimuli pass the mystic with no apparent effect, the researchers enhanced the natural noisy environment with artificial stimuli of various sorts—photic (strong lights), auditory (loud banging noises), thermal (touching the skin with a red-hot glass rod), and vibratory (tuning fork). Two master yogis sat wired to an EEG. Before meditation began the lights, noises, and other sensations registered squarely in each yogi's brain, causing heavy beta-wave activity, and feelings of anxiety pressure. Then the bombardments were stopped, and each man began meditating. After only a few minutes the EEGs showed heavy alpha waves and occasional theta ripples indicating a deep meditative trance in both, and then the researchers flicked on the artificial stimuli. But this time neither EEG showed any change whatsoever. The recording chart curves continued to be smooth immense alpha ripples. The intensity of the bombardments was increased again and again to a point where they drove the researchers from the room, but the two mystics never displayed any measurable perception of the torture. Glaring lights that flashed in front of their open eyes, gongs in their ears, the thermal applications—none had any effect. It was as though the two men were sitting in the middle of 42nd Street and Times Square, being blasted by car horns, bumped by impatient pedestrians, and blinded by flashing neon lights, yet not reacting to any of it. Not that they were unaware of the artificial laboratory stimuli, for each claimed he had a peripheral awareness of the bombardments, but the stimuli were absolutely meaningless to him.[6] How marvelous, how healthful to be able to turn off the din of wakeful life and yet know in a vague, dreamy sense what is going on. Here we see the great mental mastery accompanying true mystic consciousness. The yogis were able to retain a remnant of wakeful perception, but the information was relegated to an auxiliary mental file. The bulk of the mind was soaring above the real world.

During the same research project two other yogis were subjected to a different type of test. A pail of ice water kept just above freezing was placed in front of each yogi. Before beginning meditation each man, wired to an EEG, plunged his hand into the ice water. There was an immediate jump in brainwave output and ensuing electrical frenzy while their hands remained in the pails. Neither man could keep his hand immersed for longer than about a minute without experiencing severe discomfort. Their hands were then removed from the icy water, and each yogi was asked to enter a meditative state. When both EEG's showed strong alpha patterns the researchers plunged each yogi's hand back into the ice water. The alpha patterns proceeded without variation. Their hands remained in the pails for almost an hour; their eyes were open all the time looking at the ice encrusted water, but each man was completely oblivious to any sensation of coldness.[7] They had transcended the freezing experience.

What mental state were the men in? Dr. Erich Fromm describes it beautifully:

> I would say that it is a state in which the person is completely tuned to the reality outside and inside of him, a state in which he is fully aware of it and fully grasps it. *He* is aware of it—that is, not his brain, nor any other part of his organism, but *he*, the whole man. He is aware of *it*; not as of an object over there which he grasps with his thought, but *it*, the flower, the dog, the man, in its or his full reality. He who awakes is open and responsive to the world, and he can be open and responsive because he has given up holding on to himself as a thing, and thus has become empty and ready to receive.[8]

Ready to receive what? Enlightenment, for one thing, and psi communications for another. Although the ultimate goal of the mystic is never the acquisition of parasensory talents, in the normal course of deep meditation psi occurrences are spontaneous. In "Psi in Communities and Other Interpersonal Situations in the Eastern World," Dr. Ramakrishna K. Rao, a psychologist of Andhra University in Waltair, India, relates many such incidences between disciples and their swamis. One young man, for example, well known to Dr. Rao, asked his swami why he had not heard from a certain relative for a long period of time. He got the paternal answer, "We will give you the answer at the appropriate time." Of course, the young man had complete faith in the swami, and two nights later he had a vision of the swami in a dream in which the master explained that the relative was safe and on a trip. The following morning the man arrived at the swami's home. As the master opened the door, the first words out of the master's mouth were, "Your question was answered. We hope the response was satisfactory."[9] Rao has found that such communications between a swami and his disciple are not at all infrequent. The bond forged between them through intense meditative exercises is strong enough to support telepathic impressions. "When asked by my friend," says Rao, "how he exercised these paranormal powers, the swami said that he does not exercise them, but these experiences occasionally *flow* out of him without any effort on his part . . . these are spontaneous occurrences . . . facilitated by the rapport that exists between the guru and his disciples."[10]

Dr. Lawrence LeShan has made the same observations, to a somewhat lesser degree, of his students engaged in intense meditative exercises. Several times a year LeShan takes individuals who have been screened for their sincerity and determination to learn Eastern meditation to a secluded resort area in upper New York State. For five days the group, usually ten people, is immersed in a twelve-hour-a-day meditation program devised by LeShan. "Quite often," he says, "by the third day certain people are receiving telepathic messages from others in the group. This is not our goal, but it just happens in the natural course of the week's training."

During one seminar in late 1972, a businessman and a young psychologist, after almost forty hours of round-the-clock meditation exercises, became extraordinarily psychic, even being able to read each other's thoughts when they separated for meals and at bedtime. In fact, LeShan claims that when they held their hands out flat, separated by a few inches, they experienced a buzzing sensation that traveled back and forth—what LeShan calls a "zap."[11] This does not happen with everyone, but only between certain people who develop a special meditative rapport. Considering the intensity of the training and the fundamentals of yoga principles, the phenomenon is not surprising, says LeShan.

Indeed, Dr. Rao points out that there are three important implications for parapsychology in the eight limbs of yoga: "First, there is inhibition of particular cerebral functions through physical exercises. Second, there is activation of the psyche through concentration. And third, the expansion of concentration sought in the final stages reverses the role of the psyche from one of receiving impressions through the somatic senses to one of entering into direct communication with nature."[12]

In discussing mystic consciousness one pit of confusion must be avoided. Since the psi-conducive feature of mystic mentation is transcendence and since this is also the salient feature of other ASCs, one might be tempted to lump them together qualitatively. This would be a mistake, for mystic consciousness, although it opens the doors to the paranormal world, is unique. Laying aside for the moment its physiological correlates, which will be discussed latter, one essential difference between mystic consciousness and other ASCs is the technique used to attain it. This is an important point, argues Dr. Rao. In hypnosis, for example, or dreaming or drug-taking, there is no intentional orientation toward the features which facilitate psi. An ASC is produced in each of these cases that contains a measure of transcendence as a nondeliberate consequence. However, the very core of the yogic method, from its earliest stages, is a deliberate, self-directed move toward a liberation of mind from body. In fact, the very motivation which sustains a student through the arduous years of training is a desire for transcendence (or, to use its Eastern name, spiritual enlightenment).

This difference between the yogic route to a psi-favorable ASC and those paths leading to other desirable mentations is greatly emphasized in the writings of Gopi Krishna. He says, "There is no confusion or distortion [in mystic consciousness] as happens with drugs and no loss of memory as happens in hypnosis. The intellect remains unaffected, and there is no overlapping or aberration. The inner and outer worlds stand side by side, but with one momentous difference: from a point of consciousness the soul now seems to stretch from end to end, an ineffable and intangible Intelligence present everywhere."[13]

Needless to say, to stretch the soul from end to end, whether it be to glimpse the Beatific Vision or to send a telepathic message across the treacherous Himalayas, is no easy task. Often yogis on their way to Samadhi or Zen monks reaching Satori (enlightenment) can have a bad trip. They do not call it a "bummer," though that's what it is; they refer to it as having gone to "The Devil Land." There are some ascetics in India who can perform all the eighty-four Asanas (positions) to perfection and continue performing them all their lives but never attain enlightment or have so much as one paranormal experience. Krishna writes that some master the breathing exercises so thoroughly that they can be placed in hermetically sealed chambers and buried underground for days without suffocating. When they are exhumed, they arise as from a deep sleep, dazed, but not transcendental.

Some ascetics in India, who desperately desire mystic consciousness, resort to brutal self-torture and even mutilation to assuage their burning thirst for spiritual liberation. They lie with naked flesh on beds of nails or keep one of their arms constantly upraised until the limb becomes atrophied and withers to a stump. Some hang from trees with their heads downward inhaling acrid fumes from burning herbs. Others stand on one leg for weeks at a time, and there are even those who gaze fixedly at the sun until their eyesight is burned out. All this to have one mystical experience. Is it worth it? Is it worth traveling to the top, opening the doors to the paranormal world, and passing through and beyond? Gopi Krishna describes the spectacular view from the summit:

For a short time we are invincible, eternal—immune to decay, disease, failure and sorrow. We are but drops in an ocean of consciousness in which the stormy universe of colossal suns and plants looks like a reflection that has absolutely no effect on the

unutterable calm, peace and bliss that fill this unbounded expanse
of being. We are a wonder, an enigma, a riddle; even those who
have access to it some time in their lives cannot describe mystical
experience in a way others can understand. For the soul belongs
to another realm, another state of existence, another plane of
being where our senses, mind and intellect flounder in the dark.[14]

Krishna's description, like those of other illuminati who have written
on the subject, is riddled with superlatives, hyperbole, and grandiose meta-
phors—"colossal suns," "unutterable calm," "oceans of consciousness"—
all attempts to articulate verbally that which can only be experienced. One
is reminded of Wittgenstein's sagacious warning, "All philosophy is a battle
of the intellect against the bedevilment of language."
    But the psychic plunges into "oceans of consciousness" as does the
mystic; the psychic soul too "belongs to another realm . . . another plane
of being." Yet the psychic does not lie on beds of nails, stare fixedly at the
sun, or hold an arm erect until it withers to a stump—and, psychical
encounters outside this meager four-dimensional space–time cage are never
painted in flowery, hyperbolic language like the mystic's. Why? Compare
for a moment Krishna's quote with Mrs. Eileen Garrett's words on her
transcendental experiences:

Not all of them are dependent on the flow of imagery, but may
occur in the unaccountable appearance of a strange picture in
which one sees through and beyond barriers that would completely balk our ordinary sensory vision. A road may wind among
hills for any distance. One sees the hills, and as the road reaches
away, perspective operates and its farther dimensions diminish, as
they would diminish to our sight or in any picture. Nevertheless,
at the same time one sees the entire road completely, regardless
of the intervening hills, and its farther reaches are as meticulously
discernible as the areas that lie close to the spot from which one
is seeing. Each rut and stone is individually seen and can be
described with precision. The leaves of trees and the blades of
grass are countable throughout the landscape.[15]

Obviously, Mrs. Garrett's vantage point and that of Gopi Krishna are
both "out of this world"; both experience things telepathically, clairvoyantly, catch glimpses of the future; but are the mystic and the psychic
standing on the same cosmic plateau? Perhaps if we look to that turn-of-the-

century Harvard prophet, William James, then turn quickly to a contemporary psi researcher, Rhea White, we will have the answer. James, in his extensive study of mystics, listed four universal characteristics of the mystical experience: (1) ineffability; (2) noetic quality (certainty that the knowledge gained is veridical); (3) transiency of the state; and (4) passivity.[16] On the other hand, Rhea White of the American Society for Psychical Research, who has studied gifted psychics, listed the following common characteristics: (1) deep mental and physical relaxation; (2) passivity; (3) freedom from outside distractions; and (4) lack of strain.[17] The overlap between the two comparisons is only partial. The psychic is seldom ineffable; in fact, often he is difficult to quiet. And the psychic is never truly certain of the information he perceives; there is always that residual equivocation—"I think the target picture is red," "I can't be certain, but I believe the card is a queen of hearts."

It appears that the supreme mystical experience lies beyond the psi event. The latter, in fact, is a subset of the former. The mystic passes the psi plateau of consciousness on his way to Satori or Samadhi. The mystical experience is more profoundly religious than earthly, more a communion with "God" than with fellow humans. The mystic is a psychic, but the psychic is not a mystic. In bringing the mystic into the laboratory, psi researchers are not only opening the doors to the paranormal but also entering the very vestibules of religion.

The Mystic Body

To the people of Trinidad, Lalsingh Harribance is a mystic. He gives health readings. A middle-aged woman stands before him; by closing his eyes and meditating he gives her a medical diagnosis as thorough as a whole battery of clinical tests could provide. She had chicken-pox as a child, and mumps. Although she looks healthy, she has chronic gastric problems and an enlarged heart. But Harribance goes one beyond a hospital diagnosis. Shortly the woman will develop a small tumor in the uterus, which, if left unattended, will become malignant within two years. A doctor might give a prognosis, and then with some reservation, but never a seemingly blind forecast. Harribance does forecast, and more often than not he is right.

For the last few years Harribance has been studied by psi researchers with quite positive results. For six weeks in 1969 he was the guest of Drs. W. G. Roll and R. L. Morris at the Parapsychology Research Foundation in Durham, North Carolina. Twenty people, ten men and ten women, all of them strangers to Harribance, participated in a series of experiments in which the West Indian psychic had to "read" them one by one. All the subjects were college students or adults living in the Durham–Chapel Hill area. During the first experiments Polaroid pictures and a detailed personal history were taken of each subject, and a piece of the person's hair was clipped. The photograph and the lock of hair were sealed in an opaque envelope and eventually given to Harribance.

Holding one envelope he described the physical appearance of a woman: the color of her hair, her eyes, a scar; he gave details of her family life and medical history. He was wrong. With another envelope he conjured the image of a man: his age, height, appearance, business activities, married life, his general health. He was wrong. Another woman, and he was wrong again. Another man, another miss. But something strange was happening, for the information triggered by the second woman's envelope fit the woman of the first. His description of the first man matched well with another man in the group. Harribance wasn't so much wrong as out of synchronization. The problem, says Roll, seemed to be "psychical contamination," a phenomenon reported by several other researchers. The envelopes had been stored one on top of the other, and somehow, as an unwrapped onion in the refrigerator can leave its distinctive taste in a piece of pie, the psychical properties of one picture and hair lock contaminated another. Clearly, if the experiment was to proceed Roll and Morris would have to change the experimental procedures.

It was decided that each day at ten o'clock in the morning a subject would come to the Parapsychology Research Foundation Library, be photographed, have a lock shorn, and fill out the personal-history form. There would be no collection of target envelopes, but a fresh, new one each day. At 9:45 A.M., Harribance was locked in a laboratory room with one researcher; the room had no windows and was in a building removed from the library. Since Harribance felt he worked best with people who needed his help, each subject was asked when he or she arrived to write a personal problem on an index card. This the researchers thought would put the subject in the frame of mind of "seeking help" and thereby help Harribance to make contact. The envelope containing the index card, the "undeveloped" photograph, and the lock of hair was taken to Harribance's room and slipped under the door. Now, Roll found, with the problem of contamination solved, Harribance's descriptions matched the correct people. Of course, he was not always right, and if on a rainy day he said the mystery person was wearing a raincoat, the remark was ruled out. But statistically the experiment was a success, and there were several direct hits.

A pattern emerged from Harribance's readings. With both men and women he could give accurate physical descriptions—color of hair and eyes, height and weight. With men he was best on details of family life—number of children, type of house, wife, financial problems; with women he was best on details of their love life—number of marriages, contentment, sexual problems, and lovers. In all the various tests eventually conducted with the West Indian psychic, his EEG showed high alpha-wave production when he was performing a psychical feat. In fact, the stronger the alpha rhythms, the more certain was Harribance of his information.[18] The researchers wondered—Is there really a relationship between alpha strength and psi accuracy?

During the mid-1960s researchers had shown that the strength of alpha waves in mystics was related to the number of years spent in meditation. Two Japanese neurologists, Akira Kasamatsu and Tomio Hirai, worked with forty-eight Zen monks of the Soto and Rinzai sects. The men were divided into three categories based on their years of meditative experience: at least five years, five to twenty years, and greater than twenty years. Not surprisingly, the monks with the most training produced much higher amplitude alpha waves than those with less experience. Some of the more adept men were able to generate intense alpha even with their eyes open, a condition which is not amenable to alpha production because visual input insists that the brain immediately process the information. The researchers found that the monks with more than twenty years of training were such masters of the mind that for several minutes after meditation ceased alpha production lingered on.[19] Other studies, some of which we will examine, support the premise that the greater the alpha density the more successful the paranormal feat.

When the mind of the mystic and the mind of the psychic are in an alpha state, whether one is striving for Nirvana or the face of a playing card, what is taking place in the individual's body? Is it too optimistic to suppose that researchers can construct a list of major bodily functions and, adjacent to each, detail the exact changes induced by meditation? This precise study has been done quite thoroughly with a meditation technique called Transcendental Meditation (TM). Parapsychologists are interested in the physiological correlates of meditation because of its apparent psi-favorability.

The landmark scientific inquiry into the effects of TM on human physiology is Robert Keith Wallace's "The Physiological Effects of Transcendental Meditation."[20] His findings constitute what has been called the "psychobiology of consciousness." Transcendental Meditation is quite different from the extreme yogic methods mentioned earlier. It was developed for the busy modern man by Maharishi Mahesh Yogi in 1958 and is a practical, easy-to-learn technique with almost immediate benefits. TM was publicized most in the 1960s by the Beatles, Mia Farrow, and a host of other luminaries. Not surprisingly, the idea of cramming years of arduous training into twenty minutes a day of pleasant meditation caught on like a brush fire throughout the Western world. Since 1965 an estimated 200,000 individuals in the United States alone have become TM students and today many major universities offer TM seminars. The TM philosophy can be simply stated by saying that the meditator begins on the surface level of ordinary thought and, through breathing and body positions, follows the thought through finer and finer stages to its ultimate source, like the inverse action of an air bubble expanding in water as it rises to the surface. The meditator moves from "I am acting" to "I am thinking," eventually to "I am." Dr. Wallace, and others, have been able to show that measurable physiological changes accompany TM after only a few weeks of training.

Writing in the March 27, 1970, issue of *Science,* Wallace reported a study he conducted with students at the UCLA Meditation School:

> ... oxygen consumption, heart rate, skin resistance, and electroencephalograph measurements were recorded before, during, and after subjects practiced a technique called transcendental meditation. There were significant changes between the control period and the meditation period in all measurements. During meditation, oxygen consumption and heart rate decreased, skin resistance increased, and the electroencephalogram showed specific changes in certain frequencies. These results seem to distinguish the state produced by transcendental meditation from commonly encountered states of consciousness and suggest that it may have practical applications.[21]

Wallace ended the article by stating, "Physiologically, the state produced by transcendental meditation seems to be distinct from commonly encountered states of consciousness, such as wakefulness, sleep, and dreaming, and from altered states of consciousness, such as hypnosis and autosuggestion."

The finding are provocative, and important for parapsychology. For, with a minimum of time and effort, major alterations in brainwave emanations and body metabolism are possible—changes which are psi-conducive.

In 1971, Wallace, working with Harvard's Dr. Herbert Benson, tested thirty-six men and women from seventeen to forty-one years of age living in the Boston area. Their experience with TM ranged from less than a

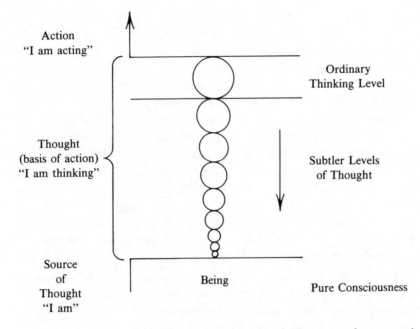

Action
"I am acting"

Ordinary
Thinking Level

Thought
(basis of action)
"I am thinking"

Subtler Levels
of Thought

Source
of
Thought
"I am"

Being

Pure Consciousness

month to nine years, with the majority having had two to three years' experience. Wallace and Benson found that during TM, oxygen consumption fell by sixteen percent and carbon dioxide elimination by fifteen percent; blood pressure and lactate levels in the blood both decreased; skin resistance to electrical current increased markedly (in some cases more than fourfold); heart rate decreased, and there was an increase in alpha rhythms in the frontal and central regions of the brain.[22]

These changes bear little resemblance to those encountered in other states of consciousness. Whereas oxygen consumption drops rapidly within the first five or ten minutes of TM, hypnosis produces no such change, and during sleep the consumption of oxygen decreases appreciably only after several hours. Skin resistance commonly increases during sleep, but the rate and amount of the increase are on a much smaller scale than they are in TM. And, EEG patterns characteristic of sleep are quite different, consisting predominantly of strong activity in waves at twelve to fourteen cycles per second and a mixture of weaker waves at various frequencies—a pattern that does not occur during meditation. Moreover, brain waves during hypnosis have no relation at all to those typical of TM. In a hypnotized subject the brainwave pattern takes the form characteristic of the mental state that has been suggested to the subject. If he or she is told to relax, the brain waves slow down. If the subject is placed in an aroused state, beta waves appear. The same is true of changes in heart rate, blood pressure, skin resistance, and respiration. All these visceral parameters in a hypnotized person reflect the suggested state. Ostensibly, mystic consciousness, even in its relatively simple TM form, differs greatly from other psi-favorable ASCs.

At the winter meeting of the Institute of Parapsychology in North Carolina on December 29, 1966, Dr. Soji Otani presented a paper entitled "A Possible Relationship Between Skin Resistance and ESP Response Pattern." In a psi experiment Otani hooked himself to a polygraph to measure galvanic skin response (GSR) and guessed a series of random numbers. He found that hits correlated with increased skin resistance to electricity. The polygraph measures how easily an electrical current passes across the skin, usually on the palm of the hand. When a person is relaxed, the skin is dry and the current passes relatively slowly. The resistance to its flow is high. However, when tension increases, sweating occurs and because of the moisture, the resistance drops and the current moves more easily. Thus a high GSR value indicates a high level of relaxation and calm. Otani found that most of his psi hits would have gone completely unnoticed if it had not been for the GSR detection, a fact that Douglas Dean's plethymograph studies and Dr. Berthold Schwartz emphasized earlier.

And while the GSR value increases significantly during a psi experience, it skyrockets during TM. Wallace and Benson found that the GSR showed an average increase of about 250 percent during TM, going as high as 500 percent, as opposed to a 100 to 200 percent increase during sleep. Psi researchers are beginning to realize that a few months of TM training for their subjects might make a world of difference in the outcome of a psychical experiment.

We know that dreaming is necessary for mental and physical health. A subject awakened at the onset of each REM cycle and thus deprived of the experience of dreaming rapidly develops psychotic symptoms such as hallucinations, disorientation, and uncoordinated mental activity. He becomes irritable and tense. A dream relieves stresses and strains, pent-up feelings, and frustrations. Dreaming is also a psi-favorable experience. TM, writes Dr. Demetri Kanellakos, senior research engineer at Stanford Research Institute in California, "relieves the strains and stresses accumulated on the nervous system itself more efficiently than during either dreaming or sleeping." It seems that more sensitive areas of the nervous system are enlivened and rejuvenated by TM. Thus, "deprivation of the state of transcending leaves the nervous system filled with deep-rooted stresses which deprive a man of the opportunity to use his full range of capabilities."[23]

Dr. Kanellakos uses an example to emphasize the point that tensions stored within the body are a mental poison as deadly as accumulations of mercury in the blood and a barrier to psi perception:

For example, suppose I am crossing a street and suddenly a car comes hurtling at me out of nowhere, screeching on its brakes and stopping a few inches before it hits me. My heart begins to beat fast. I sweat. Adrenalin and cholesterol rush through my whole system preparing me to flee from danger. But there is no reason to run. The car didn't hit me after all. So I just walk on. However, my nervous system was overwhelmed with sensory inputs and a lot of strain was stored biochemically in the nerves—in the same way that information is stored in a computer. That part of my nervous system in which this stress is stored is no longer available for me to use. Furthermore, let's say that two weeks later I am sitting in my living room reading the paper and a car outside slams on its brakes. The stored memory of the earlier experience, triggered by the outside noise, causes my heart to beat fast and my adrenalin and cholesterol to rush through my system, just as it did before. It is twenty minutes before I can settle back to reading my paper again. This not only wastes time and energy; it also stores *new* strain in my nervous system.

The more dramatic the experience, the more deeply it is stored in the nervous system—on more unconscious, sensitive, and subtle levels where the rest gained from sleep and dreaming cannot get at it. But during TM, the physiology of the whole body settles down to a lower and lower level, giving the body a more deep, profound rest, while the mind remains alert. Eventually I reach the level where this particular stress is stored . . . it is released painlessly, usually without my even being aware of it. The body, given the appropriate restful condition, will automatically throw off stress . . .

Let's say that the next day I am sitting in my living room reading a paper and a car outside slams on its brakes. I look up from the paper and think, "A car outside has just slammed on its brakes like that time when one almost hit me" and I calmly go back to reading the paper. Not only have I not wasted any time or energy being upset, but also I have not stored new strain for a future time.[24]

Figuratively speaking, every day we are hit or almost hit by hundreds of cars under the guise of disappointments, financial hardships, emotional problems, sexual frustrations, and fights, along with the other stresses and strains that are part of modern living. As Kanellakos points out, simple relaxation, cat naps, and evening sleep do not get at the root of these anxiety vines to release the poison, and the more poison, the less chance of experiencing a paranormal event. This seems to be the reason that of all the altered states of consciousness known to man, mystic mentation appears to be one of the most favorable in terms of psi occurrences. Psi researchers are just now beginning to investigate this auspicious area, and undoubtedly, the eventual rewards are going to be impressive. One study that already hints at what is coming was performed at the University of Houston.

Dr. William G. Braud of the Psychology Department at Houston and his wife Lendell at Texas Southern University were familiar with the success of dreaming and hypnosis experiments. Their goal though was to test a person's enhanced psychic ability after deep-rooted stresses and strains were shed through deep relaxation. To accomplish this they used the Jacobson's progressive relaxation technique. The procedure (not the same as the TM format) involves alternately tensing then relaxing each part of the body in sequence until a profound state of muscular relaxation is achieved. The toes are curled tightly and held in that state for a count of ten and then released. Then they are bent upward toward the face and held again. Working up the body to the forehead, this procedure is followed until a person's entire musculature is in a calm, tenseless state. After achieving body relaxation, each of the Brauds' subjects underwent mental relaxation by first conjuring imagery of pleasant and restful scenes, then blanking his mind and becoming as passive as possible. Before achieving this relaxed state, a subject was instructed to "keep somewhere in the back of his mind" the fact that a particular target picture would be transmitted and that he or she was to try to receive impressions of it.

Between November, 1969, and January, 1972, the Brauds worked with twenty-two persons, some of whom were students of Transcendental Meditation. Remarkably, by using the relaxation technique, nineteen people repeatedly scored hits, while only three could not experience psychical impressions. Many of the hits were amazingly exact, so much so that the judging panel had no real judgments to make.

The subject in one experiment was a twenty-seven-year-old male assistant professor of psychology at the University of Houston who had no history of psychic experiences, but was firmly convinced of the reality of psi.

While he underwent the relaxation procedures in one room, an agent in another room on a different floor of the building was given a randomly selected target picture taken from a pool of art prints and magazine clippings. In addition to relaxing the percipient, the Brauds gave definite instructions to the agent; he was told to "concentrate . . . upon the selected target picture in terms of its 'raw sensory information' (shapes, colors) and [to] avoid . . . 'intellectualizing' the picture (he did not attempt to put the parts of the picture into words, did not try to associate to the picture, etc.). In addition to looking at the picture, the agent traced the outlines of the major shapes in the picture with his finger and also attempted to hallucinate textures, tastes, odors, and sounds that were portrayed in the picture but could not be directly sensed. This was done in an effort to involve all sensory modalities, not merely vision."[25]

One target picture was a Coca-Cola advertisement showing two bottles of Coke surrounded by ice cubes and an insert in the upper center of the picture of an old-fashioned car and a man on a motorcycle. The psychologist who served as percipient gave this report (excerpt):

> . . . two crossed . . . lines . . . the "X" appeared . . . in the center upper left . . . I vividly saw a glass, a frosted glass filled with Coca-Cola. This glass appeared to be in the upper right-hand area . . . Some secondary images . . . a road in the center of the photo . . . Dominant colors: brown, green, tan, white and silver . . .[26]

In this first series of experiments involving ten subject, *all* of them scored hits, and seven were direct hits. The Brauds duplicated this experiment with equal success. At present, they are trying to determine whether there is a preferential sexual combination between percipient and agent, as the Maimonides group has found.

Maharishi Mahesh Yogi stresses in his teachings that a person can best tap psychic energy, and put it to use, when in a TM level of consciousness. The psi-favorability of meditative states versus other ASCs is an area for future research. Maharishi writes:

> Unless one produces this state for a few minutes daily, by means of Transcendental Meditation, one has no chance of providing any rest for the inner machinery of the body, which otherwise functions twenty-four hours a day for the whole of one's life as long as breath flows.[27]

For those who might like to experiment with TM, for the obvious health benefits derived from it and for the possible enhancement of psychical powers, a list of twenty-one major TM centers in the United States is available from: U.S. National Center, SIMS-IMS, 1015 Gayley Avenue, Los Angeles, California 90024. Telephone (213) 477-4537.

Biofeedback and Psi

Jack Schwarz is an unusual psychic—although he scoffs at the term: "I abhor it; it makes the things I do sound like something supernatural, something outside our understanding." According to Schwarz, whom Dr. Elmer Green of the Menninger Foundation regards as "one of the greatest talents in the country and probably the world in the realm of voluntary bodily controls," every man, with the proper training, can do what he does.

What does he do? To the amazement of physical scientists and physicians and the delight of parapsychologists, he feels no pain. During his demonstrations, he will hold the burning ash of a cigarette against his flesh for ten to twenty seconds. Then he might thrust a rusty bicycle spoke through the palm of his hand or skewer his bicep with a long dirty needle —all with a look of detachment and nonchalance. And in addition to an absence of pain, Schwarz does not contract tetanus or infections and he does not bleed from the open wounds or scar. He has been tested and retested; EEGs, GSRs, EKGs, and temperature sensors all indicate that when he performs his "magic" he is in a state of deep meditative consciousness. And Jack Schwarz also performs psychic healing.

With Schwarz it was always so. At the age of nine he could pass his hands over the local ailments of his family to ease their particular pains. His mother attributed her recovery from tuberculosis to his healing powers, and friends and neighbors called upon him to heal themselves, their children, and even their pets. During those early years Schwarz claimed no spectacular cures, but he could alleviate pain and this stirred his intellectual curiosity. By twelve he was devouring texts on Indian and Oriental philosophies and the works of great mystics and psychics.

From his study of Eastern metaphysics he concocted a meditation procedure which he practices to this day, and to which he attributes his seemingly superhuman talents. Once he began the daily meditation, something quite similar in nature to TM, he noticed a sharpening and broadening of his powers. He could perform many of the feats of the Indian fakirs he was reading about. While working in a clothing store in the Dutch town of Dordrecht, he kept his lapel full of pins, and one day a young girl came up to him and playfully slapped him on the chest. A dozen pins pierced his flesh, but he found that he could immediately shut out the pain. He ran to the rest room to pull out the pins. What happen, and what followed, are told in Schwarz's words as he recounted the incident for *Esquire* magazine (December, 1972):

There were little holes, but almost no blood. So, I thought, maybe I'm a fakir. To find out, I selected one of the largest pins and pushed it straight into my wrist, right through one of the veins. It went in about two inches, right down to the head. There was no pain. I was an egotistical little brat then, just sixteen, and I wanted to show everybody I could control the bleeding, too. So I went out and called the shopgirls over to watch me pull out the pin. And I managed to do it without any bleeding.

I was so excited by all of this that I ran home and asked my father to build me a bed of nails just like the ones I'd seen in some of the books. He refused, so I got a carpenter friend to do it. Meanwhile, my friends and I put up signs all over town giving notice that in two weeks I would lie on a bed of nails. I asked the carpenter not to bring it to the hall where I was going to perform until five minutes to eight. So when the curtain opened I was seeing it for the first time, just like the audience. That was so I didn't have any chance of losing my nerve.

The thing was a piece of wood six feet long with little legs. The nails protruded up through it about four inches and were spaced seven or eight inches apart. There were about forty nails altogether, and my body rested on about fifteen of them. They were large nails but very sharp. I am told that with my body weight of one-hundred-fifty pounds, there would be about thirty-three pounds of pressure per square inch. But since the nail points are much smaller than a square inch, the actual pressure over each nail was much greater than that. That, of course, was with no weight on me. Then I would invite members of the audience to come up and stand on me. Once I had a man who weighed four-hundred-five pounds. I'd also put a fifty-five pound rock on my stomach while I was on the nails and invite members of the audience to come up and hit it as hard as they could with a large sledgehammer. I never felt any pain during any of this. The holes became less and less deep with each new performance so that, finally, they were only about an eighth of an inch deep. There was no infection, and my skin today is as smooth as a newborn baby's. The holes closed up rapidly and usually weren't visible fifteen minutes after I got up from the bed of nails.

Today, Jack Schwarz's captive audience consists of scientists and physicians. The forty-nine-year-old Dutchman, who emigrated to the United States in 1957 to be studied by the scientific community, has been run through the laboratory mill many times. As he told the researchers at the Menninger Foundation where he underwent tests that would challenge the ingenuity of any Middle Ages torturer, "I never really was on the bed of nails. Not mentally, I left my body, became detached from it. If, for a moment even, I had said to myself that I was really stretched out on a bed of nails I would have suffered like anyone else."

Schwarz, to put all doubting minds at ease, is no physiological freak; he *can* feel pain and he *can* bleed—if he wants to. This was one of the first things the medical men checked him for, suspecting that the nerve channels which relay pain stimuli to the brain were damaged or blocked. His control is mental. All EEG tests and body-function monitoring reveal unusually strong alpha wave production during his feats, accompanied by the metabolic changes characteristic of deep meditation. Although his talents lie far beyond the mean capabilities of the average individual, Schwarz emphasizes that the *potential* he displays is within all of us. Just as we are taught, explicitly or by inference, that telepathy and clairvoyance are impossible, we are educated early in life that nails cause pain and bleeding, and that a rusty nail can cause death. If the skin is pierced, we *must* bleed. If the body contacts infection, we *must* succumb. If we ingest poison, we *must* expect the worst. It's a closed issue. We are educated in our limitations rather than our boundless potential. We dwell on what is impossible rather than the infinite realm of possibilities. And, as mentioned earlier, what we believe we cannot do, we cannot do.

Jack Schwarz is also self-educated in the infinite. He can see human auras and read them to tell the mental and physical conditions of individuals. The auras that Schwarz sees are multicolored flares and spirals, as dramatic as any light show, but they are not mere psychedelic hallucinations. While he was undergoing tests at the Menninger Foundation, a psychiatrist, Dr. Peter Schram, asked Schwarz for an on-the-spot aura reading. Having no *a priori* knowledge of Dr. Schram, Schwarz, in front of a group of medical men, gave the psychiatrist a complete medical history, including an abdominal problem he had had two years earlier, a cerebral dysfunction, and a small lesion in the upper lungs. Unquestionably impressed by Jack's accurate performance, several others present asked for aura readings and got them. As one amazed psychiatrist whose aura was read put it: "I don't know that there is actually such a thing as as aura, but it seems possible that Schwarz is able to pick up information about people psychically, after which his brain projects an aura, presenting the incoming data in a sort of visual configuration."[28]

Jack Schwarz claims that he can pinpoint the year of any physical or mental problem in his aura reading much the same way a botanist determines the age of a tree—by counting "rings." Schwarz sees whirlpools of color containing concentric rings when he meditates to see an aura. The rings grow in number and size with a person's accomplishments, problems, and increasing years. He feels the rings are composed of cosmic energy which is unconsciously consumed by every person to varying degrees and becomes part of the etheric or astral body. Man can tap this energy, Schwarz told the Menninger researchers, through meditation, and he feels his daily exercises attest to this fact. Even when Jack Schwarz goes for seven to ten days without food, meditating for hours on end, he still has regular bowel movements twice a day. "It's apparent," he says, "that I'm taking in energy. Somehow it becomes chemical and is processed by normal metabolism."

What do the scientists who have studied Jack Schwarz say? That he is legitimate. Although not all of his talents are understood—especially those of telepathy, psychic healing, and aura reading—his immunity to pain, his ability to control bleeding and to close wounds are finally being grasped. A few years ago, before the dawn of biofeedback training, *all* of Jack Schwarz's talents were called paranormal. Medical science taught that there were a host of so-called "involuntary" bodily functions—heart rate, brainwave emanations, gastric secretion, body temperature, muscle potentials—which lay beyond man's wildest dream of control, although mystics had been claiming otherwise and demonstrating it for centuries. Slowly, through biofeedback research, the pendulum swung from "impossible" to "possible" broadening the recognized capabilities of man, and people like Jack Schwarz and mystics have acquired legitimacy. There is no reason to suspect that the pendulum has reached the height of its swing. As today's open-minded scientist has come to realize, it is only a matter of time before all of Jack Schwarz's talents, and those of mystics and psychics alike, will be understood. Then they will no longer be paranormal. One of the major forces pushing the pendulum of potential higher is unquestionably meditation. Schwarz himself says that it is at the very foundation of his powers, his link with the cosmic source of psychic energy.

This belief has prompted open-minded men like Dr. Elmer Green to study infinite-minded men like Swami Ramo—a true meditative adept. Swami was able to amaze, and frighten, the Menninger scientists by stopping his heart for a full seventeen seconds; he could have gone longer if the medical men present had not asked him to terminate the demonstration fearing permanent brain damage would occur. But one of Swami's most spectacular feats was to demonstrate a state of consciousness not seen in this part of the world—a perfect blend of wakefulness and deep delta-wave sleep. It was agreed that Swami would enter the delta state for twenty-five minutes, then bring himself out of it.

After about five minutes Green noticed that the EEG began to show heavy delta waves, and Swami, lying down with his eyes closed, was gently snoring. Green felt sure he was asleep; and physiologically he was. One of the research assistants then made a statement in a low voice, "Today the sun is shining, but tomorrow it may rain." Every five minutes she made a different remark, a total of five. When the twenty-five minutes had elapsed, Swami Rama promptly opened his eyes and sat up, awakened by some internal alarm. Then, to the amazement of all present, he repeated, verbatim, the statements made by the research assistant, and he mentioned other sounds that had taken place in the room, including the opening and closing of two doors.[29] How could he have been asleep, in fact deeply asleep, and fully awake at the same time? He had been in a marvelous state called "yogic sleep"—a perfect blend of two modes of consciousness. Yogic sleep, claims Swami, is so beneficial that fifteen minutes of it is more restful than over an hour of normal sleep.

If the concept of having one's mind in two distinctly different mental camps seems strange, we have only to consider the not uncommon phenomenon which the Dutch physician Frederik van Eeden termed the "lucid dream." Here, the dreamer fully engrossed in a REM fantasy suddenly realizes he or she is dreaming—clearly knows that the sequence of events is not real, but a dream. Van Eeden, in his 1913 paper, "A Study of Dreams," wrote: "In these lucid dreams the reintegration of the psychic functions is so complete that the sleeper remembers day-life and his own condition, reaches a state of perfect awareness, and is able to direct his attention, and to attempt different acts of free volition. Yet the sleep, as I am able confidently to state, is undisturbed, deep and refreshing."[30]

During a period of fourteen years in which van Eeden kept a faithful log of his dreams, he experienced 352 of the lucid variety. "I dreamt," he said in one instance, "that I was floating through a landscape with bare trees, knowing that it was April, and I remarked that the perspective of the branches and twigs changed quite naturally. Then I made the reflection, during sleep, that my fancy would never be able to invent or to make an image as intricate as the perspective movement of little twigs seen in floating by."

Van Eeden believed that the dual aspect of the lucid dream could be explained in terms of the physical and etheric bodies. The physical body was the wakeful, objective spectator of the antics of the fantasy-prone etheric body. He wrote: "In a lucid dream the sensation of having a body—having eyes, hands, a mouth that speaks, and so on—is perfectly distinct; yet I know at the same time that the physical body is sleeping and has quite a different position. In waking up the two sensations blend together, so to speak, and I remember as clearly the action of the dream-body as the restfulness of the physical body." Although van Eeden's explanation to account for the lucid dream is pure speculation on his part, many people do have them. Ostensibly, they demonstrate a blend of wakeful and REM consciousness just as yogic sleep incorporates the more beneficial combination of wakefulness and deep sleep. Besides the obvious difference between natural and yogic sleep, Swami Rama points out a further distinction. Most people let their brains go to sleep while their minds are still busy worrying over daily matters, with the result that they awaken tired. But, says Swami, it is necessary for the mind and brain to sleep at the same time. This mind-brain sleep is required to root out the stored stresses and strains that natural sleep does not reach.

The importance of Swami Rama's demonstrations, and those of Jack Schwarz and others that have been studied, lies not in the performances themselves, but rather in their implications. Few people want to be able to stop their heart from beating, poke a nail through their flesh, or burn themselves with a cigarette, but the fact that these physical feats can be done without pain or infection and with miraculous healing reinforces the fact that we consistently function far beneath our maximum human potential. The powers of the mind, as the parapsychologists are loudly shouting, and the mastery it can exert over the physical body are truly boundless. The psi research goal stemming from the works with meditative adepts is quite straightforward: Through biofeedback training man should be able to learn to produce the physical and mental parameters that the greatest mystics have spent a lifetime to master—and do it in a relatively short period of time. One psi researcher, Charles Honorton, has already successfully employed alpha feedback training to enhance the clairvoyant powers of normal subjects.

In 1971 Honorton ran twenty-five volunteer subjects through an alpha training program. Each person, wired to an EEG with the audio feedback of a beep signal, learned how to enter his or her own alpha state. Some began by conjuring pleasant, relaxing scenes—a bright yellow sunlight pouring over a deserted beach—then gradually letting the light intensify and whiten, blocking out all details until the mind was a blank. Others thought of pastoral scenes which they let grow in expanse until trees, rocks, and flowers ran off into infinity, leaving a blank green field. Each person experimented until he or she learned how to produce alpha waves voluntarily. Out of the initial twenty-five people, only two could not master alpha production and were eliminated from the experiment. The remaining subjects, fifteen men and eight women, ranged in age from sixteen to thirty-two.

For the psychical part of the experiment a subject was seated in a comfortable chair in a semidark room. He relaxed, entered an alpha state as each subject had learned to do, and attempted to clairvoyantly perceive the card on the top of a deck of randomly shuffled playing cards which rested on a table in front of an agent in a different room. No one, not even the agent, knew the sequence of the cards. When the percipient sensed an impression, he called it out over the intercom, and the agent then turned the top card over, looked at it, and scored the guess a hit or a miss.

After 100 such trials the experimental situation was altered. Now the lights were turned on fully in the percipient's room, and he was told to open his eyes. The EEG showed that there was no longer any alpha production. With a new deck of randomly shuffled cards the percipient and agent ran through the same procedure. The results were undeniable. Honorton found that the impressions the subjects received while in alpha consciousness were statistically more accurate than their calls when in the normal wakeful beta state.[31] Here, subjects had been trained to produce an ASC, at will, that enhanced their psi perception. The results of Honorton's experiment are very promising for the future of biofeedback training in psychical research.

Granted, biofeedback training is a powerful tool that is just beginning to be explored. But some scientists feel that no matter how sophisticated biofeedback techniques eventually become, we will never be able to duplicate pure mystic consciousness. They feel that there will always be subtle differences between an ASC attained through years of meditation and asceticism and one acquired quickly through electronic techniques. This belief is based on the fact that one could never know *all* the countless psychophysical variables encompassed in mystic consciousness. However, from a parapsychological standpoint it is not spiritual enlightenment, the ultimate goal of mystic mentation, that is desired, but only the penultimate parasensory effects. And these have already been achieved in several laboratories by mental states which approximate mystic consciousness. Although scientists and spiritualists may continue to argue over fine points in attempting to electronically duplicate exact mystic mentation, no one can dispute the fact that biofeedback techniques have already become an indispensable tool in psychical research.

The Dichotomous Brain

There is a horizon on the parapsychological frontier so new that psi experimentation has not yet begun, and only calculated speculation can be offered at this point. However, because of its powerful allure and undeniable auspiciousness to future psi research, it is mentioned here along with the thoughtful comments of psychologist Dr. Robert Ornstein of the Langely Porter Neuropsychiatric Institute—one of several men working in the area.

Humankind has always recognized a dichotomy in human consciousness. Reason versus passion, science versus art, the analytical and the intuitive, male–female, yin–yang are but a few of its infinite guises. The dualism can be found throughout folklore, religion, and science, and, until recently, these two antithetical modes of consciousness were believed to reflect cultural differences; never was it suspected that such plays of opposites might have a solid physiological basis. Now, however, it is becoming increasingly clear that they do.[32] There is, quite literally, a double brain in humans. One houses the logical, analytical, language-oriented faculties—the left hemisphere, the one which has become known as the dominant, major, or light side. The other houses the faculties of spatial orientation, perception, artistic appreciation—the right hemisphere, the one which has been called the mysterious, minor, dark side. The concept that the left hemisphere of the brain handles analytical functions while the right governs intuition has several spin-offs. The observation gives a physiological boost to Jung's notion of enantiodromia—the law of reconciliation of opposites —which he believed was the key to tapping cosmic energy. In a sense, it may also give a street address to psi phenomena; Ornstein suspects that they may spring from the right, and not the left, hemisphere of man's brain. Before going forward, let us first backtrack a bit.

As early as 1864, the eminent neurologist John Hughlings Jackson realized that the left hemisphere controlled language, for he observed that patients with damage to this half of the brain, diagnosed as aphasics, lost their ability to verbalize. Many surgeons and psychiatrists since that time have confirmed Jackson's observation. The big mystery for nearly a hundred years was: What does the other half of the brain do? The first clues came in the mid-1930s when, to halt the spread of epilepsy, surgeons took a dramatic step and severed the corpus callosum—the three-and-a-half-inch long bundle of nerve fibers which connects the two hemispheres of the brain. Researchers found that each hemisphere does not learn independently, but one, via the corpus callosum, transmits memories and learning to the other. Then, in the early 1960s the major breakthrough came, largely due to the pioneering efforts of Dr. Roger Sperry at the California Institute of Technology and his associates, notably Joseph Bogen and Michael Gazzaniga.

Their study began with a forty-eight-year-old veteran who had suffered head injuries during World War II, and shortly thereafter developed epileptic seizures. Over a period of years the fits came on with increasing frequency and severity until surgeons eventually had to resort to radical surgery and sever the man's corpus callosum. Not only were the lack of seizures evident, but a detailed follow-up showed that the man had a dual consciousness; quite literally, his right hand no longer knew what his left hand did. If he held a pencil hidden from sight in his right hand (which feeds the left hemisphere), he could describe it verbally as usual. But if he held the pencil in his left hand (which feeds the right hemisphere), he could not describe it at all. Another test, with another split-brain patient, involved spatial abilities; the person was required to construct a three-dimensional geometrical figure using a set of cubes, each face painted a different color. The patient's left hand could do the test quite well; the right hand could not. And the patient's left hand was unable to restrain itself from helping its bumbling partner. To show the extent of this hemispherical dichotomy, one split-brain man attacked his wife with his left hand while his right hand tried to rescue her from the attack.

The figure below is a cartoon illustration which quite accurately sums up the extent of the double brain in man as understood today. It is not difficult to guess which hemisphere may serve as the seat of psi abilities; especially from the two giveaway terms *fantasy* and *perception*. Fritz Perls, the originator of Gestalt Therapy, makes an incisive comment on the two modes of consciousness:

> Ultimate awareness can only take place if the computer (left hemisphere) is gone, if the intuition (right hemisphere), the awareness is so bright that one really comes to his senses. The empty mind in Eastern philosophy is worthy of highest praise. So lose your mind and come to your senses.[33]

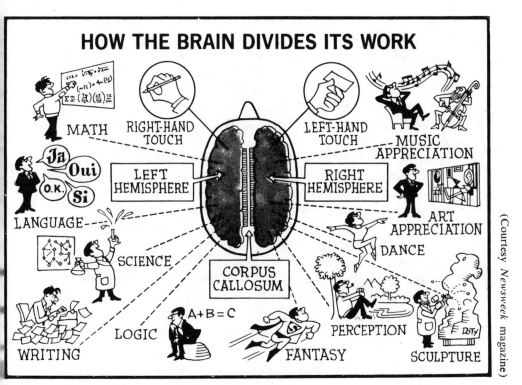

(Courtesy *Newsweek* magazine)

Perls is voicing the "let go" philosophy, the need to shed the analytical for the intuitive, the logical for the seemingly ridiculous, the stiff pattern for free-flow hallucination, all to open the senses fully—or to awaken the parasenses.

Dr. Ornstein refers to the right hemisphere as the "silent side of man" because it lacks a tongue to speak and because of the profound creative and psychical aspects it manifests. In his book, *The Psychology of Consciousness,* Ornstein writes: "When the 'silent' side is dominant, some people can receive this unusual (paranormal) form of communication . . . a shift then, to the mode of the 'night' (right hemisphere) may well enable an 'extraordinary' communication. This 'paranormal' communication can exist between different systems inside one person, or between individuals and the geophysical surround, or between two people."[34] Here Ornstein makes a neurophysiological case for psi phenomena, especially telepathy and clairvoyance.

Ah! one says, if only we could voluntarily turn off the left hemisphere and fully activate the right for a few minutes, what a world we might see.

Recall that in the Brauds' telepathy experiments, the scientists insisted that
when an agent looked at a target picture, he or she *not verbalize* its contents,
but instead, trace it with his or her fingers, conjuring the appropriate tastes,
smells, sounds, and textures of the objects pictured. We now realize that all
of this was to sensorily activate the right hemisphere of the brain while
minimizing the verbal workings of the left. This theme, whether explicitly
mentioned or not, is found throughout all parapsychological research. At
a meeting at the Smithsonian Institution on ASCs in March, 1973, Ronald
Fisher, a Johns Hopkins' pharmacologist, spoke of the hemispherical dichotomy in man. Fisher pointed out that most children's artistic impulses
start disappearing around the age of nine because they are "brainwashed"
from the school age of six onward to use their left hemisphere almost
exclusively. The "Three Big R's"—Reading, 'Riting and 'Rithmetic—are
all left-hemisphere functions. A child is never encouraged to conjure fantasies or entertain hallucination; in fact, the child who does is punished.
Music, art, dance, sculpture, all right-hemisphere appreciations, are regarded as diversions from the serious works of the Big R's, never as subjects
of serious intent *per se.* We are killing our parasenses, and we begin doing
it almost immediately after birth when we coax the infant to say "Mama."
Wittgenstein's comment that language is the bedevilment of philosophy
could just as well have been worded "language is the demise of the parasenses."

But, of course, we must learn to speak and to read and to perform
mathematical computations. Yes, we must. But in doing so we need not so
deliberately, so flagrantly, squelch the right-hemisphere functions. A harmony can be attained between the dual mentations in man. This was, quite
explicitly, the essence of Jung's life work—volumes on enantiodromia
which still have not been given their proper place in established intellectual
circles. The child, from an early age, should be taught illogic (a notion he
innately harbors) along with logic, art along with science, music appreciation with language, and fantasy, which, as Maslow said, "has its place." The
daydream, the hallucination, oneiric fantasy, eidetic and kinesthetic imagery must be encouraged in the child in order to open fully what Huxley
termed "The Doors of Perception"—only then will the paranormal be
normal.

Hemispherical dichotomy is a new frontier in parapsychological research—in fact, it is a relatively new area in all ways. Currently, Dr.
Ornstein and his associates are testing the right and left hemispheres, not
of split-brain patients, but of normal individuals. One group comprises
lawyers and scientists who are predominantly engaged in analytical work;

the other is made up of artists. With electrodes connected to their scalps, Ornstein is measuring the right and left hemisphere potentials that the people normally employ. Then, he hopes to take those in the left hemisphere "rut" and, through biofeedback training, teach them to increase the use of their right hemisphere. He will also attempt to teach the artists to voluntarily turn up the electrical generators of the left hemisphere to solve those mathematical problems which have always bewildered them.[35] Charles Honorton's successful clairvoyant experiments involved training a person to increase the overall alpha production of both hemispheres. The next step in psi research, says Ornstein, is to teach a subject to shift consciousness from one hemisphere to the other. Will psi scoring be enhanced when the right hemisphere is electrically hot and the left is virtually turned off? At the moment the answer is speculative since no experiments have been conducted, but now the speculation rests on firm ground.

8
Precognition

"I don't know what you mean," said Alice.

"Of course you don't!" the Hatter said, toss-ing his head contemptuously. "I dare say you never even spoke to Time!"

"Perhaps not," Alice cautiously replied. "But I know I have to beat time when I learn music."

"Ah! that accounts for it," said the Hatter. "He won't stand beating. Now, if you only kept on good terms with him, he'd do almost anything you liked with the clock. For instance, suppose it were nine o'clock in the morning, just time to begin lessons: you'd only have to whisper a hint to Time, and round goes the clock in a twinkling! Half-past one, time for dinner!"

Lewis Carroll, *Alice's Adventures in Wonderland*, 1865

The Illusion of "Now"

William Cox is an American researcher with an intense interest in psychic phenomena, especially precognition. He feels that every person receives precognitive flashes, but few are aware of them. About ten years ago Cox set out to investigate this possibility. Specifically, he wanted to know whether people who frequently ride trains can sense when an accident will occur. In a long-term field study, Cox collected information on the total number of people on each train at the time of an accident and compared this with the number of passengers who traveled on the same train during the seven days before the accident, and on the fourteenth, twenty-first, and twenty-eighth days before the accident. Surprisingly, he found that over a period of several years of operation—observing the same trains at the same stations—people did avoid accident-bound trains. There were always fewer passengers in the damaged and derailed coaches than would have been expected for the train at that time. The difference between expected and actual number of passengers was so great that the odds against its chance occurrence were over a hundred to one.[1]

Cox does not feel that the people who avoided the accident-bound trains did so consciously. In fact, he says they had no hint of impending trouble. For him, there is only one way to account for the data—a precognitive flash must have registered at some subconscious level and altered the person's morning routine, perhaps causing him to sleep later or have a longer breakfast, so that the normal train, which was bound for an accident, was missed that morning.

In one sense William Cox's field investigations call to mind the plethysmographic studies of Douglas Dean. Dean's subjects had the blood flow measured in their fingertip while an agent concentrated on a batch of names—some meaningful to the subject, some not. Although blood fluctuations correlated significantly with the emotion-laden transmissions, the individuals were never consciously aware of receiving telepathic impressions. Perhaps subliminal or dimly illuminated precognitive flashes influence our behavior more than we suspect.

Precognition is at once the most exciting, enigmatic, and downright frustrating of all psychic phenomena. Although, under the name "prophecy," it dates back to the Egyptian seers and the oracle at Delphi, all attempts to find a rational basis for it have met with scientific embarrassment. Parapsychology's critics are vehement over the issue. "No one, absolutely no one," insists the psychologist Dr. Albert Ellis, "is going to make me believe we can see the future. The idea is pure hogwash."[2] Even scientists standing firmly in the parapsychology camp become distraught when they contemplate precognition. Dr. Gertrude Schmeidler, a psychologist at City College of New York and a psi researcher for some thirty years, has this to say: "To be honest, I'm not at all comfortable with the concept. I know it exists; it's real enough, but at times I almost wish it weren't."[3] The uncertainty and puzzlement of critics and researchers is understandable enough, for in accepting the reality of precognition one opens a Pandora's box of scientific and philosophical dilemmas. The notion of predetermination is, to say the least, a formidable issue.

Of course, the crux of our problem with precognition is deeply rooted in our notion of time. To foresee future events implies an ability to transcend present time—and what *is* time?

Time, we say, is a rhythm, a regular beating like the heart's or the oom-pah-pah of a Strauss waltz, and we feel comfortable with the idea. Throughout history we have tracked time with sundials, sandglasses, pendulum clocks, spring watches, and now with atomic clocks. But the seconds, minutes, and hours these devices tick off have nothing to do with the intrinsic nature of time. They are, rather, the arbitrary and convenient means we have chosen to mark the passage of wakeful events. Real time, like real space, lies beyond a single mode of awareness. It is a continuous backdrop against which one scene of the watercolors of "normal" life is dilutely painted. And that sequential ordering of events into past, present, and future which strikes us as being so intuitive and real is, according to philosophers and scientists alike, an illusion, a learned habit picked up so early in life that it makes precognition seem an utter impossibility. If we are ever to understand precognition, we will have to relinquish our present notion of the passage of time. Not that we should throw away our watches and clocks. The convenience of dividing and classifying the unidirectional, forward flowing of time is unarguable. Such unidirectional time will be referred to throughout this chapter as *wakeful time.* But it is also clear that any theory of time must become much more sophisticated if we are to understand not only precognition but a number of new scientific discoveries as well.

If we pause for a moment to consider the notion we call "present," one we feel so comfortable with, we will see that it is really an ambiguous, undefinable concept. When we are forced to explain what we mean by present time, a perplexing situation arises. Is the present this hour? No, it cannot be, for already part of this hour has passed and part is yet to come. And this is true. But perhaps the interval of an hour is too long to define the present? Very well, is the present this minute? Clearly, the answer again must be no, for part of this minute is already the past and part is still the future. This continuous slicing into smaller and smaller intervals leads to a painful conclusion. But before stating the obvious, let us try a different way to wiggle off the horns of this dilemma.

You say the present is *now*—what you are doing *right now.* So let us define the present as that time during which an organism interacts with a particular event in its environment. Having assumed this definition, consider an object across the room, and the statement: "I *will* look at that object." The statement implies a future event, since you are now looking at this page. But now look up at the object. Grammatically, the expression of your action is "I *am looking* at the object," a sentence we have learned expresses present time. But, from the standpoint of interacting with the object, once your eyes focused on it, and the light stimuli registered in your brain as perception, a portion of "looking at the object" is already in the past. You may continue to look at it, but each time a new photon of light is perceived by the brain, that bit of information "has happened"; it is in your past as surely as the photons traveling across the room now still lie in your future. Certainly, we cannot define the present as that length of time you choose to look at the object, for then it would be wholly arbitrary, differing for each person and for every particular interaction. The conclusion we tried to shun earlier is unavoidable: present time does not exist. Although this seems at first shocking, it is a tenet long held by many Eastern sects, and it is clearly reflected in many primitive languages. Eskimo, for example, does not distinguish present tense. As Easterners for ages have taught, the future is an ensemble of things which have the potential of happening—really, our expectations—and the past comprises those events from the ensemble which have occurred—our memory. The transformation of potential into actuality simply cannot be ascribed a rational, unambiguous interval.

A mathematician would say that our inability to define present time stems from viewing time as a continuum, which makes it infinitely subdivisible. The alternative, of course, is to view time as discrete packets, each one in itself indivisible. Physics has adopted this system, naming the small hard packets of time *chronons,* from the Greek for time. The duration of a chronon is defined as the length of time it takes light, traveling at 3×10^{10} centimeters per second, to traverse an elementary particle of diameter 10^{-13} centimeters; or roughly 10^{-23} seconds. This is a very small number indeed, and scientists agree that it is a makeshift definition, convenient for certain theoretical calculations, but in no way descriptive of nature.

If we wish to cling to our notion of wakeful time and agree that the present is a nonexistent concept, then where in time do we exist?—for we believe that we do indeed exist. If the time axis is divided into past and future segments, we must exist on a zero-width boundary, a mathematical interface between what will happen and what has happened. In other words, we are on the crossroad between potentiality and actuality, and the road has no width. This argument is important as a prelude to a discussion of precognition because it illustrates that even for our most familiar concept, present time, we are surprisingly naive. But the modern-day assault on time goes much deeper than an attack on the present; it delivers a crushing blow to the very heart of the concept.

Assaults on Time

As a psi researcher, Cox is not terribly disturbed by precognition, for he is well aware that in the twentieth century the concept of time is no longer sacrosanct. In fact, there has never been a philosopher or scientist who truly embraced the traditional concept. Even Newton, that seventeenth-century giant who posited the idea of absolute time—a sort of objective clock ticking throughout the universe—had doubts later in life about his own creation.

The first and most famous blow to traditional time was delivered by Einstein in 1905. In his paper on the Special Theory of Relativity, Einstein showed that time is not the constant ticking of a universal clock against which we measure the passage of events, but, rather, the passage of time varies—speeding up or slowing down—depending on the velocity of the timekeeper. Simply put, the theory states that a person traveling at a velocity approaching that of light (about 186,000 miles per second) experiences an appreciable slowing down of time with respect to an observer who is at rest. This notion was dramatically crystallized in the famous age paradox. In Einstein's own words:

> If we placed a living organism in a box . . . one could arrange that the organism, after an arbitrary length of flight, could be returned to its original spot in a scarcely altered condition while corresponding organisms which had remained in their original positions had long since given way to new generations. In the moving organism the lengthy time of the journey was a mere instant, provided the motion took place with approximately the speed of light.[4]

The relativity theme is pushed to its logical limits, and beyond, in the famous limerick:

> *There was a young lady named Bright*
> *Whose speed was far faster than light;*
> *She set out one day,*
> *In a relative way,*
> *And returned home the previous night.*

Einstein's notion that time passes differently for a person at rest compared to a person in motion has been experimentally verified many times.

Direct evidence of time dilation has come from the study of cosmic-ray phenomena, cyclotrons and synchrotrons, radioactive decay processes, and a recent (1971) experiment in which atomic clocks traveled by planes in different directions around the world. In the last experiment, Dr. J. C. Hafele, professor of physics at Washington University in St. Louis, Missouri, and Dr. Richard E. Keating of the Time Service Division, U.S. Naval Observatory in Washington, D.C., placed four cesium beam clocks on jet planes heading first eastward and then westward. (The clocks had, of course, been synchronized with the standard atomic time scale of the U.S. Naval Observatory.) Hafele and Keating found that at the end of the journey, the clocks traveling eastward (with the rotation of the earth) had *lost* 59 nanoseconds;* while on their westward trip (opposing the earth's rotation) the clocks *gained* 273 nanoseconds. The figures are in excellent agreement with the predictions of relativity theory. As Hafele and Keating write, "These results provide an unambiguous empirical resolution of the famous clock 'paradox' with macroscopic clocks."[5] Or, stated in more personal terms, we could say that flying from Los Angeles to New York decreases one's age—but you will never see the difference in a mirror.**

Einstein's intuitive insight (for that is how he arrived at all his conclusions) into the relativity of time was the most damaging blow the concept had even received. It was not the last word on the subject, however. Just eleven years later, in his General Theory of Relativity, he predicted that time is also a function of the gravitational field in which it exists; that is, the stronger the gravitational field of a planet, the slower the passage of time on its surface. In our solar system this would mean that the passage of time we call a second on earth would be of slightly longer duration on the planet Jupiter, which has a stronger gravitational field. Thus, if we imagine a person from earth living on the Jovian planet, he or she would age slower than friends on earth. This astonishing gravitational prediction also has been repeatedly confirmed by studying the spectra of light emitted by a massive body.

The slowing down of time as a result of the strength of gravitational fields is an amazing fact. It suggests a way—theoretically—by which the passage of time might be brought to a halt, but this would require a gravitational field of infinite intensity. Conveniently, the requirement is somewhat

*A nanosecond is one billionth of a second.

**To appreciate how small the variation in time with velocity is: for a person traveling at half the speed of light, i.e., 93,000 miles a second, time would slow down only by about thirteen percent compared to a person who had remained at rest.

approximated in nature in that new astronomical oddity called a black hole. When the internal furnace of a large star begins to die out because of a decreasing fuel supply, the pressures within the star diminish. Eventually the star collapses under its own gravitational force. Under certain conditions the resulting entity, several times as massive as our sun yet no bigger than ten miles across, is called a black hole. The gravitational field of this super-dense mass is so intense that time within the hole virtually comes to a standstill. Any light trapped within a black hole can never escape (hence the name *black hole*). This is because light travels at the finite velocity of 186,000 miles per second, and the duration of a second in the hole is stretched out to an almost infinite interval of time. If a man descended into a black hole (an impossibility since he would be shredded to pieces by the differential forces as he climbed over the edge, but his safe descent is something we can imagine for a moment), he would virtually stop aging. While centuries passed outside and civilizations rose and fell, the man in the hole would not have aged a day.*

All of these strange features of time—its slowing down, speeding up, and almost stopping—have to do with how we track it, that is, by the passage of events whether they be the tickings of a clock or birthdays. After a lifetime of worrying about time, and having revolutionized our notions of it, Einstein arrived at a single conclusion: The passage of time is merely a feature of our consciousness, it has no objective physical significance. "For us believing physicists," wrote Einstein shortly before his death, "this separation between past, present and future has the value of mere illusion, however tenacious."[6]

Another major assault on time came in 1949. That year, physicist Richard P. Feynman of the California Institute of Technology proposed that newly found particles called positrons, the antiparticles of electrons, were not really new particles at all, but merely electrons traveling backwards in time. This notion of *time reversal* is not the intellectual fantasy of a radical scientist. The concept has proved so productive that in 1953 Feynman received the prestigious Albert Einstein Medal and in 1965 the Nobel Prize. As philosopher of science Hans Reichenback wrote, Feynman's theory represents "the most serious blow the concept of time has ever received in physics." As bizarre as the notion of time reversal sounds, surprisingly it does not violate any of the laws of nature. As mathematician G. J. Whitrow recently observed: "All the laws of motion and the laws

*The situation of time passage in a black hole is considerably more complicated than painted here. For further information see *Physics Today,* January, 1971.

governing forces and interactions in physics are just as valid if we imagine time flowing backwards instead of forwards. This is true for the laws of gravitation (both Newton's and Einstein's), of electromagnetism and of those governing the so-called strong forces between the protons and neutrons in the atomic nucleus."[7] The fact that all the fundamental laws of nature give no intimation as to a preferred direction of time should make us begin to seriously question our predilections on the matter, and should make us far more comfortable with precognition.

Outguessing Atoms

Precognitive experiments involving dice-throwing and card-guessing have always been plagued with problems of ensuring true randomness and eliminating possible fraud. Even the best die, due to an inhomogeneous density or irregular curvature of its edges, can be unintentionally biased; and card shuffling can be even more precarious. Thus for years parapsychologists have sought the ideal precognitive experiment. Not long ago, one man devised it.

Dr. Helmut Schmidt is a brilliant physicist who for several years now has been devoting his training in physics to the benefit of psychical research. Formerly an employee of the Boeing Scientific Research Laboratories, Schmidt is currently director of the Institute for Parapsychology at Duke University, a chair passed to him from Dr. J. B. Rhine. Although he has worked in many branches of psychical research, today Schmidt's primary interest lies in precognition. He harbors no prejudice toward this phenomenon, as baffling as it is to comprehend, for he clearly understands the confusion in physics concerning the nature of time.

Schmidt's precognitive experiment is the ultimate in sophistication, and is based on a physically random event: the spontaneous radioactive decay of the element strontium 90.

According to present physical theory, the decay of a radioactive element is one of the most random events in all the universe. For a given pile of strontium atoms, there is no way of predicting when particular atoms will undergo decay. All that can be said is that every twenty years (its half life) precisely one half of the intact atoms will have fallen apart—emitting energetic particles as they decay. Schmidt uses the unpredictable emanations from the radioactive material to randomly turn on one of four colored lights on a panel which rests before an experimental subject. It is the task of the subject to electronically record his "hunch" as to which light will be activated by the quantum mechanical events. As Schmidt emphasizes, until a particular light come on, no one in the universe knows which one it will be.

In one series of tests eleven individuals, university students, sat before the lights making a total of more than 10,000 "guesses." Schmidt was not surprised to find that some of the people had a definite knack for anticipating the radioactive decay; pooled, the successful predictions had a better than chance score of more than 1,000 to one odds.[8]

Three of the star subjects from the first test were run through a second experiment; this time 63,066 trials were conducted. Their average results were astronomically high: odds against chance success, two billion to one.[9] Encouraged by these results, Schmidt has conducted other experiments using especially sensitive subjects and has obtained odds against chance running over ten billion to one.[10] The very nature of the experiment precludes cheating, and all the score tallying and statistical computation is handled by computer.

Several other researchers have used Schmidt's technique and obtained impressive results. Of course, not everyone drawn from the general populace can outguess the flashing lights, and the select individuals who can are often thoroughly flabbergasted by their performance. Some who have never experienced a paranormal event find that in the laboratory, they are performing like experienced psychics. Schmidt's experiments, and those of others, clearly show that there is a small percentage of individuals who can momentarily shed the learned constraints of wakeful time, and transcend what we comfortably call the present. How they do it, and why they can do it in the laboratory and not in the gambling casino, are among the things which make psychical research so exciting.

Precognitive Dreams

Abraham Lincoln was a questioning Christian. Religious dogma repelled him, for he sought to understand things through reason, rather than accept them on blind faith. One thing which confused his common-sense mind, though, was precognition—a phenomenon which Lincoln reported having experienced several times during his life.

Ward H. Lamon, Lincoln's close friend, wrote in his biography, *Life of Abraham Lincoln* (Boston, 1872): "Assured as he undoubtedly was about omens, which to his mind were conclusive—that he would rise to power and greatness, he was firmly convinced by the same tokens that he would be suddenly cut off at the height of his career and the fullness of his fame." Lincoln held this belief for years, and a week before his death it was frightfully echoed in a dream. In *Recollections of Abraham Lincoln* (Chicago, 1895), Lamon related Lincoln's premonition of his death by assassination. This is Lincoln's own account of his dream:

> I retired very late. I could not have been long in bed when I fell into slumber, for I was weary. I soon began to dream. There seemed to be a death-like stillness about me. Then I suddenly heard subdued sobs as if a number of people were weeping. I thought I left my bed and wandered downstairs. There the silence was broken by the same pitiful sobbing, but the mourners were invisible. I went from room to room; no living person was in sight, but the same mournful sounds of distress followed me as I passed along; every object was familiar to me, but where were all the people who were grieving as if their hearts would break? I was puzzled and alarmed. What could be the meaning of all this? Determined to find the cause of a state of things so mysterious and so shocking, I kept on until I arrived at the East Room, which I entered. There was a sickening surprise. Before me was a catafalque on which rested a corpse wrapped in funeral vestments. Around it were stationed soldiers who were acting as guards; and there was a throng of people, some gazing mournfully upon the corpse whose face was covered; others were weeping pitifully.
>
> "Who is dead in the White House?" I demanded of the soldiers.
>
> "The President," was the answer; "he was killed by an assassin!" There came a loud burst of grief from the crowd, which woke me from my dream. I slept no more that night, and although it was only a dream, I have been strangely annoyed by it ever since.

Lincoln told the dream to his wife, Mary, and to Lamon. The biographer states that he related it reluctantly, "in a melancholy, meditative mood," saying of the dream that "like Banquo's ghost, it will not go down." The premonition haunted Lincoln right up until that fateful night one week later at the Ford Theater.

Precognition through dreams is its most frequently reported mode of occurrence. Lincoln's dream is only one among thousands recorded in the pages of parapsychological literature. Dr. Louisa Rhine's detailed analysis of over 10,000 spontaneous psi cases indicates that parasensory information is most frequently mediated through dreams, and many of the dreams contain precognitive material rather than telepathic or clairvoyant impressions.[11] Since the late 1960s that observation has been confirmed by several dream experiments.

During the early telepathically induced dream experiments at Maimonides, Dr. Ullman and Dr. Krippner had noticed that often a subject would report a dream unrelated to the night's target picture, a dream of a precognitive nature. Most of these were of simple events, but due to the researchers' interest in dreaming, several of the dream premonitions were followed up and later found to occur. One evening, an educational research worker, Bernard Basescu, sleeping in the dream chamber, gave this report:

> . . . There was a friend of mine, Harold, who I haven't seen for about twenty years—oh, I guess well over twenty years. And he was in the dream. He was being set up for the next experiment . . .[12]

Basescu's dream contained no elements from that night's target picture which an agent down the hall was attempting to telepathically transmit, but a few days later Mr. Basescu met Harold:

> . . . I was in a restaurant rather out of the area where I usually eat. I was sitting with an acquaintance and had just told him of the dream and that I had not seen Harold for about twenty years, since high school. . . . We got up to leave and there, standing in the line near the doorway, was Harold . . . I tapped him on the arm and informed my friend that this was the fellow I had just told him about . . .[13]

Ullman and Krippner were interested in conducting formal precognitive dream experiments, but already their days and night were brimming with telepathy studies; the formal precognitive work had to wait until 1967 when parapsychologist Charles Honorton joined the Maimonides staff.

Honorton began his precognitive experiments with the famous English psychic Malcolm Bessent, after devising a clever experimental procedure. It was decided that Bessent, who has a long history of paranormal dreams, would be studied for sixteen consecutive nights. "On the odd-numbered nights," explains Honorton, "we asked Mr. Bessent to attempt to dream about a target that would not be selected until the next day." (This was quite a twist from Ullman and Krippner's telepathy experiments.) "On the even-numbered nights we showed him the target which had been randomly selected that morning—the one he was to have dreamed about the night before—and we asked him to intentionally dream about it that night." In this way, Honorton hoped to get some idea of how Bessent's subconscious mind combined target elements with his storehouse of past experiences.

The targets for the study were not the art prints which had been used in the telepathy tests; they were more dynamic "experiences." One entitled "Birds," for example, consisted of a series of ten slides depicting various species of birds, and a tape recording of bird calls. Each audiovisual experience ran about ten minutes.

On the night of September 7, 1970, Bessent entered the soundproof dream cubicle. No target experience had yet been selected; the target would not be chosen until the next day. Bessent was wired to an EEG to monitor his REM periods so he could be awakened for dream reports. He was then given the following instruction over an intercom: "Tomorrow evening you will be shown a series of slides accompanied by sound effects. You are to try to dream about that slide-and-sound sequence tonight." With that monumental task, Bessent went to sleep. During that night he had three dreams:

[Excerpt: first dream report:] . . . I forget what you call them in the States, kind of young policemen, but a particular kind to do with campus disorders . . . I wish I could remember the names— National Guard, perhaps . . . Well, I just had this scene of a university campus with a lot of people there and, you know, they were just sitting around and suddenly all these people in motor uniform came marching into the scene . . . it was obvious that the only outcome was going to be violence of some kind. . . .[14]

[Excerpt: third dream report:] ". . . guards from the island of Rhodes plus a couple of hundred children. There were 500 National Guardsmen on this place . . . The guardsmen had white, old-fashioned Greek uniforms . . . and there seemed to be a kind of . . . garrison for them . . .[15]

The following morning, September 8, a target experience was randomly selected. To everyone's delight, it was entitled "Police," and consisted of slides of policemen on foot, on motorcycles, and in patrol cars. The police were shown arresting people, giving tickets, and enforcing the law through both violent and nonviolent means. The musical tape that accompanied the slides contained themes from James Bond movies.

That night, Bessent watched the slides and heard the film themes before entering the dream chamber. He dreamed twice, but surprisingly,

now neither dream pertained to the "Police" experience. Why he was able
to dream of the experience precognitively but not when shown the target
material is a baffling mystery. The series of experiments conducted with
Bessent, though, were phenomenally successful. In five out of the eight
nights he had precognitive dreams *directly* related to the target picture that
was randomly selected the following morning.

Honorton will gladly talk about the experiment and reveal the detailed
statistical results, but he is silent when it comes to speculation as to what
exactly is happening. "At this stage of research," he says, "it is premature,
even foolish, to offer explanations as to how precognition comes about. At
the moment we are concerning ourselves with just conducting the most
controlled, thorough experiments we can devise."

The Guesses of Hamsters and Businessmen

In 1968, two French psychologists, Pierre Duval and Evelyn Mantredon, announced the results of a highly unusual experiment; they claimed
to have observed a precognitive faculty in ordinary laboratory mice. The
researchers used a two compartment cage with a low barrier separating each
housing. The wire floor of the compartments was electrified, and activated
by a random generator. Thus, every minute one of the compartments became mildly charged and shocked any mouse that happened to be there.
Although there was no way of telling which cage would be the temporary
electric chair, Duval and Mantredon found that the mice were able to avoid
being shocked by jumping the barrier into the safe cage before the charge
was delivered.[16]

Several U.S. researchers, fascinated by the French claim, decided to try
the experiment themselves—not that they doubted their French colleagues,
for in parapsychological research one quickly learns that anything is possible. The experiment, if verified, might shed some light on the nature of
precognition. Over the last three years the experiment has been run six times
and six times it has been successful. The most sophisticated and impressive
tests have been conducted by researchers James W. Davis and L. Allen
Mayo, Jr. at the Foundation for Research on the Nature of Man in Durham,
using jirds (*Meriones unquiculatus,* an animal closely related to the gerbil)
and hamsters.[17]

The experiment is ultra-computerized; in fact, it can run for several
days without human intervention. A large metal wheel, much like an
amusement park ferris wheel, has twenty mesh wire cages, each containing

one hamster (or jird). As the wheel rotates and stops, one cage door automatically opens, and the inquisitive animal runs out into an experimental pen. The pen, as in the French experiment, is really a two-compartment cage with a low barrier down the middle and electrified floors. Once a photoelectric eye spots the animal in the pen, it signals the computer to start the test. For twenty-six minutes a random electrical generator delivers current (10 microamps, which does not harm the animal) or no current to the compartments. The animal is free to jump back and forth from cage to cage to avoid the being shocked—if he can "guess" the cage that will be charged.

In order to remove any human element, another photoelectric eye detects the animal's jumps and correlates them with the random shocks. The final statistical results are typed out by the controlling computer—a PDP 11/20. Once the researchers push the button to start the experiment, they need never enter the room again. The way the equipment is constructed, it is impossible for an animal to sense the current coming up to a particular cage once the random generator has made its decision. It takes slightly less than one thousandth of a second for the electrification—a time too short for him to run. Thus if he is going to avoid the shock, he must know in advance what the random generator will do.

At the end of the twenty-six minutes, the cage door on the ferris wheel opens, the animal, glad to escape, enters, and the wheel automatically rotates one cage and lets out the next creature.

The results of these experiments have been extremely positive. The researchers write that the tests "suggest that animals can demonstrate psi reliability at high scoring rates under certain conditions which relate to their own behavior as well as the environment."[18] They carefully point out that the results cannot be attributed to the behavioral conditioning of the animals, for the grid shocks are truly random.

So far, tests show that the hamsters score slightly higher than the jirds. Quite naturally, the researchers wonder how rabbits might score, or cats. Although the automated experiments have not been extended to include other species, this is in the making. What parapsychologists hope for is a correlation between apparent precognitive talent and species sophistication. If such a trend exists, it would do much to help us understand parasensory abilities.

If hamsters can do it, so can humans—at least we would like to think so. Researcher E. Douglas Dean feels that many business executives and stock-market sharpshooters have at least as much precognitive talent as hamsters. Several years ago Dean set out to see if the successful businessman's hunch was in fact a sort of "sixth sense." Was he receiving parasensory information about conditions that would affect a deal at some time in the future?

For ten years now Dean has been studying successful executives, a group of 107 company presidents, men who almost single-handedly run their company and whose daily actions determine the success or failure of the whole business. "Almost all of the men we studied," says Dean, "told us of numerous incidences where those around them advised them not to make a particular move, and the president had a feeling opposite that of his advisers." More often than not, the presidents' hunches paid off. By conducting tests in search of psi talents among the businessmen, Dean found that the men who had been in office about five years, and during that time had more than doubled their profits, scored significantly higher on standard psi tests. On the other hand, those who followed their hunches right to the poorhouse exhibited no significant parasensory ability.[19] Perhaps individuals with amazingly accurate hunches who repeatedly make the right decisions, turning small businesses into multimillion-dollar conglomerates, or making a fortune on the stock market, have information that other businessmen do not. The repeatedly accurate hunch may be more than just economic acumen.

If some people make their fortunes on unconscious psychic flashes, others apparently know exactly what they are doing. Mary Tallmadge is a cheerful, amiable lady in her late fifties who lives in northeastern New Jersey. Her chief hobbies are the stock market and parapsychology—combined. She makes market forecasts based on precognitive flashes, and very often her psychic hunches pay off. Business executives and corporation presidents regularly consult her for advice, and her private haul from the market attests to her repeated accuracy. Mary says: "I do it by kind of relaxing my mind and letting visions drift into it. I might see a bear riding on top of a bull, for instance, and in the background there might be a company trademark. This would show me the company's stock price is about to fall." Not long ago Ms. Tallmadge had a vision of a ship with the name United Fruit on the side and huge piles of bananas on deck. "The bananas seemed to glint like gold," says the Wall Street psychic. "I mean they seemed metallic, not just yellow." She advised her clients to buy United Fruit, which was not popular at that time, for forty-two dollars a share. Three months later the stock topped seventy dollars. Her success has been even more remarkable in forecasting the highs and lows of such big board issues as Telex, A&P, Marshal Industries, Natomas, and Cox Cable Communications.[20]

Douglas Dean has studied Ms. Tallmadge and her uncanny string of successes. With a perplexed smile he says, "She isn't wrong often. She actually does seem to see the future on many occasions. I know it sounds strange, but what else can I say?"

Hooked on Time

Today, there is no way to account for the accurate guesses of jirds, hamsters, and businessmen. Dean's and Cox's field studies will always be open to critical debate, but the quantum mechanical experiments of Helmut Schmidt, the dream research of Charles Honorton, and the animal experiments of Davis and others—to mention only a few—are beyond reproach. In some mysterious way the learned constraints of wakeful time can be surmounted. In man, at least, this accomplishment seems inextricably linked with the transcendence aspect of ASCs. But if we are unable to attack the precognition problem head on, it might be fruitful to pry open the back door.

All clocks keep track of various patterns in the occurrence of events. Now we know that these constraining patterns are only the products of a certain level of consciousness. Mathematicians express this idea through formulas;* physicists try to devise ingenious experiments to reveal the patterns as illusion, and even musicians such as Schoenberg, Webern, Berg, and Stravinsky have composed music with total disregard for our old patterns of time. This leitmotif has even been picked up by modern poets. As T. S. Eliot wrote in *Four Quartets,*

> *There is, it seems to us,*
> *At best, only a limited value*
> *In the knowledge derived from experience.*
> *The knowledge imposes a pattern, and falsifies.*

An explanation of precognition, we say, has to do with the illusory passage of time, the manner in which we perceive time's flow. Undeniably, as human beings, we are addicted to the forward, unidirectional flow of wakeful time. How did we get hooked on it?

In his famous essay on the development of our concept of time, "La

---

*For an account of the use of hypernumbers related to altered states of consciousness and meditation, see Charles Muses and Arthur Young, ed., *Consciousness and Reality,* Chapter 6, "Some New Techniques of Awareness."

Gènese de l'idée du temps," French psychologist M. Guyau argued that time should not be regarded as a prior condition, but as a consequence of our experience of the world and the result of a long evolution. He suggested that the idea of time arose when the first organism to develop the ability to think became conscious of its reactions toward pleasure and pain, and of the succession of muscular sensations associated with these reactions. A pattern of occurrence of events was established and a notion of forward movement. Thus, for the organism, as Guyau argues, it is not time that produced the idea of irreversible and undirectional flow, but the wakeful perception of events which take place in time.[21] Or as the mathematician Whitrow says: "Whereas man's spatial conceptions may have originated when he became fully conscious of, and reflected upon, his movements, the temporal concepts can be traced back to the feelings of effort and fatigue, pleasure and pain, associated with these movements."[22] What both Guyau and Whitrow are saying is that our conscious awareness of time depends on the fact that our normal level of consciousness operates by *successive acts of attention.* We separately perceive cause, then effect, and consequently feel a flowing in time. Without a consciousness which feeds on this cause–effect relationship, that is, without causality, we would not be able to say "now this," "then that," and we would lose our feeling for the passage of time.

We know that in certain ASCs our subjective feeling for time can be very different from what it is in normal consciousness; time may dilate, contract, and even vanish. In situations that hold our attention, for example, we have the feeling that time is passing faster than in situations we find tedious and boring. In dream consciousness we do not demand smooth transitions between time sequences; at one moment we might be with friends sailing on a lake, when suddenly, with no sense of ambiguity, we are cavorting with fiends in the murky depths of the lake. In hypnotic consciousness an hour can be stretched into a day, or the mathematical computations of several hours compressed into twenty minutes; time can be brought to a standstill. Or, in hypnotic consciousness, we can be regressed in time, and act and speak as we did as children. In these ASCs the strange manipulations of time are never questioned as strange by the percipient; they are natural—innate to the particular mentation. This fact suggests a "what if" situation. What if the first organism, from the very dawn of consciousness, had evolved spending its time in dream consciousness or hypnotic consciousness or some other altered state—anything but wakefulness? How would its offspring millennia hence perceive time? The unambiguous answer illustrates the arbitrariness of the unidirectional, past–present–future scheme: for the offspring of that ASC organism, the notion of time would be radically different from what it is for organisms today.

In speaking of how man got hooked on time, or, to be more exact, why we perceive it as we do, there is a possibility different from Guyau's view, one connected with our internal body rhythms.

Every system in the body, from the simplest to the most complex, is a clock in itself. These body clocks regulate such things as heart rate, respiration, gastric secretions, and enzyme release. Although we are unaware of their primal rhythms, the unconscious mind knows of them; it hears the concert so to speak, even though we cannot see the stage. One example of this is a person awakening at a prespecified time without the use of an alarm clock. How often have you told yourself on retiring, "I must get up at exactly seven o'clock, no later," and only moments before the alarm sounds, you reach over and turn it off? For some people this "head clock" works with amazing accuracy; under hypnosis it operates with uncanny precision. An order given to a hypnotized subject to perform a particular action after a stated time interval will usually be obeyed on the nose. Somehow, the person unconsciously marks time with his or her internal body clocks. It seems that our sense of time is also inherently locked into physical body rhythms. This may explain why in ASCs, when the mind transcends the body, it also leaves behind the wakeful passage of time— the living body is still ticking, but there is no one at home to read the clock.

We have mentioned two possibilities to account for our particular perception of the passage of time. But there is a third; the so-called "Three Arrows of Time"—the evolutionary, the thermodynamic, and the cosmologic.

The evolutionary arrow represents the apparent irreversibility of biological evolution. By this one means it is highly improbable that a given set of mutations and a given environment will repeat themselves so that the steps of evolution will be exactly retraced. In fact, as evolutionary complexity increases this probability grows smaller. As the authority on time direction and evolution, Harold F. Blum, has commented, "It would be difficult to deny that the over-all effect of evolution is irreversible: the Ammonites, the Dinosaur and Lepidodendron are gone beyond recall."[23]

The second arrow of time comes from the second law of thermodynamics; it states that in a closed system left alone, events tend to randomize themselves rather than maintaining or heightening their organization. A familiar example of this from everyday life is the effect of stirring when cream is poured into a cup of coffee. In a short while, we obtain a liquid of uniform color, and however long we stir, the contents of the cup never revert to their separate states of coffee and cream. Throughout the physical world this undirectional tendency toward disorganization is a dominant theme, and it serves to reinforces our notion of the unidirectional sense of time.

The third arrow is a cosmological one. Here, we are confronted with the observation that the universe is continuously expanding outward. The Newtonian universe used clocks to measure time, but this modern picture suggests itself as a clock—one always flowing in a single direction.

As many physical scientists argue, the unidirectional nature of the Three Arrows of Time supports our notion of the passage of time. However, these arrows are all based on average, macroscopic observations, and, quantum physics has taught us to be suspicious of macroscopic events—they are not the whole story. The microcosm has a reality of its own, radically different from everyday, large-scale observations, but just as real. As the brilliant theoretical physicist David Finkelstein of New York's Yeshiva University puts it: "The way has been prepared to turn over the structure of present physics, to consider space, time and mass as illusions in the same way temperature is only a sensory illusion."

In recent years it has become clear that all of our mental abilities are only potential capacities which we can realize through learning. Whereas animals inherit particular patterns of sensory awareness, we have to learn to construct all our patterns of awareness from our own experience. This is the price we pay for the privilege of thinking and, according to Bertrand Russell, it is what fouled up our perception of time. In his famous essay "Mysticism and Logic," Russell says, "There is some sense—easier to feel than state—in which time is an unimportant and superficial characteristic of reality . . ." By "some sense" Russell is referring to mystic consciousness. He goes on to say that "a certain emancipation from slavery to time is essential to philosophic thought." He could have just as well said: "A certain emancipation from slavery to time is essential to the understanding of precognition."

We speculated earlier that in certain altered states of consciousness the enclosure properties of "inside" and "outside" break down. These are spatial properties. But space, as we understand it today, is insepara- bly fused with time. It does not take much extrapolation to argue that in certain ASCs the temporal properties of "before" and "after" break down. At present, this must stand as our only explanation for precogni- tion.

Again, to quote from T. S. Eliot's profound and poetic dissertation on time, *Four Quartets:*

> *Time past and time future*
> *Allow but a little consciousness.*
> *To be conscious is not to be in time.*

9
Psychokinesis and Life Fields

The magnet loves the loadstone, but does the loadstone also love the magnet, or is it attracted to it against its will?

A twelfth-century physicist

Life Fields and the Human Aura

The sea pansy is a delicate creature about the size and color of a ripe strawberry, and just about as pulpy. It lives burrowed beneath the ocean floor as much as fifty feet under water. As biological systems go, it is relatively uncomplicated, in all but one mysterious way. When disturbed, the sea pansy sends out shimmering waves of iridescent green light in spheres about its body. The light can easily be photographed, and it is bright enough to read by, which is not unusual. What is unusual, though, is the form of the sea pansy's light—it's "cold"; it has no heat content. By contrast, most manmade light sources are "hot" and very wasteful; the incandescent bulb, for example, gives off only ten percent light and ninety percent heat. Thus, the sea pansy—and some forty other creatures of the deep—possess an incredibly efficient mechanism for light production. This phenomenon, called bioluminescence, is several million years old, but it was only recently found that the light comes from a giant photoprotein,[1] and, to this day, no one knows just how the pansy's primitive nervous system switches on the molecule. It is one of many energy systems in nature which remain a mystery.

Like the sea pansy, many of our human energy systems are just beginning to relinquish their secrets.

The human body, we know, is wrapped in a cocoon, a finely spun electromagnetic blanket. It does not shine with the brilliance of the sea

228

pansy's light. In fact, the body's electromagnetism is invisible to the naked eye, but it is there nonetheless. Every body function, from the blink of an eye to the luxury of conjuring a daydream, adds spindles of current to the cocoon. These currents, called biocurrents, are characteristic of all life forms. Attach the electrodes of an EEG to a person's scalp, and you see unequivocal evidence of the electromagnetic fields of the brain. Attach an EKG to a person's chest, and the somewhat stronger biocurrents of the heart are evident. But the invisible life fields spun by flowing biocurrents do not terminate abruptly at the surface of the skin. They extend outward, pulsating and flaring in harmony with the psychophysical state of the organism. The field generated by the beating of the human heart, for example, has been detected as far as four feet from the body,[2] and as technology improves fields will be picked up at even greater distances.

There is nothing mysterious about the body's invisible electromagnetic sheath. Whenever a current flows through a conductive material, be it a copper wire or muscle fiber, a dynamic field is generated. From the early days of Hooke's classic experiments with frogs' legs and copper wire, scientists have had every reason to suspect that all living organisms are surrounded by reactive fields. Because of their weak intensity, detecting them has been another story, one which really waited until this century to be told. The refinement in detection technology of the last three decades has permitted great strides.

Yale University's Dr. Harold S. Burr, one of the pioneering researchers in the area of life fields, has repeatedly demonstrated how humans wear their physical and mental states like suits of invisible clothes draped about the body. Burr developed a sensitive high-resistance voltmeter equipped with silver-chloride electrodes that can measure many subtle changes in body fields. The electrodes never come in direct contact with the person, but measure the fields at a distance. In a year-long test with women college students, measurements of their electromagnetic fields were taken each day. Burr found that each woman showed small daily fluctuations, and that once a month each one showed a huge increase in voltage,[3] sharp flarings directly correlated with ovulation. Thus, each woman, quite unknowingly, projected an invisible corona characteristic of her physiological state. The field was always there to pick up; it only required a detector of the appropriate sensitivity to reveal it.

Body fields have even been used to detect disease. In an experiment at New York's Bellevue Hospital the fields of 1,000 women were studied. In 102 cases, researchers found abnormal voltage gradients when measurements were made between the abdomen and the cervix. Medical examinations showed that ninety-five of these women had cancer of either the cervix or the uterus.[4]

If body fields are a reality, and if they are being used diagnostically, can certain people of gifted sensitivity perceive such fields, and in doing so, accurately and fluently make medical diagnoses? Are psychics, like the fairytale child, able to see the emperor's new clothes? Virtually all healers studied claim this to be the case, but they go a step further: They claim to *see* the psychophysical drapings as a dance of colorful and pulsating lights whirling in vortices about a person. And these claims are made even though the radiations, which unmistakably are there, lie outside the visible portion of the electromagnetic spectrum. The question is thus: Do certain individuals who can see auras possess retinas which are sensitive to the known, invisible electromagnetic fields of the body ("visual extension")?—or, is the human body surrounded by *another* field, one composed of *visible,* albeit faint, light?

The argument long favored in parapsychology has centered on the theory of visual extension, and it has received continual support since all attempts to detect a *visible* body field have ended in darkness. But the theory of visual extension, although appealing, is an intellectual embarrassment whose full ramifications border on the ridiculous. To have eyes that are visually sensitive to infrared radiation or other portions of the nonvisible spectrum would not only permit one to look out the window and see a crowd of people as vibrating, cigar-shaped cocoons all but wearing their problems on their cuffs; such a sensitive person would see an entirely different world. Since all objects emit infrared (heat) radiation, the person so endowed would live in a world which knew no darkness. When the lights of a room were shut off at night, the bulbs, lamp shades, and furniture would glow brightly until they were swamped out by the morning sunlight. And, on a hot summer day, a black asphalt road would rage with the brilliance of a fiery furnace. Such visual extension would be a curse, not a blessing. Yet despite these real complications, the theory of visual extension has repeatedly been used by parapsychologists to account for sightings of the human aura; when you have only one theory, there is a great tendency to clutch it like a life raft. Else, the phenomenon it purports to explain falls into an occult abyss.

All of that was true until late 1972 when a sophisticated experiment made visual extension unnecessary as an explanation for seeing the human aura. The body, stripped of its clothes, *does* have a *visible* glow! And what's more, the encompassing halo appears to be brightly colored (as psychics have always insisted), to pulsate at definite frequencies, and to assume geometric configurations which are presumably correlated with specific psychophysical states.*

The discovery story is interesting in itself.[5] Dr. Richard Dobrin was in a quandary. He had a close friend (whom he regarded as level-headed, intelligent, and honest) who claimed that he could see his own body cocoon. What's more, the man, named John, an established and highly regarded M.D., claimed both voluntary control over the the flaring and ebbing of his field, and an ability to discern its vivid colors and sculptured shapes. As a radiation physicist at the New York University Medical Center, Dobrin was well acquainted with the known radiations characteristic of living matter. He knew that they were invisible to the human eye. Thus, his friend's claim offered an interesting challenge—either John had a unique pair of eyes, he was hallucinating, or there was a new, undiscovered energy field which surrounded the human body. In any case, Dobrin reasoned he had something significant to learn about his friend. Should the experimental odyssey lead to a new energy field, so much the better for diagnostic medicine. Working in the evenings at the Institute for Bioenergetic Analysis in New York City, Dobrin and an interdisciplinary team of physicians and physical scientists set out to study John.

The task was unusually difficult. The radiations John emitted would be weak at best, and if any energy lay in the visible band, a totally *dark* room, free from all stray light, would be required to detect it. In constructing the lightless room the researchers made several startling discoveries. Certain construction materials, for instance, could not be used. Ordinary sealing putty, for example, which was needed to fill in cracks, threw off too much radiation, as did certain types of paint. After three months of laboriously picking, testing, and eliminating dozens of materials, the room was ready. It had an ambient dark current of less than one billionth of an ampere. But now, with a room almost totally black, and containing ultrasensitive detection equipment, another problem arose: Certain articles of clothing, due to their electrostatic discharge and the fluorescence of certain dyes, could not be worn in the room. Nylon, for example, was a forbidden garment. After another month of clothing tests the experiment was ready to begin. At this point Dobrin felt that he had the most sensitive light detection laboratory in the country. If the human body had a visible aura,

*Here, we are not talking about the ill-understood Kirlian displays of colorful, flaring coronas. In the Kirlian process an external electric charge is delivered to the body to produce an image that is captured on film. But other recent research reveals that the body, without being externally sparked, naturally emits its own *visible* aura.

it was not going to get out of the room undetected.

One evening in December of 1972, John entered the room bare-chested and the door was sealed. He stood about twenty inches in front of a photo-multiplier tube—a device which detects small quanta of light and amplifies them to readable currents. The detection equipment was wired to a record-ing chart outside the dark room. Over an intercom John was asked to increase and decrease his fields—the instructions were randomly inter-changed. Sometimes he would have to increase his emanations three times in succession before he was told to decrease them. What the research team found was profound. Quite simply, John glowed! His body emitted a *visible* field, and by turning himself on maximally, he could increase his "shine" by more than 500 percent.

This is the first proof of a human aura composed of light falling between the blue and red portions of the visible spectrum, and, it is the discovery of a wholly new energy field characteristic of humans.

Since that eventful day, the Energy Research Group (ERG) at the Institute for Bioenergetic Analysis has worked at a feverish pace to explore their new find. The group, headed by psychiatrist Dr. Carl Kirsch, has found that John's performance is not always consistent. When he arrives at the laboratory in the evenings feeling exhausted or worn out from a hard day's work, his visible field is not so bright as on those days when he feels perky and fit. So far, his field has been a barometer of his moods.

One question the researchers immediately attacked was that of how John controlled his emanations. Did he tense his muscles? Wrinkle his forehead? Grit his teeth? Certainly, these things would increase the electro-chemical potential in his body cells and add spindles of current to his *invisible* electromagnetic sheath. But did they also increase his visible aura? Did he conjure thoughts of anger and hate? Did he work himself into a psychological and physical frenzy? "No," says Dr. Kirsch, "John is able to increase his body field through breathing exercises. He never works himself up into a state of anger. In fact, if anything, that would decrease his emanations." Kirsch, Dobrin, and the others are quick to point out that the idea of increasing one's visible aura through rhythmic breathing is linked to the yogic notion of prana—the psychic energy that a person taps through breathing exercises—but they are cautious not to take the correlation too far, for the research is still in its early stages. "Right now," says Dobrin, "all we can say is that we are detecting a new radiation field which sur-rounds the human body; one that may have great diagnostic potential. We know that the radiation lies in the portion of the electromagnetic spectrum which theoretically makes it visible to the human eye. To my knowledge, in the past this visible field has only been reported by psychics, never experimentally proven."

The next question was a very human one: Does everyone have this visible aura? Dobrin and Kirsch readily give an affirmative answer, but they quickly follow it with the qualifier that not everyone's aura is of equal strength, and certainly not everyone has equal control over its pulsations. One night Dobrin tested his own aura. Stripping, he entered the dark room only to find that his "glow," despite his years of yogic training, was badly wanting. It was hardly higher than the room's ambient dark current. Kirsch, on the other hand, shines in the dark room, and can control his field to some degree. Others who have been tested also show mixed results. As with any human characteristic, different people possess it to different degrees. Is a strong glow a sign of health? Is it evidence of inner peace and contentment? Do the halos of lovers pulsate in unison? Do the colors in a person's field reveal his personality?

Obviously, many questions now confront the Energy Research Group. Eventually, they hope to place yogis, Zen monks, and psychics in their chamber, and one teammate, Dr. Myron Kolov, a psychologist, is interested in seeing how a person's aura is affected by various ASCs. What happens to an individual's glow when he or she is dreaming? Hypnotized? On drugs? Alcohol? One long-term goal of the group is to understand the colors, pulsations, and shapes of the visible aura as they relate to mental and physical disease. "I think that what we have here," says Dobrin, "is the first stage of a revolutionary new diagnostic tool. Perhaps one more powerful than X rays, EEGs, and other techniques used today."

When that inevitable day finally arrives, and M.D.s are making diagnoses via the human aura, psychics may chide them for their tardiness.

From Russia with Love

Parapsychologists in both the United States and the Soviet Union have been studying body fields for an obvious reason—in the life forces lie the missing pieces to the psi puzzle. If we pause to consider the significant role fields play in our psychophysical constitution, we catch a glimpse of the secrets they hold.

Earlier this century atoms were regarded as tiny planetary models with electrons orbiting around a small hard nucleus which consisted of protons and neutrons. It was a convenient picture then, and is even now for some educational purposes, but the model is a naive one. More recently it has become clear that electrons more resemble hazy clouds of electricity vibrat-

ing with wavelike patterns around the nucleus. Virtually all of the mass and
the energy of the atom are contained in this hard, dense core. Proportion-
ally, there is more empty space inside an atom than there is in our entire
solar system. If all that empty space were squeezed out of a person, the
amount of solid matter remaining would be no larger than a speck of dirt.
This space of which we are almost entirely composed is filled with three
types of fields—electromagnetic, nuclear, and gravitational. In the words of
the biologist Dr. Lyall Watson, "We are hollow men and our insubstantial
bodies are strung together with electromagnetic and nuclear forces that do
no more than create the illusion of matter."[6] It is little wonder that every
psychophysical change we experience can be detected in alterations of our
body fields.

The importance of body fields today has made them a prime candidate
for attempting to explain certain psychic phenomena. Suggestions have
been made that telepathic information might ride on the biocurrents generated by the brain, and that these currents may be intensely focused like
sunlight through a magnifying glass to move an object psychokinetically.
The idea is appealing because it provides a familiar carrier, electromagnetic
waves, to cart information back and forth between sender and receiver.
Classical materialists argue that if the brain generates an invisible electromagnetic field which can be picked up by an EEG, and a *visible* field (even
one below most people's vision threshold), why can't these forces extend out
across space like radio or television waves, and in similar manner carry
audiovisual messages? In fact, the radio–television analogy has been a favorite paradigm of many parapsychologists ever since Upton Sinclair published
his psychical work, *Mental Radio.*[7] But if an idea became a fact merely by
its popularity, psychical phenomena would long since have been satisfac-
torily explained in terms of the body's known biocurrents. To the contrary,
if anything is clear from parapsychological research, it is that known electromagnetic carriers are not the messengers of paranormal information. All
attempts to understand psychic events in terms of the well-known body
fields have intrinsic and intractable problems.

The human brain weighs less than a pound and contains over
90,000,000,000 cells. The cells are arranged in an intricate communications
network, firing off electrical impulses. Every time the brain is called upon
to regulate a body function, biocurrents are generated. But even considering
the astronomical number of brain cells, the electrical potential of the brain
is extremely weak, on the order of five to fifty microvolts, or a radiative
power of ten to twenty watts. This is barely enough to power a small light
bulb, let alone transmit a telepathic message over several miles or levitate

an object. Even during the electrical frenzy of an epileptic fit, the brain's power does not appreciably exceed twenty watts.

Many admirable efforts have been made to salvage the electromagnetic model to account for psi occurrences. The main impetus for this effort is the fact that electromagnetic theory is the solidest and best understood mathematical cornerstone of modern physics. It must apply! has been the cry of many researchers. One of the most comprehensive attempts to apply it to psi phenomena has been made by the Soviet cyberneticist I. M. Kogan. But even his titan efforts have borne a single disappointing conclusion: Known electromagnetic radiation originating in the human body is too faint to support the simplest psi event, even under the most ideal conditions.[8] We must face the fact that man is not a good physical power station.

Even though electromagnetic radiation is not the bearer of paranormal messages, it does play a tantalizing minor role in those events, and as such it may be an excellent index of psi occurrences. Just as the heat energy generated when a block is pushed across a rough surface is an excellent indicator of the magnitude of the mechanical energy exerted by one's arm in moving the block, so too may the swelling and ebbing of the body's visible and invisible electromagnetic sheath be an excellent indicator of a yet undetected psychic energy field. And there is every reason to believe that all these fields are in some way connected. One of several studies that dramatically demonstrates the electromagnetic barometer of a psychical event was conducted on the Russian psychic, Nelya Mikhailova.[9]

At the Utomskii Institute in Leningrad, neurophysiologist Dr. Genady Sergeyev rigorously studied Mikhailova's extraordinary talent for psychokinesis. Mikhailova was wired to an electroencephalograph and an electrocardiograph, and measurements were made of her physiology while she was resting calmly. Sergeyev discovered that even in a relaxed state she had a magnetic field around her body that was one tenth as powerful as that of the earth's. He also found that she had an unusual brainwave pattern. Fifty times more voltage was generated at the back of her head than at the front. Amazingly, all this energy was generated before she attempted any psychokinetic feats.

In one of the most difficult psychokinetic tests ever contrived, a raw egg was broken into saline solution in a large aquarium six feet in front of Mikhailova. Her task was to separate the white of the egg from the yolk and move the two apart. While the demonstration was taking place, closely monitored by cameras, her EEG showed intense emotional excitement and great activity in the deep levels of the brain which coordinate and filter information. As the white and yolk were separating, the electrocardiograph showed an irregular action of the heart which is characteristic of crises. Her pulse soared to 240 beats a minute, four times its normal level, and high percentages of blood sugar were recorded together with other endocrinal disturbances characteristic of a stress reaction.[10]

The tests lasted thirty minutes, and during this time Nelya lost over two pounds in weight. At the end of the day she was very weak and temporarily blind. Her ability to taste was impaired; she had pains in her arms and legs; she felt dizzy; she was unable to sleep for several days thereafter.

The high readings of all physiological processes monitored indicate that Nelya's body was working hard to increase its natural biocurrents. Everything was functioning at peak output. During the experiment Sergeyev also detected a synchronization of physiological processes which gave an increased overall body field. With a field-effect detector placed near Nelya during the test, he found that at the exact moment she began separating the white from the yolk, there were sudden changes in the electrostatic and magnetic measurements of her field. As she strained to bring her influence to bear, the electric field began to pulse until it was undergoing a regular fluctuation at a rate of four cycles per second. This beating was precisely synchronized to a pulse rate of four beats a second, and finally brainwave action fell in at the same rhythm. Her fields were throbbing in unison, and they seemed to produce a field that was concentrated on the spot where her eyes were fixed, a psychic field which eluded detection.[11]

What must be noted here is that the egg white and yolk were definitely separating, but the division was not a direct action of the electromagnetic fields which Mikhailova was generating and which the detectors were picking up. The electrostatic and magnetic activity occurred very close to her body, which was six feet from the water tank containing the egg. As little as a foot in front of Mikhailova, the detectors showed that the electromagnetic field had already dropped, quite predictably, to a level so faint it was below the threshold of the equipment. Clearly, no appreciable amount of this energy was reaching the tank; certainly not enough to separate the egg. As the scientists concluded, the electromagnetic energy was an indicator, a sort of measurable side effect, of a powerful, mysterious field which was stretching from Nelya to the egg.

Around Nelya, Sergeyev detected vibrations that *acted* like magnetic waves. He reports, "The moment these magnetic vibrations or waves occur, they cause the object Mrs. Mikhailova focuses on, even if it is something nonmagnetic, to act as if magnetized. It causes the object to be attracted to her or repelled from her."[12] As Dr. Smith had observed in her enzymatic studies with Mr. Estebany, the *net effect* of the action was what one would expect from a magnetic field, even though no ostensible field could be detected en route from sender to object.

This fact that no electromagnetic field has ever been detected traveling between the sender and the object undergoing psychokinetic motion does not merely imply that the field is too weak for even the most sensitive equipment. Instead, it says that no known field is present. To *push* a physical object, or to *levitate* it, requires a respectable amount of energy. In sliding a book across a table top, for example, the force of friction must be overcome before the book will move, and in levitating it there is the ubiquitous force of gravity to be overridden. Further, in psychokinetically moving a compass needle, the earth's magnetic field must first be overpowered. The forces of friction, gravitation, and geomagnetism holding an object are easily calculable, and the energy needed to overcome them is well within the limits of good detection equipment. If anything seems clear about psychokinesis, it is that no form of known radiation passes from the human body to the object acted upon.* All evidence to date seems to say that the synchronization of body fields in a person performing psychokinesis is a peripheral or auxiliary effect accompanying a process not yet discovered. That process, say parapsychologists, seems to be the generation and propagation of psychic energy. If such energy is ever to be detected, they feel that psychokinetic phenomena are undoubtedly the best place to look. For it is in psychokinesis that the energy would be most highly concentrated and focused.

Poltergeists

Tropication Arts, Inc. is a novelty and souvenir company with a wholesale warehouse in Miami, Florida. Most of its items are inexpensive imports from the Far East, handpainted ashtrays and vases depicting palm trees, parrots, and flamingos, for sale to tourists in the Sunshine State. Until late 1966 Tropication Arts went happily along, enjoying, with hundreds of other gift firms, Florida's booming tourism. But then something happened. Around mid-December, the owners, Alvin Laubheim and Glen Lewis, noticed an unusual amount of breakage. Alligator and sailfish ashtrays,

---

Sergeyev has recorded electrical fields as high as 10,000 volts per centimeter in the vicinity of the object at the time of motion. However, detectors reveal nothing in the intervening space between subject and object. ("PK in the Soviet Union,"* Montague Ullman, delivered at the Parapsychological Association meeting, Virginia, September, 1973.)

cocktail and shot glasses, and beer mugs were increasingly found broken on the floor of the large warehouse. The breakage never occurred at night when the warehouse was empty, only during working hours. At first the owners attributed it to carelessness on the part of the shipping clerks, but as the weeks progressed it became clear to everyone that something peculiar was going on. And it was becoming costly to the small firm.

Shortly after noon on January 13, a box of daggers fell off its shelf. A few minutes later a shot glass fell in the aisle and other items just seemed to pop off the shelves. One box fell a few feet in front of one observer, Mr. Sinclair Buntin. The box, he says, "fell at an angle which it could not have been at if it had just been pushed off—about a thirty degree angle out away from the shelf." He picked up the scattered items, put them in the box, and replaced it on the shelf. But he had only taken a few steps away when the box was flung at his heels. No one was near the shelf. Just then a newspaper reporter arrived. As he walked down one aisle, a beer mug, which had been stacked on its side, leaped off its shelf, traveled several feet in the air, and landed with a thud. Mr. Buntin picked it up and returned it to its proper place only to have everyone see it defiantly fly into the air again.

On January 14, the Miami police were called in. Patrolman William Killam arrived at the warehouse certain he had been selected for a bum assignment dealing with "a lot of nuts." The complaint clerk at the station had told him "this person who called said that he had a ghost in his place of business . . . going around breaking ashtrays and he said they were just coming up off the floor and breaking." Perfunctorily Killam made his rounds of the warehouse, shaking shelves and stamping on the floor to see if this would knock an object to the floor. As he began to walk down aisle four, he was shocked. A Zombie highball glass, which was sitting next to several others, suddenly lifted itself into the air, landed several feet away on the floor, and shattered. There was no one anywhere near the shelf. Killam shook the shelf roughly several times, but no glass even fell over. Owners, shipping clerks, policemen, an insurance agent, and psychical investigators who were called in all came to share the same opinion: there was a poltergeist in the warehouse.[13]

But the story does not stop here. The Tropication case is different from many others on several accounts. In most poltergeist cases people see objects travel through the air, or strike the ground, but it is highly unusual to see an object actually start to move from rest. In the Maimi warehouse, thirteen items out of an eventual 224 that mysteriously fell were seen by one or more people to go from a stationary condition, into the air, and onto the floor. Two psi researchers, Dr. William G. Roll of the University of Virginia and Dr. J. G. Pratt of Duke, arrived at the scene in early January. With a staff of workers they recorded every incident, and themselves witnessed seventy-eight happenings. They were looking for a common denominator, a clue to the breakage mysteries, and they found one. Although various shipping clerks, painters, and clerical help came and went during the days of the poltergeist occurrences, one young man, a nineteen-year-old refugee from Cuba named Julio Vasquez, was present for every breakage. Julio was not near the items when they fell, but he was always in the large room. Once Roll and Pratt had catalogued all the events and their locales, they noticed that certain spots in the warehouse were favored by the poltergeist. As an experiment, "decoy" items were securely placed in the favored spots and observed. Whenever Julio was taken out of the room the items never budged, but when he was brought back, little time would pass before a decoy flew through the air. With the area observationally under control, there was no chance of trickery. And, the breakage continued. In his 1967 case report Roll writes: "No evidence was found in connection with any of the disturbances indicating that an object was ever moved by any magical means or trick devices or was pushed or thrown with the intention to deceive anyone about the nature of the event."[14]

Was Julio unconsciously moving the objects by psychokinesis? Was he, in effect, the warehouse poltergeist? If so, with 224 incidences carefully recorded in greatest detail, could Roll and Pratt find some clue to the type of energy Julio used?

The two researchers, joined by Dr. Donald S. Burdick, a Duke mathematician, and Dr. William T. Joines, an electrical engineer, turned up some interesting facts. When they plotted the length traveled by each item and the angle of rotation it went through to land where it did, the data showed that the energy which moved the items did not follow the standard inverse square law applicable to all forms of electromagnetic radiation. Instead, it diminished by the *law of exponential decay*—the diminution process found in such natural processes as bacterial and radioactive decay. In two of three poltergeist cases Roll had studied prior to the Miami incident, he also observed this exponential law. In a purely physical sense it means that the energy that moves the objects dies out at a faster rate than it would if it were electromagnetic in nature; it's shorter-lived. The interdisciplinary team also found that almost all the incidences occurred when Julio's *back* was toward the object, not when he was facing it. And, the items that moved were on Julio's *left* side, not his right. Whatever the nature of the energy, it seemed to exhibit a preferential direction with respect to Julio's body. From the deviations of where a shelf item was found on the floor, Roll determined that the energy must have moved in a *counterclockwise* direction, swinging the items in the direction from south to north. And, they moved *away* from Julio.[15]

The curvilinear nature of the energy field was an interesting observation. If the psychokinetic energy possessed a linear field, it would have hit an item like an oncoming train and knocked it off the shelf in a straight line trajectory. The interaction between the item and the energy would have been a one-shot, hit-and-run affair. But from the rotations found, it appeared that the energy captured an object, carried it along in a curved fashion, then dropped it when the beam became too weak or was instantaneously shut off at the source. There was no question in the researchers' minds that Julio was the warehouse poltergeist.

The psychoanalyst Nandor Fodor has described the poltergeist as a "bundle of projected repressions" that sometimes lash out at an object like a reflex reaction. In one of the Miami disturbances, immediately after an alligator ashtray had broken, Roll detected a noticeable change in Julio—he was less tense and angry. Roll asked him how he felt at that moment. "I feel happy; that thing [the breakage] makes me feel happy; I don't know why," the boy responded. After each incident Julio always felt relaxed, as though a great weight had been taken off his body. Was it purely a psychological reaction, or was it due to a physical release of energy pent up in Julio?

Psychologist Dr. Gardner Murphy says in his book *Personality* that "the ultimate elements in personality structure are the needs or tensions." Tension, as anyone knows who has had a headache or been under emotional stress, is a concentration of energy in particular tissues. These tensions are connected and spread from one region of the body to another in successive wavelike collisions. "The result," writes Murphy, "is a *tension system* whose lawful structure is expressed in terms of the relative strengths of the tensions and the relative rigidity of barriers to their diffusion." It seems that for Julio the poltergeist breakages were literally a means of releasing tensions.

If there is one common factor found in almost all poltergeist cases, it is the presence of a teen-ager. It seems that the level of emotional adjustment associated with adolescence is directly related to recurrent spontaneous psychokinesis (RSPK). Witness just a few cases:

At the Seaford, Long Island, home of Mr. and Mrs. James Hermann, sixty-seven mischievous events occurred, from objects flying across the room to broken bottles. They have a son, thirteen, and a daughter, twelve.

The Beck family in Indianapolis, Indiana, suffered fourteen mysterious arm and leg punctures which resembled bat bites; some invisible energy pricked their skin like needles. The Becks have a thirteen-year-old daughter.

The home of Mrs. Pearl Howell in Clayton, North Carolina, was illuminated nightly by sudden and brilliant flashes of energy. Glowing flares exploded like flash bulb lights without warning. Mrs. Howell's nineteen-year-old daughter was always on the scene.

At her Newark, New Jersey, home, Mrs. Maybelle Clark watched helplessly as some of her most precious possessions were destroyed by fifty-nine poltergeist visits. Mrs. Clark's thirteen-year-old grandson lives with her.[16]

The literature is filled with such incidents involving adolescents. Many times poltergeist activities show a measure of intelligence or purpose, as when objects are aimed at particular persons. In one family case involving a young teen-age girl, only articles belonging to her mother were broken. One evening, from a collection of thirty-five phonograph recordings, two mysteriously fell out of their jackets on the shelf and and broke on the floor. The titles were "My Mother" and "At Home with Me."[17] The periods of puberty and adolescence appear to be critical for poltergeist phenomena.

But we all have tensions, and we all have gone through the emotional and sexually frustrating times of adolescence without causing ashtrays and kitchen plates to fly about the room or unexplained lights to flash on and off. Is there something special about people with "poltergeist personalities" that might explain their unconscious psychokinetic ability?

Determined to find an answer, Dr. Roll brought Julio to Duke University. On February 10, 1967, Dr. John Altrocchi began a personality study of Julio. First Julio took the standard Minnesota Mutiphasic Personality Inventory (MMPI) test. It was clear that he was not a very happy person. Dr. Altrocchi found evidence of "anger and rebellion, feelings of not being part of the social environment, a feeling that he doesn't get what is coming to him and lack of strongly pleasant experiences in life." Also, there had been problems in Julio's homelife in early December, just ten days before the onset of the warehouse incidences. His stepmother had insisted that Julio move out, and a series of bitter arguments had ensued. He had had horrible nightmares during December that had grown worse in January; he would see himself brutally killed and attending his own funeral. Up to this point in his life Julio had never experienced such morbid and lifelike dreams. Altrocchi found that Julio's unhappiness resulted not only in anger but also in suicidal tendencies.

Roll thought a brainwave examination might reveal some anomalies, so Julio was taken to Dr. Walter D. Obrist, an EEG expert. The results, however, were negative. He found that awake and sleeping Julio had brainwave patterns typical of a nineteen-year-old boy. Determined to get more answers, Roll took Julio to Dr. Harvey T. McPherson, an endocrinologist and professor of medicine at Duke University. If puberty and adolescence are prime times for RSPK, reasoned Roll, perhaps there was an imbalance in Julio's endocrine system. Although McPherson could only find a slight case of acne and slightly overactive adrenals in Julio, one strange fact emerged which could be significant. During the three months just prior to the onset of the warehouse disturbances, Julio had had no less than three childhood diseases: chicken pox, measles, and mumps—one right on top of the other.[18] Something was occurring in his system.

On February 1, Julio had terminated his employment with Tropication Arts, Inc.—he had little choice in the matter. Since that day, and to the time of this writing, there have been no further poltergeist incidents at the warehouse. Also, since Julio's emotional life has stabilized, he is no longer "possessed by a ghost." In his presence no objects fly through the air, even though now he has tried to consciously perform for scientists. As with all poltergeist activity, it seems to come during a critical phase in a young person's life, last from a few weeks to a few months, then vanish like a ghost.

Roll and his Sherlock Holmes team of a psychologist, a mathematician, and an engineer have developed a sophisticated and rigorous procedure for analyzing poltergeist cases. Their observation that the items in the Miami disturbances moved *behind* Julio, to his *left,* and always *away* from him, and the fact that the energy field moved in a *counterclockwise* direction and followed the *law of exponential decay* are all valuable clues at this early stage of scientific investigation. To continue their studies, Roll and his sleuths must patiently wait until some other teen-ager, in the throes of an emotional crisis, develops a poltergeist personality. Unfortunately, there is no way to tell when, where, or to whom that will happen.

The Smaller, the Better

Unconscious psychokinesis, as seen in poltergeist activity, is a seemingly effortless task. The person, with no noticeable strain, emits a sudden burst of energy; it is always short-lived, usually undirected, and knocks over or captures the first object in its path. Ostensibly, pent-up tensions in certain individuals generate the requisite psychic energy to move objects, or, as some parapsychologists believe, during the period of adolescence a person is unconsciously "tuned" through a highly active endocrine system to an internal source of psychic energy. But *conscious* psychokinesis is a different matter entirely. It virtually always involves herculean effort and results in mental and physical exhaustion—if not more serious symptoms. Where the poltergeist person feel relieved and relaxed after a psychokinetic feat, a person like Nelya Mikhailova feels drained.

If we contrast the energy requirements of psychokinesis with phenomena such as clairvoyance and precognition, we see a striking difference. PK involves mental anguish while the latter two require mental passivity. But the difference is deeper and more profound than this. Clairvoyance and precognition are information acquisition processes. A person obtains information from a sealed letter or from the future. But in both cases he is a *receiver* and *passive*. The person initially directs his thoughts to the particular task at hand, then sits back, relaxes, and clears his mind to transcend space and time for the desired information. In telepathy, we see a dual role, and a more vital distinction. Again, the telepathic *receiver* is *passive,* opening his consciousness to psychic waves. But the sender does have to concentrate on the target, working hard to transmit the thoughts. Of course, a telepathic sender never need undergo the physical torture that someone like Nelya Mikhailova endures to muster energy for a psychokinetic feat. However, to explain this difference in effort by saying that to levitate an object is more difficult than to transmit a thought—although possibly true—is to miss an important distinction between the psychic energy requirements for telepathy and psychokinesis.

The point is this: A telepathic sender is primarily concerned with transmitting *information,* while an individual engaged in psychokinesis is concerned with transmitting *energy.* But isn't telepathic information really energy? The answer is a flat no. Information and energy are two entirely different things. As Norbert Wiener, the pioneer of cybernetics, said, "The mechanical brain does not secrete thought as the liver secretes bile . . . nor does it put it out in the form of energy as the muscle puts out its activity.

Information is information, not matter or energy. No materialism which does not admit this can survive at the present day."[19] An analogy should serve to distinguish the important difference between energy and information. If you are taking a camera picture in a fairly dark room, your flash bulb must provide a considerable amount of light *energy*. Here, the quantity of energy is the important feature. However, a warning buoy anchored in the ocean at night can convey its *information* as long as you see the faintest glimmer of light. Here, the quantity of energy is secondary to the information that the energy carries. This same principle can be seen in normal sensory hearing. If a room is quiet and someone softly utters the phrase "Today is sunny," as long as you clearly hear it, the information has been conveyed. Shouting, that is, using more energy, does not increase your reception of the phrase. Thus, although levitating an object may be more difficult than transmitting a thought, it should be remembered that telepathy is primarily concerned with the transmission of *information*, while psychokinesis is *only* concerned with transmitting sheer *power*.*

This fact has opened up a new line of research. Psychokinesis apparently suffers because people cannot muster the required psychic energy to overcome environmental forces of electromagnetism and gravitation. If this is so, perhaps PK can more easily and reproducibly be demonstrated by using micro-sized objects. Obviously, the lighter the object, the easier it is to move. In fact, why not descend the ladder of weights to the world of subatomic particles, which have virtually no mass? They should be a cinch to move. Well, almost.

This has been the approach of several recent experiments. Dr. Helmut Schmidt has modified his strontium 90 precognitive experiment to accommodate PK testing in an experiment that uses the radioactive decay of strontium nuclei to turn on a circle of nine lights one at a time in either a clockwise or counterclockwise direction. The task of the PK subject is to force the lights to flash in the direction of his choice. As a strontium nucleus decays, it gives up its energy by emitting a beta particle. Several beta emissions, "lumped" together, are of sufficient strength to activate the lights. The mass of a beta particle is 10^{-27} grams, hardly even a weight, and the manipulation of these particles would apparently require much less energy than, say, levitating a book.

*For theoretical attempts to handle psi phenomena in terms of Information Theory see Chari, "Remarks on some Statistical and Informational-Theoretic Models for ESP," *JASPR*, April, 1966. Chari, "Some Generalized Statistical Models for ESP," *JASPR*, Oct. 1969. Robert Taetzsch, "Design of a Psi Communication System," from the Parapsychology Foundation, Inc., N.Y.C.

Schmidt worked with fifteen different subjects, none of whom claimed to possess psi talents. As seems to be the pattern in most psi experiments, not all the subjects achieved positive results, but those few who did racked up odds against chance of 1,000 to one.[20] Although they could not make a pencil roll across a table top, levitate a glass, or spin a compass needle, they could, much to their surprise, apparently manipulate the subatomic particles.

The lighter-than-air philosophy underlying Schmidt's experiments has also been used at Stanford Research Institute by Dr. Harold Puthoff and Russell Targ working with the incredibly gifted Ingo Swann. Besides Swann's clairvoyant and alleged out-of-the-body abilities, he is a superb artisan of psychokinesis.

In one experiment he was placed in a large laboratory. In the center of the room was a giant magnetometer, a device which produces a uniformly decreasing current from a radioactive source deep within a well. The magnetometer was anchored for stability to the concrete foundation of its building, and it was shielded with *mu* metals, the best known magnetic shields. For three days and nights the device had been running smoothly, giving out a continuous wave which was recorded on a moving chart. Nothing had disturbed its rhythm. In fact, when Puthoff and Targ wheeled in an enormous magnet, enough to drive an unshielded magnetometer crazy, this one did not stir.

Swann was shown blueprints of the internal workings of the device and told of its heart, a radioactive core. Swann's task was to perturb that core by altering its subatomic emissions.

No sooner had Swann concentrated on the core when the graph recorder changed from its three-day rhythmic pattern to abrupt high frequency spikes. As long as he stared at the magnetometer, directing his thoughts to its core, the high frequency output continued. At one point Dr. Puthoff engaged Swann in conversation, to see what would happen when his concentration was broken. As they spoke of other things, Puthoff noticed that the graph returned to its smooth-wave output and stayed there. But as soon as he mentioned the magnetometer in the course of the conversation, the sharp spikes returned.[21] It seems that after establishing initial contact with the device Swann had only to think of it in order to produce effects. For Swann, the lightweight task was indeed as easy as the physicists had hoped.

The use of micro-sized objects in PK experiments opens up a whole new area of research, one that seems to offer great promise. Mentally juggling a subatomic particle may not be as visually dramatic (or as comprehendible) as psychokinetically fetching a book from a library shelf, but it may offer something better—experimental repeatability, which, after all, is the crux of the scientific method.

The SRI experiment with Swann and the PK balance scale experiment with Uri Geller were designed to be cheat-proof, and indeed they were. But they do suffer from one flaw which needs be mentioned, even though the point does not invalidate the demonstrations of psychokinesis for either man. The point leaves open to question just what Swann and Geller affected. Did Swann interact with the heart of the magnetometer and Geller with the pan of the scale to cause the anomalous readings, or did they interact with the recorders that plotted the data? The question is fundamental, for if one starts with the hypothesis that an individual can interact with laboratory equipment, and then uses laboratory equipment to measure the interaction, there exists a closed loop of ambiguity. Swann and Geller influenced something, that is sure, but was it the target or the arm of the pen-and-ink recorder? Future experiments now in the planning stage will attempt to overcome this tricky problem.

The reality of psychokinesis—that certain individuals *can* consciously or unconsciously interact with laboratory equipment—presents a serious dilemma to experimentalists. It is quite conceivable that an experimenter's strong desire for particular results might be enough to bias the experimental outcome, not just in parapsychology but in every science. A bacteriologist's disgruntled mood might kill her prize fungus culture. An enthusiastic chemist might unintentionally accelerate the rate of reaction of a solution because that is the result he has his heart set on. And a physicist's anger might dangerously increase the critical mass in a nuclear reaction. Admittedly, these cases are extreme, but they serve to make the point that this is what the reality of psychokinesis means. One day, objectivity in science may mean not only unbiased equipment but also unbiased researchers.

The Psi Menagerie

If a nineteen-year-old boy can by mentation lift a ceramic ashtray and knock over a beer mug, if a fourteen-year-old girl can psychokinetically force two phonograph records from their album jackets, can species lower down the evolutionary ladder—monkeys, cats, and chickens for instance— also perform PK feats? In 1971 James Davis pondered the question. To some scientists it sounded like a harebrained idea. After all, it is hard enough to believe one's eye's in viewing the PK feats of the likes of Geller, Swann and other psychics, but the notion of a chicken controlling a compass needle was ludicrous. Ludicrous to all except Davis. He had already performed his precognitive experiments with hamsters and jirds, and obtained significant results. Here, with the PK phenomenon, he saw an even better chance of success. Is an animal's instinct for survival, he wondered, strong enough to influence laboratory equipment when that equipment is programmed to jeopardize the animal's survival? Animals in the wild routinely encounter severe environmental and predatory hardships. Is at least part of their endurance due to psychical factors rather than to instinct and behavioral conditioning?

Davis first secured a group of young chickens from a farm, all of them between one and two weeks old, a time when constant warmth is essential for their survival. The young chicks were placed under a large heat lamp which was connected to a random generator. Under normal conditions the light would be on for a total of only twelve hours out of every twenty-four-hour period, providing an environment that was too cool for the chicks. If they wished to grow normally, perhaps even to continue living, they would somehow have to psychokinetically perturb the random generator to keep the light on longer than its statistical program called for.

Davis found that the young chicks could indeed do this. Although the light-generator system was tested and retested with the chicks out of the housing and always functioned perfectly, when the chicks were placed under the lamp the light shone with a higher frequency.[22]

Encouraged by the results, Davis decided to go a step further. His next idea sounded so preposterous that it was best not mentioned until the experiment was underway. If young chickens who were dependent on warmth for survival could affect laboratory equipment, could the same results be had by placing fertilized eggs under the lamp? Here, the need for heat would be even more crucial. He obtained a dozen chicken eggs that had been incubated and were only seven days from hatching. Another dozen were placed in a kettle of boiling water and cooked for half an hour until they were hard-boiled. These would serve as the control group. Each batch would in turn be placed in the chamber one foot beneath a 150-watt heat lamp. If the lamp behaved differently for the viable eggs than for the hard-boiled ones, the only apparent reason could be that PK was at play. By now this experiment is well known throughout the parapsychological community, for there is something both eerie and beautiful about the results. The light behaved exactly as it was programmed when the hard-boiled eggs were beneath it. But strangely enough, it kept coming on, and on again, more than it should have, to warm the fertilized eggs to hatching.[23] Did the life force in the eggs fight the generator and win? Davis believes that is precisely what happened, and he is at a loss to come up with an alternative explanation. The equipment functioned flawlessly throughout the entire experiment.

Electronic gadgets—washers, dryers, lamps, ranges, heat combs, toothbrushes, and the rest—although designed to be our slaves are more often our masters. Our almost helpless dependency on machines makes this so. For the mechanically minded person reared in a world of electronic gadgetry, it is somewhat spooky to see a simple, ordinary heat lamp fall under the influence of an embryonic life form. Yet, at the same time the experience is refreshing and reassuring, for it says something about the precious quality of life. Some parapsychologists see in Davis's experiments a glimmering of what physicians commonly call "the will to live"—survival in the face of impossible medical odds. They cite the countless cases on the medical books in which therapeutic procedures, regardless of how modern and how extreme, just cannot be credited with a patient's "miraculous" cure. Does the will to live, in animals and man, broadcast itself into the environment in the time of crises?

Davis's experiments with animal PK are not the only ones that have been performed. Helmut Schmidt has successfully duplicated Davis's work using not a chicken or an egg, but a cat,[24] and others have worked with hamsters, rats, and lizards.[25]

In one experiment, electrodes were implanted into the pleasure centers of the hypothalamus of rats' brains. For many years now Dr. Neal Miller of Rockefeller University has demonstrated that white rats rewarded by electrical stimulation to the pleasure regions of the brain can be trained to regulate their heartbeat and blood pressure, and to blush in only one ear and not the other. But here, in the Miller-type psi experiment, the rats learned to psychokinetically control the very equipment that provided them with pleasure shocks. First, a rat was taught that by stepping on a bar he would be rewarded with a quick, pleasurable high. Typically, an educated rodent soon was frantically dancing up and down on the bar, pressing it several hundred times an hour. In fact, so pleasurable was the experience that he refused food, water, and even sleep in favor of shock stimuli. Then, a random generator was placed in the electronic circuitry. Now half the time the rat jumped on the bar he was greatly disappointed; there was no pleasure shock. At least this is the way the equipment should have worked, but it did not. After initially following its statistical pattern of on-off, soon it was providing the rat with more shocks than it should have, a fact that pleased the experimenter even more than the rat. What had happened? Again—and that hedging word *somehow* must be used—the rat had learned (consciously or unconsciously) to influence the generator in his favor.[26]

Miller's autonomic training experiments with rats have shown that when it comes to receiving pleasurable stimuli, even at the risk of death, the animal still goes for the temporary treat. White rats with electrodes implanted in the pleasure centers of their brains have been known to lower their heart rates in order to get the shock reward to the point of stopping their hearts. Apparently the desire for pleasure can override the instinct for survival. Perhaps this is one reason why the psi experiments with implanted electrodes have yielded such favorable results. Even more than the chicks and eggs that wanted to live, the hedonistic rodents wanted more and more pleasure; so much so that they psychically interacted, and overpowered, the laboratory equipment. Admittedly, animal PK is harder to accept than human PK for many people. But if one is true, the other is not far behind. Psi researchers are actively engaged in both types of PK experiments.

How does the PK interaction occur? What do rats, chicks, eggs, and, for that matter, Geller, Swann, and Nelya Mikhailova broadcast from their own desires to the target object? Currently, the only answer is psychic energy and it may be many years before we learn exactly what that is.

An Environmental Balance

Dr. Gertrude Schmeidler, professor of psychology at City College of New York, has been in parapsychological research for thirty years. She entered the field in the days when ESP was thought to be more a magician's stage trick than the avocation for an eager young Ph.D. But that did not stop her. Over the years she has amassed scores of technical papers, respected association chairs, and the distinction of being a world authority on personality variables as they relate to psychic ability. Those years have also brought a marked change in the attitude of her stolid psychology peers toward parapsychology. "They all are not completely won over yet," says this charming woman, "but before they looked on the field with amused tolerance, now they view it with amused interest." With considerable enthusiasm she adds, "To me, parapsychology seems the most exciting and promising research area there is today. But then I've always felt that way."

Lately, the tireless Dr. Schmeidler has been pursuing a different route to parapsychology. Although as a psychologist her primary interests lie with the personality factors influencing psi, she has begun to investigate its physical nature, and one of her latest experiments, performed in 1972 with Ingo Swann, lays important groundwork for future research.

Normally, when we think of energy, we also think of heat. The two are related. Anyone who has hammered a nail and felt its head grow hot knows that some of the mechanical energy exerted driving the nail into the board is lost through heat. This everyday observation gave Schmeidler an idea. If psychic energy seems to elude detection, perhaps heat is a generated by-product at both the source and the target. Could this heat be measured? Specifically, she wanted to know whether during one of Ingo Swann's PK feats temperature sensors could detect an increase in the surface temperature of his hands, and if they picked up a temperature change at the target. This would not be psychic energy, but it would be heat energy related to it. It was a start.

In a City College laboratory Schmeidler enclosed a thermistor—a very sensitive temperature detector—in a thermos bottle and ran a lead to a chart recorder. This would be the target. Two other thermistors were connected to the palms of Swann's hands. On random command from Schmeidler, his task was to psychokinetically raise and lower the thermistor in the thermally insulated bottle which was twenty-five feet across the room. But the experiment contained an element unknown to Swann. Another thermos containing a thermistor was located several feet to the side of the target and out of sight. Would his energy be directed in a perfectly straight line to the target, or would a broad energy beam also sweep across the secondary bottle?

As Schmeidler suspected, with enough concentration Swann was able to influence the target thermistor. She would say, "Heat the target" and the arm of the recorder would move upward, and continue until she said, "Cool it down," and then the arm would gradually slide downward. "I found concurrent changes on Ingo's skin," says Schmeidler. "It would actually cool down and heat up." However, the biggest surprise was the control thermos sitting out of view. It too heated and cooled, but *opposite* to the direction of the target. When Swann raised the temperature of one target thermistor, for instance, the other one cooled down.[27] "It appears that a thermodynamic balance was achieved," says Schmeidler. "Rather than Ingo transferring all of his energy to the thermistor target, it appears that he drew on energy from the environment, and when he cooled the target, he transferred that energy back." If so, this says something important about a psychic's source of energy. Although he may draw some of it from himself, he might also collect and concentrate it from the environment. Uri Geller, and other psychics, strongly believe this to be the case. Although the ostensible temperature equilibrium observed in Schmeidler's experiment is rich fodder for the speculative mind, one thing is absolutely certain: Swann did not project normal heat energy, not the type that flows from a lamp bulb or an oven, across the room to influence the thermistors: they were too well insulated. The measured heat was an effect secondary to the action of an undetected type of energy.

Dr. Schmeidler's experiment leads to several important questions which only future research can answer. For instance: Was the amount of heat energy imparted to the target thermistor exactly equal to the decrease in energy in the control? How does the temperature of Swann's hands quantitatively correlate with the changes in the target and the control? And if several thermistors were spaced at varying distances from the target in a definite matrix, would a temperature pattern be observed throughout the field?

In the past, "mind over matter" was usually associated with images of rolling or levitating sizable objects. Someone who had psychokinetic ability was suppose to be able to open a book or lift a card table by will alone. Today, some of the modern PK experiments refine that image to include very subtle interactions with nature. As a result, PK ability is being found in an increasing number of individuals, people who can muster the energy to influence a minute atomic process, but not to swing a compass needle or roll a tumbler. In this sense the phenomenon is becoming less alien. Alien? Perhaps that is the wrong word, for we should realize that nothing could be more natural, more an everyday occurrence, than psychokinesis. Once we accept the definition of PK as the mind directly influencing matter, we are immediately confronted with an infinite number of personal PK experiences. Nobody would question the fact that a person's mind controls every action of his physical body. But the mind, we say, is a nonmaterial, intangible entity. How then can it influence the material body? The answer, by definition, is through psychokinesis. PK is the bridge that connects the insubstantial mind to the chemistry of the brain. Thus, we have circled back some 2,500 years to that nagging philosophical question that has defeated the world's greatest thinkers: What is the relationship between mind and body? Perhaps present-day experiments in psychokinesis will begin to unravel the mystery.

Epilogue

In seeking to understand new and unusual phenomena, scientists search for models, theoretical frameworks which will embrace their observations. Only when a model can be constructed which houses the phenomena is the scientist comfortable with them. Only then does he have an intellectual grasp of their nature, a means of predicting their occurrence and a margin of control over their behavior.

Up until the mid-1800s many scientists thought they had the ultimate, all-embracing model of the physical world in the mechanics of Isaac Newton. It was a powerful formalism which in its simplicity rendered the reeling of heavenly bodies around the celestial sphere no more mysterious than the falling of an apple to the ground. Newton's mechanics survived two hundred and fifty years and fostered a smug, if somewhat naïve, confidence that was eventually shattered by the atomistic views of Max Planck and Einstein's notions on cosmology. Shortly after the turn of the century, Planck and Einstein showed that the Newtonian model of the physical world was really only an approximate paradigm, fine when used to explain and predict common, everyday interactions between relatively large objects moving at slow speeds, but totally inadequate to handle the extremes of size and speed found in the subatomic and super-cosmologic worlds. These realms had their own canon of laws and logic.

As we know, the twentieth-century model of the physical world houses some arcane concepts: space is not Euclidian but curved so that parallel lines intersect; mass is not a solid, tangible constant, but a property that increases as a body is accelerated; time, under various conditions, appears to slow down, speed up, stop, and flow backwards; even the notion of cause-and-effect, the commonsense cornerstone of the Newtonian model, simply does not hold in the subatomic world. In building the modern physical edifice, scientists of this century learned an important lesson: reality has more than one meaningful face; what we observe is not necessarily what really is. Planck summed it up when he said:

> Modern Physics impresses us particularly with the truth of the old doctrine which teaches that there are realities existing apart from our [normal] sense perceptions, and that there are problems and conflicts where these realities are of greater value for us than the richest treasures of the world of [normal] experiences.

In this century we have witnessed a total restructuring of our views of nature, and now we are beginning to see a complete revamping of our views of ourselves. It comes with the willingness of scientists to study, for the first time in history, human beings in altered states of consciousness, and to observe and record systematically the events which spring naturally from these mental states.

In the past, Western science's model of consciousness was a narrow one indeed, made up of two states, wakefulness and slumber. The mentation of a child who sees "hidden analogies between cabbages and kings" was regarded as pure nonsense. The visions and voices reported by Eastern mystics were called delusions. Hypnotic consciousness was looked upon as a curious but uninformative state. Dream consciousness, a universal experience, was regarded as a nonsensical succession of flashbacks, bizarre and improbable incidents, really no more than a collection of subliminal paraphernalia.

Today's scientists realize that these seemingly irrational mentations, with their peculiar logics and strange distortions of space and time, offer a wealth of information on the nature of humans and their untapped potential. This broader model of human consciousness, which includes the continuum of altered states, has provided a home for parapsychological phenomena.

In 1902 William James made a plea for an expanded notion of consciousness. The plea fell on deaf ears then, but it is enlightening now to compare James's words with those of Planck quoted above, for the physicist and the psychologist, each in his way, was saying the same thing:

> Our normal waking consciousness . . . is but one special type of consciousness, whilst all about it, parted from it by the filmiest of screens, there lie potential forms of consciousness entirely different. We may go through life without suspecting their existence; but apply the requisite stimulus, and at a touch they are here in

all their completeness . . . No account of the universe in its totality can be final which leaves these other forms of consciousness quite disregarded . . . they forbid a premature closing of our account with reality.

We have come to realize that in this larger paradigm of consciousness our paranormal side is just as much a part of human nature as any of our other faculties. We are more than the mere composite of our wakeful perceptions, for the purely "wakeful person" is only half human. Perhaps as research into the paranormal accelerates, the day will come when the prefix *para* will be dropped altogether. After all, it is only an admission of our present inability to grasp the full spectrum of things that are humanly possible.

Notes

Impossible Things

1. J.B. Watson, *Psychol. Rev.* 20 (1913): 158–167.
2. C.D. Broad, *Religion, Philosophy and Psychical Research* (London: Routledge & Kegan Paul, 1953).
3. Rosalind Heywood, *The Sixth Sense* (London: Pan Books, 1956), p. 156.
4. G.N.M. Tyrrell, *Science and Psychical Phenomena* (London: Methuen, 1938).
5. W. Carington, *Telepathy* (London: Methuen, 1945).
6. Heywood, *Sixth Sense*, pp. 170–171.
7. B.F. Skinner, *Science and Human Behaviour* (New York: Free Press, 1953), pp. 30–31.
8. B.F. Skinner, *Beyond Freedom and Dignity* (New York: Alfred A. Knopf, 1971), p. 12.
9. Stanford Research Institute, press release. March 9, 1973 (Menlo Park, Calif.).
10. Sheila Ostrander and Lynn Schroeder, *Psychic Discoveries Behind the Iron Curtain* (Englewood Cliffs, N.J.: Prentice-Hall, 1970), p. 20.
11. *Ibid.*, p. 21.
12. *Ibid.*, p. 7.
13. Dr. Eugene B. Konecci, paper delivered at the Fourteenth International Astronautics Federation Meeting. Sept. 26, 1963 (Paris).

1—The Dream Scene

1. Ostrander and Schroeder, *Psychic Discoveries Behind the Iron Curtain*, p. 118.
2. C. G. Jung, *The Structure and Dynamics of the Psyche, Collected Works*, Vol. 8, tr. R. F. C. Hull (London, 1960), pp. 9, 420.
3. Louisa E. Rhine, *ESP in Life and Lab* (New York: Collier, 1967).
4. S. Freud, *Int. J. Psychoanalysis* 3 (1922): 283–305. S. Freud, *Int. J. Psychoanalysis* 24 (1943): 71–75. J. Ehrenwald, *Psychiatric Quarterly* 24 (1950): 726–743.
5. Personal communication.
6. *Proceedings of International Conference on Hypnosis, Drugs, Dreams and Psi* (New York: Parapsychology Foundation, Inc., 1967).

7. S. Krippner, "The Implications of Contemporary Dream Research," part 2, *Journal of the American Society of Psychosomatic Dentistry and Medicine,* Vol. 18, No. 3 (1971): 133.

8. M. Ullman and Stanley Krippner, "Dream Studies and Telepathy: An Experimental Approach," Monograph No. 12 (New York: Parapsychology Foundation, 1970), pp. 32–33.

9. David Foulkes, *The Psychology of Sleep* (New York: Scribners, 1966).

10. J.R. Smythies, editor, *Science and ESP* (London: Routledge & Kegan Paul, 1967), pp. 30–31.

11. M. Ullman and Stanley Krippner, "Experimentally Induced Telepathic Dreams," *International Journal of Neuropsychiatry,* June 1966: 444.

12. *Ibid.,* pp. 444–445.

13. *Ibid.,* p. 445.

14. *Proceedings of International Conference on Hypnosis, Drugs, Dreams and Psi,* 1967: 141.

15. Personal communication.

16. Ullman and Krippner, "Dream Studies," p. 73.

17. Personal communication.

18. *Ibid.*

19. S. Krippner and Richard Davidson, "The Use of Convergent Operations in Bio-Information Research" (New York: Maimonides Medical Center), p. 9.

20. "A Dream Grows in Brooklyn," *Psychic,* Jan./Feb. 1970.

21. *Proceedings of International Conference on Methodology in Psi Research* (New York: Parapsychology Foundation, 1968).

22. *Ibid.,* p. 50.

23. Personal communication.

24. Foulkes, *The Psychology of Sleep,* pp. 190–191.

25. *Ibid.,* pp. 53–54.

26. Rhine, *ESP,* p. 95.

27. Personal communication.

28. Personal communication.

2—Hypnosis and Psi

1. Charles T. Tart, ed., *Altered States of Consciousness* (New York: Wiley, 1969), pp. 268–269. (The name and age of subject are fictitious in this dramatization of an actual experiment.)

2. *Ibid.,* p. 253.

3. L. LeCron, "Hypnosis and ESP," *Psychic,* July/Aug. 1970: 20.

4. Robert Van de Castle, "ESP through Hypnosis," *Psychic,* Jan./Feb. 1972.

5. *Ibid.*

6. C. Honorton and Stanley Krippner, "Hypnosis and ESP Performance: A Review of the Experimental Literature," *Journal of the American Society for Psychical Research* 63 (July 1969).

7. Burton S. Glick and Jonathan Kogen, "Clairvoyance in Hypnotized Subjects:

Some Positive Results," *Journal of Parapsychology* 35 (Dec. 1971). (Also to be published in *Psychiatric Quarterly.*)

8. Personal communication.
9. Glick, "Clairvoyance," 1971.
10. Personal communication.
11. Personal communication.
12. Milan Ryzl, "A Method of Training in ESP," *International Journal of Parapsychology* 8 (Autumn 1966).
13. *Ibid.,* pp. 505–506.
14. L.E. Levinson, "Hypnosis—Key to Latent Psi Faculties," *International Journal of Parapsychology* 10 (Summer 1968).
15. Lawrence LeShan, "Toward a General Theory of the Paranormal," Monograph No. 9 (New York: Parapsychology Foundation, 1969).
16. *Ibid.,* p. 28.
17. Levinson, "Hypnosis."
18. *Ibid.*
19. *Ibid.*
20. D. Gibbons, *Beyond Hypnosis: Explorations in Hyperempiria* (South Orange, N.J.: Power Press, 1973).
21. Charles Honorton, "Significant Factors in Hypnotically-Induced Clairvoyant Dreams," *Journal of the American Society for Psychical Research* 66 (January 1972): 95.
22. *Ibid.,* p. 96.
23. Leslie M. LeCron, "Hypnosis and ESP," p. 21.
24. Robert Masters, "Consciousness and Extraordinary Phenomena" (Pomona, New York: Foundation for Mind Research, 1973).
25. *Ibid.*
26. *Ibid.*
27. *Time,* Dec. 4, 1972, p. 68.
28. Russell Noyes, Jr., published in *Psychiatry.* (See *Time,* Dec. 4, 1972.)
29. *Time,* Dec. 4, 1972, p. 70.
30. John White, ed., *The Highest State of Consciousness* (New York: Doubleday/Anchor, 1972), p. 128.
31. A. H. Maslow, *The Farther Reaches of Human Nature* (New York: Viking, 1971), p. 269.
32. *Ibid.,* p. 270.
33. Karlis Osis, "Deathbed Observations by Physicians and Nurses," Monograph (New York: Parapsychology Foundation).
34. Kenneth Keeling, "Telepathic Transmission in Hypnotic Dreams: An Exploratory Study," *Journal of Parapsychology* 35 (Dec. 1971).
35. Personal communication.
36. Personal communication.
37. The experiments in mutual hypnosis presented here are from two sources: Charles T. Tart, "Psychedelic Experiences Associated with a Novel Hypnotic Procedure, Mutual Hypnosis," in Tart, *Altered States of Consciousness*—and from personal communications with Dr. Tart.

3—Psychic Healing

1. Personal communication with Dr. Lawrence LeShan, who worked with the healer in question.
2. *Ibid.*
3. William A. Tiller, "Radionics, Radiesthesia, and Physics," Proceedings of Interdisciplinary Symposium on Psychic Phenomena in Healing, Academy of Parapsychology and Medicine, October 30, 1971.
4. *Ibid.,* 68.
5. *Ibid.,* 69.
6. Duke Marc, *Acupuncture* (New York: Pyramid House, 1972), pp. 2–3.
7. Tiller, "Radionics," p. 69.
8. Personal communication with Douglas Dean of the Newark College of Engineering, who has studied Ethel E. DeLoach's healing talents.
9. Douglas E. Dean and Ethel E. DeLoach, "What Is the Evidence for Psychic Healing?" *The Osteopathic Physician,* Oct. 1972.
10. Thelma Moss and Kendall Johnson, "Is There an Energy Body?" *The Osteopathic Physician,* Oct. 1972.
11. "Scientists Hope a Photo Process May Bring Gains in Several Fields," *Wall Street Journal,* July 24, 1973.
12. Stanley Krippner, ed., *Kirlian Photography, Acupuncture and the Human Aura* (New York: Foundation for Parasensory Investigation, 1973).
13. Ostrander and Schroeder, *Psychic Discoveries Behind the Iron Curtain.*
14. Moss and Johnson, "Energy Body?" p. 43.
15. Moss and Johnson, "Energy Body?" p. 44.
16. Dean and DeLoach, "Evidence for Psychic Healing?"
17. Personal communication with Dr. William Tiller.
18. Justa M. Smith, "Paranormal Effects on Enzyme Activity," Professional Paper No. 2 (Buffalo, New York: The Human Dimensions Institute).
19. *Ibid.*
20. S. Schwartz and James Bolen, "Interview: Ambrose and Olga Worrall," *Psychic,* March/April 1972.
21. Robert N. Miller, "The Positive Effect of Prayer on Plants," *Psychic,* March/April 1972.
22. Schwartz and Bolen, "Interview."
23. Graham K. Watkins and Anita M. Watkins, "Possible PK Influence on the Resuscitation of Anesthetized Mice," *Journal of Parapsychology* 35 (1971).
24. Otto Rahn, *Invisible Radiations of Organisms* (Ann Arbor, Michigan: Edwards Brothers, 1944).
25. Bernard Grad, "The 'Laying on of Hands': Implications for Psychotherapy, Gentling and the Placebo Effect," *Journal of the American Society for Psychical Research* 61 (1967): 286–305.
26. Bernard Grad, "Some Biological Effects of the 'Laying on of Hands': A Review of Experiments with Animals and Plants," *Journal of the American Society for Psychical Research* 50 (1965): 95–127.
27. Dolores Krieger, "The Response of In-Vivo Human Hemoglobin to an Active

Healing Therapy by Direct Laying-on of Hands," Professional Paper No. 3 (Buffalo, New York: The Human Dimensions Institute).
28. *Ibid.*

4—Intimate Communications: Telepathy

1. Matt Mahoney, A. Sutton, and C. Panati, *Digital Communications.* New York, RCA Institute For Professional Development, 1968.
2. Ostrander and Schroeder, *Psychic Discoveries Behind the Iron Curtain,* p. 32.
3. Berthold Eric Schwarz, "Family Telepathy," *Psychic,* March/April 1972.
4. T. D. Duane and Thomas Behrendt, "Extrasensory Electroencephalographic Induction between Identical Twins," *Science,* October 1965.
5. Personal communications from Dr. Roberts Rugh, Columbia-Presbyterian Medical Center, New York.
6. Vincent Gaddis and Margaret Gaddis, "Natural Born Telepathists?" *Psychic,* July 1972.
7. *Ibid.*
8. C. Wilson, *The Occult* (London: Hodder & Stoughton, 1971).
9. K. Raudive, *Breakthrough* (New York: Taplinger, 1971). Peter Bander, *Voices from the Tapes* (New York: Drake, 1973).
10. Arthur Koestler, *The Roots of Coincidence* (New York: Random House, 1972).
11. Sir Cyril Burt, "Psychology and Parapsychology," in Smythies, *Science and ESP.*
12. Douglas E. Dean, "Plethysmograph Recordings as ESP Responses," *International Journal of Neuropsychiatry,* 1966.
13. Vivian Fletcher, "Plants Discovered Turning in on Us." *Catalyst* 2 (1973).
14. *Ibid.*
15. John White, ed., *The Highest State of Consciousness.*
16. Fletcher, "Plants."
17. Marvin Karlins and Lewis Andrews, *Biofeedback: Turning on the Power of Your Mind* (New York: J.B. Lippincott, 1972).
18. Lyall Watson, *Supernature* (New York: Doubleday, 1973).
19. Robert Creeley, *Words* (New York: Scribners, 1967).
20. Banesh Hoffmann, *Creator and Rebel: Albert Einstein* (New York: Viking, 1972).
21. Smythies, *Science and ESP.*
22. V.A. Frisoff, *Life, Mind and Galaxies* (Edinburgh and London: 1967), pp. 102–103.
23. Karlins and Andrews, *Biofeedback.*
24. Ostrander and Schroeder, *Psychic Discoveries Behind the Iron Curtain.*

5—The Twilight Mind

1. "Parapsychologica III," Publication of the South African Society for Psychical Research, No. 8 (Johannesburg, South Africa, 1968), pp. 14–24.
2. F.W.H. Myers, *Human Personality* (London: Longmans, Green and Co., 1903).
3. Stanley Krippner, "An Experiment in Search of Psi-Favorable States of Consciousness." (paper presented at Duke University, Durham, N.C., Oct. 10, 1970.)
4. *Ibid.*
5. *Ibid.*
6. "Interview: Thelma S. Moss," *Psychic,* July/August 1970.
7. Jess Stearn, *In Search for a Soul* (New York: Doubleday, 1973).
8. Mary Leader, her account of writing *Triad* in the *Enquirer,* Sept. 16, 1973.
9. Myers, *Human Personality.*
10. Kenneth Walker, *The Extra-Sensory Mind* (New York: Harper & Row, 1961).
11. George Sand, *A Winter in Majorca,* quoted in Andre Boucourechliev, *Chopin* (New York: Viking, 1963), p. 100.
12. C. D. Broad, "The Notion of 'Precognition'," in Smythies, *Science and ESP.*
13. Anthony Storr, *The Dynamics of Creation* (New York: Atheneum, 1972).
14. A. Maslow, "The Creative Attitude" (New York: Psychosynthesis Research Foundation, 1963), p. 15.
15. Scott Rogo, *NAD* (New York: University Books, 1972).
16. C. G. Jung, *Contributions to Analytical Psychology* (New York: Harcourt, Brace, 1928).
17. Desmond Morris, *The Biology of Art* (London: Methuen, 1962), pp. 124–125.
18. Robert Crookall, "Out-of-the-Body Experiences," *Psychic,* March/April 1973.
19. Robert A. Monroe, *Journeys Out of the Body* (New York: Doubleday/Anchor, 1973).
20. Personal communication.
21. Personal communication.
22. Monroe, *Journeys.*
23. Personal communication from Dr. Karlis Osis, American Society for Psychical Research, New York.
24. Foulkes, *The Psychology of Sleep.*
25. Personal communication.
26. Montague Ullman, "Psi and Psychiatry: The Need for Restructuring Basic Concepts" (New York: Maimonides Medical Center).
27. Personal communication.
28. Personal communication.
29. Charles Tart, "Between Waking and Sleep: The Hypnagogic State," in Tart, *Altered States of Consciousness.*

6—*Dialogues with Nature: Clairvoyance*

1. W. G. Walter, *The Living Brain* (London: Penguin, 1961).
2. Watson, *Supernature,* pp. 92–93.
3. Albert Krueger, "Are Negative Ions Good for You?" *New Scientist,* June 14, 1973.
4. E.M. Dewan and Rock Dewan, *American Journal of Obstetrics and Gynecology.* Gay Gaer Luce, *Body Time* (New York: Pantheon, 1971).
5. Ostrander and Schroeder, *Psychic Discoveries Behind the Iron Curtain.*
6. Andrija (Henry) Puharich, "Electric Field Reinforcement of ESP," *International Journal of Neuropsychiatry,* 1966.
7. *Ibid.*
8. Ostrander and Schroeder, *Psychic Discoveries Behind the Iron Curtain.*
9. Harold C. Schonberg, "Mysticism and Melancholy, Scriabin and Rachmaninoff," *The Lives of the Great Composers* (New York: Norton, 1970), p. 497.
10. Ostrander and Schroeder, *Psychic Discoveries Behind the Iron Curtain,* p. 179.
11. *Ibid.*
12. Thelma Moss, "Eyeless Sight," *The Osteopathic Physician,* October 1972.
13. Gay Gaer Luce, *Body Time.*
14. Woodburn Heron, "Cognitive and Physiological Effects of Perceptual Isolation," *Sensory Deprivation* (Cambridge: Harvard University Press), pp. 7–33.
15. Chicago *Sun-Times,* Aug. 27, 1966.
16. Brad Steiger, *The Psychic Feats of Olof Jonsson* (Englewood Cliffs, New Jersey: Prentice-Hall, 1971).
17. *Ibid.*
18. Charles Tart, "Models for the Explanation of Extrasensory Perception," *International Journal of Neuropsychiatry,* 1966.
19. Russell Targ and David Hurt, "Learning Clairvoyance and Perception with an Extrasensory Perception Teaching Machine," *Parapsychology Review,* July/August 1972.
20. Personal communication.
21. Alan Vaughan, "The Phenomena of Uri Geller," *Psychic,* May/June 1973, p. 15.
22. "Interview: Uri Geller," *Psychic,* May/June 1973.
23. Brendan O'Regan, "Now you see it, now . . . ?" *New Scientist,* July 12, 1973.
24. Stanford Research Institute, press release. March 9, 1973 (Menlo Park, Calif.).
25. Results of SRI experiments with Geller were presented at a physics colloquium at Columbia University on March 9, 1973.
26. *Ibid.*
27. *Ibid.*

7—The Mystic and Psi

1. J. Pearce, *The Crack in the Cosmic Egg* (New York: Julian Press, 1971), p. 101.
2. J. Hoening, "Medical Research on Yoga," *Confinia Psychiatrica,* 11 (1968): 74.
3. Alexandra David-Neel, *Magic and Mystery in Tibet.* (Baltimore, Md.: Penguin, 1936).
4. Walter Gibson, *The Key to Yoga* (Bell Pub., 1958).
5. Swami Vishnudevananda, *The Complete Illustrated Book of Yoga* (New York: Julian Press, 1960).
6. Anand, Chhina, and Singh, "Some Aspects of Electroencephalographic Studies in Yogis," *Encetroenceph. Clin. Neurophysiol.* 13 (1961):452–456.
7. *Ibid.*
8. Anand, Chhina, and Singh, "Electroencephalographic Studies."
9. Ramakrishna K. Rao, "Psi in Communities and Other Interpersonal Situations in the Eastern World." *Conference on Methodology in Psi Research* (New York: Parapsychology Foundation, 1968).
10. *Ibid.*
11. Personal communication with Dr. L. LeShan.
12. Rao, "Psi in Communities."
13. Gopi Krishna, "The True Aim of Yoga," *Psychic,* Feb. 1973, p. 13.
14. *Ibid.*
15. Lawrence LeShan, "Toward a General Theory of the Paranormal."
16. William James, *The Varieties of Religious Experience* (London: Longmans, Green and Co., 1928), p. 3.
17. R. White, "A Comparison of Old and New Methods of Response to Targets in ESP Experiments," *Journal of the American Society for Psychical Research* 63 (1964):21–57.
18. W. G. Roll and R. L. Morris, et al., "Free Verbal Response Experiments with Lalsingh Harribance" (Durham, N.C.: Parapsychology Research Foundation, Duke University, 1969).
19. Akira Kasamatsu and Tomio Hirai, "An Electroencephalographic Study on the Zen Meditation," *Folio Psychiat. & Neurolog. Japonica* 20 (1966):315–336.
20. R. K. Wallace, "The Physiological Effects of Transcendental Meditation," *Science* 167 (1970).
21. *Ibid.*
22. R. K. Wallace and H. Benson, "The Physiology of Meditation," *Scientific American,* Feb. 1972.
23. Jack Forem, *Transcendental Meditation* (New York: Dutton, 1973).
24. *Ibid.*
25. William Braud and Lendell Braud, "Preliminary Explorations of Psi-Conducive States: Progressive Muscular Relaxation" (New York: American Society for Psychical Research).
26. *Ibid.*
27. Forem, *Transcendental Meditation.*
28. David M. Rorvik, "Jack Schwarz Feels No Pain," *Esquire,* Dec. 1972.

29. Elmer Green, et al., "Biofeedback for Mind-Body Self-Regulation: Healing and Creativity," *Fields Within Fields* 5:1 (1972).
30. Frederik van Eeden, "A Study of Dreams," in Tart, *Altered States of Consciousness.*
31. Charles Honorton, et al., "Feedback-Augmented EEG Alpha Shifts in Subjective States, and ESP Card-Guessing Performance," *Journal of the Amer. Soc. for Psychical Research* 65 (July 1971).
32. Roger Sperry, "The Great Cerebral Commissure," *Scientific American,* Jan. 1964, pp. 42–52. Michael Gazzaniga, "The Split Brain in Man," *Scientific American,* Aug. 1967, pp. 24–29. Maya Pines, *The Brain Changers* (New York: Harcourt Brace Jovanovich, 1973).
33. F. S. Perls, *Gestalt Therapy Verbatim* (Lafayette, Ca.: Real People Press, 1969).
34. Robert E. Ornstein, *The Psychology of Consciousness* (New York: Viking, 1972).
35. Personal communication with Dr. R. Ornstein.

8—Precognition

1. B. Steiger, *ESP: Your Sixth Sense* (New York: Award Books, 1966).
2. Personal communication with Dr. Albert Ellis.
3. Personal communication with Dr. Gertrude Schmeidler.
4. G. J. Whitrow, *The Nature of Time* (London: Thames and Hudson, 1972).
5. J. C. Hafele and Richard Keating, "Around-the-World Atomic Clocks: Observed Relativistic Time Gains," *Science,* July 14, 1972, pp. 168–170.
6. In a letter dated March 21, 1955, to Michele Besso, the surviving child of Einstein's lifetime friend, Michael Besso.
7. G. J. Whitrow, *Nature of Time.*
8. H. Schmidt, *Journal of Parapsychology* 33, 2 (June 1969).
9. H. Schmidt, *Journal of Parapsychology* 33, 4 (Dec. 1969).
10. H. Schmidt, *Journal of Parapsychology* 34, 3–4 (1970).
11. Rhine, *ESP.*
12. S. Krippner, M. Ullman, and E. Honorton, "A Precognitive Dream Study with a Single Subject," *Journal of the American Society for Psychical Research* 65 (April 1971).
13. *Ibid.*
14. Stanley Krippner, M. Ullman, and C. Honorton, "A Second Precognitive Dream Study with Malcolm Bessent," *Journal of the American Society for Psychical Research* 66 (July 1972). [For the first study with Bessent see, C. Honorton, "Automated Forced-Choice Precognition Tests with a Sensitive," *Journal of the American Society for Psychical Research* 65 (Oct. 1971)].
15. *Ibid.*
16. American Society for Psychical Research, New York City.
17. W.J. Levy, et al., "A Precognitive Test with Hamsters," *Journal of Parapsychology* 37 (June 1972). Also see: Levy, et al., "An Improved Method in a Precognitive Test with Jirds," *Journal of Parapsychology* 37 (June 1973).

18. *Ibid.*
19. Personal communication with D. Dean. (The results of the study are to be published in 1974.)
20. Max Gunther, "An Occult Guide to the Stock Market," *Esquire,* April 1973.
21. Whitrow, *Nature of Time.*
22. *Ibid.*
23. *Ibid.*

9—Psychokinesis and Life Fields

1. Larry Dendy, "Chemiluminescence: Nature's Own Light," University of Georgia, Research Report, Vol. 7, No. 1, Fall 1972.
2. W. Schafer, "Further Developments of the Field Effect Monitor," Life Sciences, Corvair Division of General Dynamics, Report GDC-ERR-AN-1114, Oct. 1967.
3. H. S. Burr, *Blueprint for Immortality* (London: Neville Spearman, 1972).
4. H. S. Burr and L. Langman, "Electromagnetic Studies in Women with Malignancy of Cervix Uteri," *Science* 105 (1947):209.
5. The work presented here was conducted by the Energy Research Group of the Institute for Bio-Energetic Analysis, New York. It was obtained through personal communication with physicist Dr. Richard Dobrin and psychiatrist Dr. Carl Kirsch, two members of the research team. Journal publications are due in 1974.
6. Watson, *Supernature.*
7. Upton Sinclair, *Mental Radio* (New York: Collier Books, 1930).
8. I. M. Kogan, "Is Telepathy Possible?" (A paper presented on July 3, 1965, to a meeting of the Bionics Section of the Scientific Council for Cybernetics of the Presidium of the USSR Academy of Sciences.)
9. Ostrander and Schroeder, *Psychic Discoveries Behind the Iron Curtain,* pp. 407–411.
10. *Ibid.*
11. *Ibid.*
12. *Ibid.*
13. W. G. Roll and J. G. Pratt, "The Miami Disturbances," *Journal of the American Society for Psychical Research* 65 (Oct. 1971).
14. *Ibid.*
15. W. G. Roll, et al., "Radial and Tangential Forces in the Miami Poltergesit," *Journal of the American Society for Psychical Research* 67 (July 1973).
16. W. G. Roll, *The Poltergeist* (New York: Doubleday, 1972).
17. *Ibid.*
18. *Ibid.*
19. Chari, *International Journal of Parapsychology* 8:540.
20. H. Schmidt, *Parapsychology Review* (New York: Parapsychology Foundation).
21. Presented by H. Puthoff and R. Targ, March 9, 1973 at a Columbia University physics colloquium.

22. Walter J. Levy, "PK in Chicks," *Journal of Parapsychology* 35 (1971).
23. Walter J. Levy, et al., "A Potential Animal Model for Parapsychological Interaction between Organisms." (Paper presented at the Parapsychological Assoc. Convention, Virginia, Sept. 1973.)
24. *Human Behavior,* Sept./Oct. 1972, p. 58.
25. *Journal of Parapsychology,* 35 (1971).
26. Walter J. Levy, et al., "Possible PK by rats to receive pleasurable brain stimulation." (A paper presented at the Parapsychological Assoc. Convention, Virginia, Sept. 1973.)
27. G. Schmeidler, "PK in Temperature Records, and Suggestions about How It Occurs," City College of New York.

Further Reading

1—The Dream Scene

Dream Studies and Telepathy: An Experimental Approach. M. Ullman and S. Krippner. Monograph No. 12, 1970. Parapsychology Foundation Inc., 29 W. 57th St., New York, N.Y.

Dream Telepathy. M. Ullman, et al. Macmillan, 1973.

ESP in Life and Lab. L. E. Rhine. Collier, 1967.

The Psychology of Sleep. D. Foulkes. Scribners, 1966.

The New Psychology of Dreaming. R. Jones. Grune & Stratton, 1970.

2—Hypnosis and Psi

Altered States of Consciousness, Section 5, "Hypnosis." Ed. C. T. Tart. Wiley, 1969.

Psi and Altered States of Consciousness: Proceedings of an International Conference on Hypnosis, Drugs, Dreams and Psi, 1967. Ed. R. Cavanna and M. Ullman. Parapsychology Foundation Inc., 29 W. 57th St., New York, N.Y.

Abnormal Hypnotic Phenomena, Vols. I, II, III, and IV. E. Dingwall. Churchill, London, 1967.

Deathbed Observations by Physicians and Nurses. K. Osis. Monograph. Parapsychology Foundation Inc., 29 W. 57th St., New York, N.Y.

3—Psychic Healing

The Medium, the Mystic and the Physicist: Toward a General Theory of the Paranormal, Part 2: "Testing the Theory"; "Psychic Healing." L. LeShan. Viking, 1974.

The Varieties of Healing Experiences: Exploring Psychic Phenomena in Healing. The Academy of Parapsychology and Medicine, 314 A Second St., Los Altos, Calif., 1971.

The Kirlian Aura. Ed. S. Krippner and D. Rubin. Anchor/Doubleday, 1974.

We Are All Healers. S. Hammond. Harper, 1973.

Psychic Discoveries Behind the Iron Curtain. S. Ostrander and L. Schroeder. Prentice-Hall, 1970.

4—Intimate Communications: Telepathy

The Roots of Coincidence. A. Koestler. Random House, 1972.

Science and ESP. Ed. J. R. Smythies. Routledge & Kegan Paul, London, 1967.

The Extrasensory Mind. K. Walker. Harper, 1961.

The Highest State of Consciousness. Ed. J. White. Anchor/Doubleday, 1972.

Voices from the Tapes. P. Bander. Drake, 1973.

Biofeedback: Turning on the Powers of Your Mind. M. Karlins and L. Andrews. J. B. Lippincott, 1972.

ESP and Personality Patterns. G. Schmeidler and R. McConnell. Yale University Press, 1958.

Supernature. L. Watson. Doubleday, 1973.

5—The Twilight Mind

Proceedings of an International Conference on Psi Factors in Creativity, 1969. Parapsychology Foundation Inc., 29 W. 57th St., N.Y., N.Y.

The Act of Creation. A. Koestler. London, 1964.

The Dynamics of Creation. A. Storr. Atheneum, 1972.

Human Personality. F.W.H. Myers. Longmans, Green & Co., 1903.

6—Dialogues with Nature: Clairvoyance

Body Time. G. G. Luce. Pantheon, 1971.

Sensory Deprivation, Harvard University Press (collected papers), pp 7–33.

The Center of the Cyclone. John C. Lilly. Julian Press, 1972.

The Human Biocomputer. John C. Lilly. Julian Press, 1968.

7—The Mystic and Psi

The Medium, the Mystic and the Physicist: Toward a General Theory of the Paranormal. L. LeShan. Viking, 1974.

Magic and Mystery in Tibet. Alexandra David-Neel. Penguin, 1936.

Mysticism. E. Underhill. Dutton, 1911.

The Psychology of Consciousness. R. Ornstein. Viking, 1972.

8—Precognition

The Nature of Time. G. J. Whitrow. Thames & Hudson, Ltd., 1972.

Jung, Synchronicity and Human Destiny: Non-Causal Dimensions of Human Experiences. I. Progoff. Julian, 1973.

9—Psychokinesis and Life Fields

The Poltergeist. W. G. Roll. Doubleday, 1972.

Blueprint for Immortality. H. S. Burr. Neville Spearman, 1972.

Consciousness and Reality. Ed. C. Muses. Dutton, 1972.

Subject Index

Author Index